Manchester to Galway and Leitrim via Iran

Maureen Farazian

authorHOUSE®

AuthorHouse™ UK Ltd.
500 Avebury Boulevard
Central Milton Keynes, MK9 2BE
www.authorhouse.co.uk
Phone: 08001974150

© *2009 Maureen Farazian. All rights reserved.*

No part of this book may be reproduced, stored in a retrieval system, or transmitted by any means without the written permission of the author.

First published by AuthorHouse 6/25/2009

ISBN: 978-1-4389-8728-6 (sc)

This book is printed on acid-free paper.

Chapter One

IN A MOST BEAUTIFUL PICTURESQUE area of green fields, hills and valleys and enclosed by distant mountains lies Glencar in County Leitrim on the west coast of Ireland, this is where Annie was born and went to school, and lived with her family until she was twenty five years old..

Due to the lack of employment in Ireland, my mother Annie moved to England in 1938, in the hope of finding a job. She was nervous, and with all of her belongings in a small bag, she boarded the Liverpool ferry, taking her into an unknown world away from the security and familiarity of her parents and the nine siblings she had left back at their Manorhamilton farmhouse. On her first trip outside of the county of Leitrim, even though her nerves were getting the better of her, she had to catch that ferry. As she was the eldest in the family, she was therefore the first to leave home, so she had to appear to be brave.

Annie used to read a book kept on the mantelpiece in the farmhouse. Called 'East Lynne' by Mrs Henry Wood, the book was about the Earl of Mount Severn and Lady Isabel, who lived in a beautiful stately home in wonderful gardens. Annie had read this book several times and now visualized this as the sort of house she would get a job in, as she thought everybody in England lived in houses like that.

Annie had an aunty Molly who had gone to live in England many years earlier, so she would have someone to meet her off the boat and somewhere to stay until she could find a live-in job. Then, as was usually the case, she would probably send for other members of the family and she in turn would be able to help with their migration.

Aunty Molly was married to an Irish man called Jack whom she had met in England and they had a large brood of children, including three sets of twins though only one set had survived.

Annie eventually found a live-in job as a cook, working for a Doctor and his wife on Wilbraham Road in Manchester. Doctor and Mrs Partington a couple in their thirty's had a large detached house. The doctor was the local GP and drove around in a big old Rover, which gave him and his wife grandeur unheard of in Annie's farmhouse back home, reminding her of the characters in the book. She felt very proud to be working for the Partingtons and living in this beautiful house.

Annie eventually sent for her sister Tess, as Mrs Partington needed a cleaner. The doctor and his wife became like parents to the two girls, and the girls were very happy in this family atmosphere. Mrs Partington taught Annie how to cook, how to set a table, and how to cut the top off a packet of cornflakes with scissors instead of ripping it open; she also taught Tess the correct way to do the cleaning.

Annie and Tess would go to the Irish dance hall on a Sunday night, after not eating any food in the evening so as they would look thin. Each of the girls would have a night off during the week, when they would have to go out separately, as one of them would have to remain on duty in the house. On one of these separate nights out, a young man walked Annie home, but did not reveal his name. Then on Tess's night out she also was walked home by a young man who did not give his name. Both girls called their man the quiet man, as both said he talked very little and they started to wonder if it might be the same man. Eventually Annie found out her man was called John; whilst Tess declared her man was called Jack.

Annie always being the more crafty one, decided to spy through a upstairs window when Tess was due home, and saw that her John was also Tess's Jack.

Annie being the older and considered the wiser one of the two girls decided she would keep the quiet man for herself and warned Tess she must not see him again.

So John, the quiet man, would become my father.

His proposal to my mother went "if it's cold in October will we get married?" They were, as my father would put it "a bit long in the tooth "as he was now twenty-four. Most people of their age had already fallen in love and married, so even though she was not in love as she so often told me and that girls were expected to marry in those days. At twenty-seven, Annie said yes. They got married on 21st September 1940. Annie's sister Kate, whom her family had recently dispatched to join her sisters in this, their land of plenty, was her bride's maid. John my father chose his friend Chris as his best man and on the wedding photos, the bride and groom were a very good looking couple, and beautifully dressed, my mother wearing a gorgeous long white dress and veil, and carrying a beautiful bouquet of lilies. The wedding was a small affair, however as the war was on and money was not too plentiful.

Nine months later I arrived into this world on July 12th 1941 at 1.10am. I was delivered in a second storey flat on Upper Brook Street, Manchester, by my mums best friend Rose Donlon, who was to be my godmother, and known to me throughout my life as aunty Posy, a nickname I gave her as a young child. Posy was a nurse in the local hospital and in those days was considered to be as good as any midwife would have been.

With no love in the marriage I must have become a burden. My mother later told me that as we were on the second floor she could not get the pram downstairs, so she would have to go out shopping and leave me on my own. The first thing I managed to do wrong was at six months old; I must have been very energetically bouncing up and down, my mother came back from the shops to find that I had upturned the pram, so she used to tie the pram to a chair with a rope. After a few months of this she decided to try to find a house to rent.

Posy was always special to me, she was small and slim, so a little rose, which I knew was a posy, so Posy became my special name for her. I always felt very privileged when Posy would remind me that she had delivered me into this world. Posy remained in my life and was a very dear friend for almost six decades until she passed away, shortly before I was sixty.

Posy was working as a nurse, so we looked after her son John, who was three months older than me. Put out to play in the back yard of our rented house in Norwood Street we would upturn two old kitchen chairs and pretend they were cars. We spent a lot of nights in my cot, whilst our parents went out together but that all came to a end in August 1944 when my sister Anne was born, I was really excited at the arrival of my new baby sister.

As the war was raging, my mother took Anne and myself over to Ireland, as she thought we would be safer over there. This was my second visit to the emerald isle, and as I was now four years old, I remember lots of things clearly such as, the one and only light in the cottage, an oil lamp placed on the kitchen table. I would often sit on the table next to the lamp, especially when we had visitors, which we called the ramblers, as they would always walk up to the house. The ramblers used to keep asking me where my father worked, just to hear my English accent, as I replied "my daddy works in the coalmines". The ramblers loved to visit the McHugh family cottage and would stay until the early hours of the morning. I can still remember some of the ghost stories they would tell, as there was no radio or TV, so stories were the main entertainment. Plenty of tea would be drunk and I would watch one of the ramblers eat tealeaves with a spoon from his mug. I would lie in bed later and listen to the crickets in the fireplace, remembering the stories I had just heard, and feeling a bit frightened in case one of the ghosts would appear to me.

At daybreak, I would awaken to the cock crowing. My grandfather would go out to milk the cows, and I would be by his side, as I was at every opportunity.

A few days a week, we would take the dog on the horse and cart and go to the creamery to sell the milk, after my grandmother had taken what she needed to make butter and cheese.

Some days we would go to the quarry on our farm and I would sit on the edge as my grandfather dug out stones to sell to the council to build what was to be the N16 road, from Enniskillen to Sligo. Granddad would talk to me about the giant's grave which was a few yards away from the quarry, and he told me that there were lots more of the historical giants grave sites situated in a place called Carrowmore in County Sligo dating back some 5000 years or more, he said we were quite privileged to have one on our land. Granddad pointed out that the graves were usually marked by a large boulder, and no one is allowed to dig around them or near them, and that ours is marked on the land registry with Leitrim County Council.

Quite a bit of my education regarding farms and animals, as well as giants graves took place on these occasions. The rest of the time would be spent on the farm ploughing, haymaking and so on. I was truly my granddad pet, and truly happy.

My grandmother, who had brought up ten children, looked after the geese, and turkeys, as well as doing the cooking and cleaning. My aunty Liz was in charge of the hens and chickens. The whole family would be fed from a black pot held on a hook over the turf fire and we also enjoyed delicious home made bread with thick homemade butter.

My grandmother's life was not easy. As there was no running water, the washing was carried down to the river, and was washed there summer and winter. She would also stand for hours in front of the front door churning the butter and making cheese. I remember her chasing the chickens around the farmyard and when she caught one she would wring its neck and then cut its throat with a knife. The headless chicken would continue to run around for a while and she explained to me that the nerves were still alive, and that it would soon stop running.

There was no such thing as a bathroom, and the toilet was a hole in the ground outside in the garden. Our drinking water came from a well, which was situated in a field next to the farmhouse. Aunty Liz used to wash her long red hair in the river; she would lie on the riverbank with her head in the water, to let the waves of the water flow through her hair. She used to say it was relaxing and good for her. My grandma was not allowed to carry the water, as it was too heavy, so granddad's rule was that one of the boys must always fetch the buckets of water for the household. My grandparents were very happy together, and no one had ever heard a wrong word between the two of them.

The farmhouse stood on fifty-five acres of land. It consisted of a kitchen, an upper bedroom, a lower bedroom, and another bedroom which had been built on at the back in later years. Ten children had been brought up here in this small but happy house, my mother being the eldest.

Life was hard for most people in England because of the war, but being on the farm in Ireland, life felt rich and full to me. My granddad fed me a spoonful of his boiled egg and a large lump of butter each morning and I would then have a bowl of porridge and a glass of milk.

I called my grandfather 'my daddy that goes to the creamery' to distinguish him from my daddy in England. Life was wonderful and fascinating for me, to be able to watch the chickens hatching by cracking the shells and popping out, the new calves arriving in the large herd of cows, and the two big horses ploughing the fields.

We spent six months in this idyllic world, and then my mother took us down to my father's home in County Galway to stay with my other grandparents Michael and Mariah Connor.

I was now four and a half. After a long train journey, we arrived in Shanbally in a taxi. As the taxi stopped I alighted, spotted a ginger cat and proceeded to chase it into a neighbours cottage, up to the bedroom and under the bed, for which I was severely scolded, and told I must never go into any cottage uninvited, and certainly never go up to a bedroom. This was a sign of things to come, as I was regularly in trouble in the months we were to remain there. (This cottage, which I was scolded for entering, was to become mine later in life, as I purchased it some fifty-three years later as a holiday home).

The Connors were a relatively poor family with only one field and one cow, so when I would reach for the butter it would be pushed to the back of the table, as food was not as plentiful as it had been in Leitrim. Even so, my grandparents appeared to be very happy and contented people.

Michael my grandfather originated from County Kerry, and together with his brother John had come to Galway in search of work as there were a lot of farms there. I am not sure how he and my grandmother met and fell in love, but my grandmother being an only child, her mother had hoped she would marry well, so raised strong objections to her daughter marrying this young farmhand. They must have been a very brave young couple for their day, as they ran away to England to be married in St Helens, here they tied the knot in secret, then returned home where all was forgiven. They were happy with each other and went on to rear seven children, my father being one of them. (Many years later, I also ran away to secretly get married.)

There were thirteen cottages in the hamlet of Shanbally and the feeling was of one big family. My grandmother's name was Mariah, but she became affectionately known as Muddy, as the children could not pronounce Mariah. Although not qualified my grandmother acted as the nurse in this small hamlet, which lead nowhere, making her an important person in this tiny community. She took her role very seriously and was approached with everything from a scraped knee to an upset stomach, or sometimes more serious injuries. She was known as the Hatcher and Dispatcher, as she would deliver the babies and also lay out the dead.

Once a year some families would kill a pig, which they would then share out. I remember after our pig had been killed, it being cut up then hung from hooks in the ceiling, and later being cured in wooden cases of salt.

On occasional afternoons, my mother would go to the next-door cottage, and play the accordion, also known as the melodeon. Some of the others would play the fiddle or sing, and then the dancing would start. I would be left in our cottage, behind what was known as a half door, designed to keep the hens out. On a few occasions, I would climb over the half door with the aid of a chair, and once at least fell on my head. When I could get over the half door I spent my time peeping in through the window of the cottage to watch the gaiety, but would not be allowed in.

The only one blip in this family was my fathers youngest brother Martin, now a spoilt teenager, and very jealous of any attention my grandmother would pay me.

He would put his hands in his pocket and hit me on the head with his elbow at every opportunity; if I shouted ouch he would look innocent, as his hands were secure in his pockets and he would then smirk at me behind his mother's back.

On another occasion the cat jumped up onto the dresser and Martin stuck its head in grandma's best jug. The cat panicked and jumped to the floor, so of course the beautiful green jug was shattered, Grandma's pride and joy gone forever, and guess who got the blame, me of course. Only one cow to be milked, no trips to the creamery, no quarry, no ramblers. I was really missing my other granddad.

I must have wandered off one evening, as I remember being brought home by a neighbour, who said he had found me face down in the stream, so he had actually saved my life. My only excuse was that I was walking back to Leitrim to see my other daddy, (my granddad that goes to the creamery). If this walk had it taken place it would have been sixty-eight miles.

We finally bade farewell to these nice kind people, and I regret to say I never saw them again.

Back on the train to Leitrim life was wonderful and rosy again, until my father came over from England to visit us. Every night after I settled in my bed, my grandfather would bring a bottle of milk to me to drink before I would go to sleep. On this occasion my father bought up the bottle of milk, only to be told by me "I want my other daddy to bring up the milk.

My father had not been educated and could neither read nor write, so would probably have been embarrassed by this, but all I know is that from then on, every time I did anything wrong I got a smack on the bottom. I do remember my grandfather telling my father, "a girl should never be hit in such a place, and that his hand was too heavy to hit a child." I was never hit in my grandfather's presence again, my father would take me out to the barn to be hit, and leave me there until I stopped crying. Thankfully after his two weeks holiday my father returned to his job in England, so no more smacks, and life became happy and normal again.

As granddad had always said what a good little helper I was, I now decided to get on with the jobs on my own. To my granddads horror, he found me in the byre where the cows or bulls are sometimes kept. I was trying to milk a bull, saying, "you have no milk, you haven't". Granddad then sat me on his knee and explained the difference between a cow and a bull, and as if to make me remember his words, he told me that I was very lucky to not to have been trampled to death.

On another day when I thought I was being helpful, I climbed up on to a cow's back and onto a haystack. Whilst everyone was running around looking for me, I was calmly in a world of my own, pulling the hay and throwing it down on to the ground thinking I was feeding the animals, but a cow kept eating it, so I was wasting my time and fell asleep. I later got a good talking to for my trouble. It was explained to me that as we had a river on our land, and they knew that I was busy, but I was sure they had meant 'helpful', that if I went missing they get worried in case I had fallen into the river and been swept away. Apparently a neighbour had suffered this fate; a young boy had fallen into the river, his father had jumped in to save him and they had both drowned.

I always think of my granddad when I see a rainbow, as on one of our many walks, he pointed out my first beautiful rainbow, and told me all about the pot of gold at the end of it.
In our garden at the front of the house, I had witnessed beautiful colours, which reminded me of the rainbow, whenever my uncles used oil or petrol and spilt a small amount. Being the helpful little child that I was, I took the gallon can up the hill at the back of the house, as I thought it would be so lovely to have our very own rainbow with the pot of gold at the end of it. When I explained why I had done this, my kind and gentle grandfather seemed to understand and did not reprimand me.

The day finally came when it was time to go back to England, as the war was now over. A few of our many ramblers, on hearing that we were going back, gave me a penny or a halfpenny. On the morning of our departure, I cried for my granddad to come to England with us. He explained he could not come as he had to look after the cows, and he did not have a ticket, so I gave him my few coppers and asked him to buy himself a ticket. He told my mother that I was a very special child and had a very kind nature, that I needed special handling. My aunty and uncles still remind me of this to this day.

I was never to see this granddad again as he passed away some four years later.

Chapter Two

Back in England my parents seemed to argue all the time and my mother seemed to cry from morning until night. I learnt the reason why when I was a bit older.

My mother took Anne and myself to Whitworth Park. She was soon due to have the next baby. We sat by the rhododendron bushes and my mother who always talked to me like a adult, sobbed deeply and kept saying "this is what your daddy has done to me".

I felt so guilty because he was my daddy, and heartbroken because she was so upset, and until this day I do not know if she meant he had made her pregnant, or was it the other thing that they were always arguing about.

A woman who shall remain nameless, lived in our upstairs front room as a lodger. My mother was a very telepathic person, and whilst we were in Ireland, my mother had dreamt that my father had something going on with this woman.

When my father came over to visit us in Ireland, my mother confronted him. My father admitted he had "caught her by the arse a few times". So this was the reason for my mothers crying and obvious heartache, and it was also the time when my father hitting me became a regular event.

I was given the job of tidying the kitchen table and washing up after meals, and as I was still young and not tall enough to reach, I placed a chair at the table, a chair at the cupboard to put the food away, and a third chair at the sink in the scullery, as there was no light in the scullery, someone would light a candle for me, until one night I knocked the candle over and set fire to the net curtain, so from then on I had to wash up in the dark.

The lodger eventually left our house to get married. My mother then found new lodgers, Mr and Mrs Carroll but my mum was not very fond of Mrs Carroll being in our house, as she said "when Mrs Carroll brings down the ashes in the mornings before lighting her fire, she stays in the kitchen talking for too long". My mother did not like this sort of intrusion, but after a few months the Carroll's found a house of their own and we now got a new lodger called Mary Tighe.

Mary worked as a waitress in the restaurant in a department store called Pauldens at All Saints. I remember her inviting me and my mother there for afternoon tea. Mary met and started courting a man called Luke McDermott, who was lodging with the family next door, my mother's sister Tess.

Mary stayed with us until just before she and Luke were married. They found a house in Ossary Street in Rusholme, settled down to wedded bliss as my mother put it, and Mary Tighe became Mary McDermott. Luke also had a sister called Mary Mc Dermott, so to distinguish between the two Mary's we called Luke's sister single Mary. Single Mary later went on to get married herself, but was always still referred to as single Mary.

The McDermotts and my mother always remained close friends; she went up to help deliver some of their six children, and was always known to them as Aunty Annie.

On October 27th 1946, my sister Elizabeth was born and the nurse named her 'the doll', as she was a very beautiful baby, with a mass of red hair. We had lots of visitors. All the aunties and uncles called to look at Elizabeth and great discussions took place regarding the red hair, it was decided that she had defiantly taken after the McHugh's side of the family.

In 1947 I started school, at six years old instead of five as, with her depression and the new baby to look after, my mother must have been lacking in energy and motivation to take me the five minutes walk to Dover Street school each day, plus I was a good help to her at home.

I loved going to school and I drew pictures of flowers on a small blackboard with chalk, for my mother, but when my mother came to pick me up I was really upset when the teacher would not let me take my work home.

1947 was a very severe winter, with very heavy snow and burst water pipes. The milkman could not deliver our milk as his horse and cart could not get around our cobbled streets.

I stood up in the class, told the teacher and classroom of pupils that we had burst pipes because of the snow, and the kitchen ceiling had fallen down. When I got home and told my parents what I had said, I immediately got strapped and sent to bed. I remember my pain and confusion at being strapped for telling the truth.

On August 17th 1948, my sister Jacqueline was born. I remember Anne, Elizabeth and Jacqueline all learning how to walk. Me or our mother would give Jacqueline a bottle of milk and something to eat, but there were no walks in the pram to the park or anywhere else. My mother only went out when she went to Mass, or out into the back yard where she and her sister Tess who lived next door would chat over the back wall.

As the eldest of the family I was always very grown up and responsible. We never had toys to play with, but I used to love making a doll's house out of a cardboard box for my sisters. I used to cut out the windows and door, then draw in curtains with a pencil and draw slates on the roof. I now realize this must have been the first signs of a homemaker.

I remember one day when the priest came to the school to talk about us making our first Holy Communion and first confession, I must have been six or seven years old.

The priest asked me what I would like to do when I am grown up, and without even having to think about it I replied, "I want to be a kind mammy, and have six children." The priest said to me "that can easily be achieved," and I came away feeling as if I had revealed my soul, and had confided my private thoughts, but felt as if they had not seemed important enough to the priest. Thank God I had not told him about my dream of standing on the alter rails in my first Holy Communion dress, and a boy from our infants class looking up at me admiringly and wanting to marry me!

When my mother and Tess were having one of their chats, if any of us children went out into the back yard we would be sent back inside. I had learnt at a very early age that if they gossiped about someone and she was O-F-F or was S-I-C-K these words were spelt out; it meant she was pregnant and a baby would soon be arriving.

On Sunday July 9th 1950, at the age of sixty-eight, my dear grandfather died of high blood pressure. My mother and I were at eleven o'clock mass in St Josephs Church on Plymouth Grove Longsight. At twelve o'clock we were walking down the church isle coming out of mass, when my mother started to cry. I asked "what is wrong mammy?", and she replied "I am walking behind my father's coffin".

It was not until the next Tuesday that someone delivered a message that my grandfather had died at twelve o'clock on Sunday. He had been buried on Tuesday morning, which meant that no one in the family in England had a chance to see him before he was buried.

People in those days did not have a telephone so one of my mother's family would have to go into town and telephone Patterson's the shop on the corner of our street. This was a dreadful time for me and my mother. They had bought me a doll for my ninth birthday, which was the next day but I remember sobbing and saying that anyone could have my doll if they would bring my granddaddy back.

My grandfather as a young man had gone to work in Scotland; he wanted to earn the money for his boat fare to America, which was three pounds. Having eventually earned the fare he sailed on a ship called The Furnessia and arrived in New York on April 25th 1905 to join his brothers Patrick, James, Owen, and Michael and his sisters, Mary Anne, Kate, Roselyn and Bridget.

One brother worked in Sing Sing prison; they were called key turners in those days, the other brothers worked as policemen, and his sisters worked as seamstresses.

My grandfather got a job down at the Grand Central Station, and continued to work in New York for six years. In 1911, on one of his trips back to Ireland to see his parents and brother John Jo, he saw some farmland for sale, near to where he was brought up. He had already bought a ticket for his return journey to America on a ship called The Titanic. He decided to purchase the farmland, and he then sent a matchmaker to visit Kate who lived at the Manor; he had met Kate in the past, and wanted to find out if she was still single. The matchmaker returned to report that she was single, so granddad told him to go back and offer her a proposal of marriage on his behalf, which she accepted, so the match was set.

My grandfather then sold his ticket for the titanic and bought the first cattle for the farm, He and Kate were married in 1912. My mother was born on January 22nd 1913.

She was called Bridget Anne but was nick-named 'baby'. Her brother Paddy was born exactly one year later on January 22nd 1914 and he was nick named 'Sonny'. My grandparents had ten children in total, five girls and five boys. Five later went to live and work in England, and five remained in Ireland, five got married and the other five remained single.

Now that my grandfather had died, we all knew we would never see him again. My mother had always talked of her great love for her father, and kept praying that his spirit would turn up to visit her. This used to frighten me.

Life was really tough now, as the parents never stopped fighting. My father on his summer holidays from the coalmine would go and work with my mother's brother Paddy who worked for a demolition firm called Connell and Finnegan. Every evening after work on the demolition site, all the men would go to the pub. On these two weeks of the year, my father would come home drunk every night, whereas the rest of the year he would only be drunk on Friday and Saturday nights

My mother who was not a drinker would get upset and angry. My father would start by opening the back door and kicking the cat and the dog out; sometimes he would kick them so hard they would bounce off the back yard wall.

My father never hit my mother, but me and my sister Anne would get it instead. Anne would answer back and stick up for herself, where as I would not dare to.

Being the eldest, I would have all the housework to do. When he came home he would look up at the clothes rack on the ceiling, where the washing would be drying and if the toes of the white socks were less than white, they would be put back in the sink, and

I would be thumped until they were clean.

He would then take each of the pans down from the hooks on the shelf to check if the bottoms of them were clean; if not, he would hit me with each one before throwing them into the sink.

My father had a cruel habit when he was telling me off, of clenching his fist and thumping me on the shoulder, as if to drum everything he was saying into me.

On one of these occasions, I had my first Holy Communion dress on, to have a photo taken, so I would have only been seven at the time. My father told me to get the washing up done and I said I would as soon as I take my dress off. He tore into me, ripping my beautiful white dress down the back, and pulled it off me. When I look at my Holy Communion photo, all I see is a beautiful young girl with a sad face, and sad, sad eyes.

One Saturday lunch time my sister Anne who was about ten years old was out collecting money for May Day. She was crossing Oxford Road when she got hit with a motorbike. She suffered a fractured scull and a broken collarbone, so ended up on a medical ward in the Manchester Royal Infirmary. Even though the hospital was only two streets away and Anne was unconscious, my mother did not visit Anne until later that night as she said she had to wash her hair. She then kept me up all the rest of Saturday night, so that at six a.m. I could go down to enquiries desk at the hospital and check how Anne was. I remember they said she was comfortable.

After Anne came out of hospital, one day she got a beating, so she threw the poker at my father. He then beat her until she passed out, or pretended to pass out, I am not sure which. When my mother heard about this, she informed my father that because of Anne passing out, and the head injury, she must not be beaten again. I remember thinking

I wish I had been hit by the motorbike, and then I would not get beaten again.

In 1952, my mother was once again pregnant and this time she went to St Mary's hospital for the birth. My three sisters were sent down to Ducey Street to my mother's sister Kate, who also had a few children of her own. Us four girls usually slept in one double bed but to my horror my mother instructed me to sleep in her bed with my father to keep him company. At eleven years old to have to sleep in the same bed as this man who had so often beaten me, was very uncomfortable and embarrassing, but she made the rules so I did as I was told and slept in her bed, with my nose up against the wall.

The next evening I saw my father cry for the first time ever. This was St George's day, and he was looking in the dressing table drawer for a bed jacket for my mother. He called me into the bedroom to tell me, "mammy had twins and they are both dead, and they were boys as well". The last part was the worst, as both of my parents had always wanted boys, and had until now only had four girls. So I understood my father's heartache but could not do anything about it, and would not know what to do, as I had never been shown any affection, not a kiss or a cuddle ever in my life from either of my parents.

My poor mother came home from hospital in an ambulance on Saturday afternoon. I was at the Gaelic League, as I used to go Irish dancing, and sometimes enter the competitions; I still have some of my certificates for the dancing.

The ambulance driver delivering my mother home from hospital had knocked on our front door, but my father did not hear him, so the driver had to knock again. My father later said he did not hear anyone at the door, as he had been out in the scullery peeling an onion. Until the day my mother died, she would throw this incident at my father, saying that he cared more about his belly and his onions than he did about her, when she had just lost her twins.

The twins had not been baptized because they were stillborn, so according to the church rules they had to be buried in unconsecrated grounds in a communal grave in Moston cemetery, as this was the only catholic cemetery at that time. It was bad enough to have lost their twins, but with not even a grave to visit this was a cruel way for my parents to be treated. My parents especially my mother would in this day and age have been offered counseling, but of course in those days it was not available.

For a lot of the rest of her short life, (dying at the age of sixty three,) my mother lived with severe depression. The only thing she was offered was Valium tablets, which she became addicted to, to keep the pain at bay. These were also taken every time my father was due home from the pub, in case of any argument, which would inevitably develop. The Valium became a major crutch for the rest of my mother's life and she also developed a compulsory hand washing disorder, where she would wash her hands hundreds of times a day. We also had to wash our hands every time we touched money, keys, or opened the front door, as we were told that my father touches the front door when he comes home from the pub, and that men go to the toilet and do not wash their hands.

Only on a rare occasion would we see our mother happy and she more or less took to her bed. If one of her sisters or friends were having a baby, or would become ill, she would go to help them, then come home and go back to bed.

On an odd occasion she and I would go to the Savoy, an Irish dance hall, as in her better days she had loved to dance and to sing. The ladies would sit on chairs around the edge of the room; no alcohol was allowed, only soft drinks. After the pubs closed at 10.30pm, the men would start to roll in and quite often there would be a fight between some of them. Luke McDermott, a family friend, was a doorman at the Savoy and would soon have the men put outside, where they would usually continue the fight.

My father would sometimes work the night shift at the coalmine, so my mother would lie in bed and after I had finished all my jobs, I would sit on a stool next to the coal fire in her bedroom. She would talk and talk until two or three o'clock in the morning, about her father, her childhood, and lots about the old days. I would keep falling asleep, and she would keep shouting at me to "wake up and don't fall into that fire."

My father would come home from work just after six in the morning and get me out of bed, to clean the ashes out of the fireplaces and light the fires. If I were not quick enough, due to being so tired because of being kept up most of the night, he would kick me in the bottom to hurry me up. Of course it usually happened that when he was in these moods, the fire would not light, so I would sneak some sugar and throw it on the fire, as I had seen my mother do on occasions. If I got caught, I would then be in trouble for wasting the sugar, but if the fire did not light I would be in trouble anyway.

I have a awful memory of one morning being to tired too get up and my father coming into my bedroom, pulling the blankets off me, and throwing a pan of cold water on me.

My mother was advised by her friend Posy that she must pull herself together. This fortunately triggered something in my mother, which was to help her for a while. I remember my mother saying, "I will show her. If Posy can be a nurse, then I can be a nurse". My mother joined the Red Cross, attending one evening a week and seemed to be a natural. She was full of enthusiasm and passed all her exams, and was then allowed a nurse's uniform, with a long hat, a bit like the nuns wore, and a red cross on her apron.

She was told to do her practical work at the Manchester Royal Infirmary in the casualty department. She was very excited about the job in casualty, as she said you never know what will come in next; it could be a road traffic accident, a drunken fight or a suicide.

I do not remember ever seeing her so enthusiastic and happy. She would sometimes be on first aid duties at the fetes and live shows, or at the Free Trade Hall, so whilst I was up on stage, doing my Irish dancing in my white blouse, green pleated skirt, and gold shawl pinned across my shoulder, my mother would be standing at the back in her uniform.

I felt so proud of her. She was also on duty when the premier of The African Queen starring Katharine Hepburn and Humphrey Bogart, came to Manchester. A film she talked about for years to come was 'The Egyptian'. This and the few mornings a week she had to work seemed to bring her alive again even if not for very long. She visited all her friends and relatives, as everyone had to see the uniform.

Eventually some of the enthusiasm wore off when she was sent to Whittington hospital and had to work on the men's ward, where all the Chester's beer drinkers were being nursed, which she reminded my father about regularly as he was a Chester's beer drinker.

She was then moved to a geriatric ward full of confused old people. She used to come home and say she had missed her lunch hour as someone had died, and she wanted to lay them out herself, as she would make them look nicer than the other nurses would. However, her world seemed to crumble again when she was transferred to a psychiatric ward under a male ward sister, called Sister Jackson. Sister Jackson had been caught a few times with his belt off, beating confused patients. This upset my mother dreadfully; she now sunk into a deep depression at work as well as at home, so she left the job.

After that, one thing that cheered her up was when she heard that Sister Jackson had been involved in a fatal accident and had been killed when he crashed his motorbike. She kept saying it served him right for beating those poor old people.

I often wondered when she was so upset at the patients being beaten, why she did not get this upset when I had been beaten. But the fact was that it would very often be something that my mother would tell him that would cause my father to beat me in the first place.

I always had a longing to be my mother's friend, and when my father would be out or at work and we were alone together, I would try to get her to sing. I taught myself to play the paper and comb and sometimes she would sit on the toilet and sing 'kisses sweeter than wine', or The Donkey Cart. I would be in my bedroom of course as soon as my dad came in she would be back in bed all depressed again.

One day I remember my father was out so my mother came into the kitchen in her nightgown. I was in the scullery doing the washing. I was a shy girl so could talk better when she could not see my face and I told her the dirty jokes that the girls at school were telling each other. These were very mild in comparison to what is told today.

A few days later my mother got up, got dressed, and then came down to the school. The headmistress Miss Hewarth called me into the office. I was then forced to tell the jokes to her in front of my mother, and then got a good strapping on the hands for telling them. This was my mother's idea of bringing me up properly, as she used to say!

All the pupils were terrified of Miss Hewarth; she had a very sinister looking face, she had potholes in her skin and wore dark glasses. Miss Hewarth had the pleasure of strapping me on several occasions, as I was regularly late for school in the mornings, and after lunch breaks. A few times she forced me to tell her why I was late, which was due to me having to light the fire, bring mammy her breakfast to bed and give my sisters the porridge which I had made the night before. During the lunch break it was more likely to be, go to the shop for bacon potatoes and cabbage, get them ready and put them in a pan on a low light for when my dad would come home from work. If he was on mornings he would be home for three o'clock, if on afternoons it would be 10.30pm. On occasions Miss Hewarth would check this out with my mother, who would totally deny everything, which made me look a liar, for which I would be strapped again, then go home and get belted by my father for having told our business to the head teacher. Cruelty at school, then go home to more cruelty.

Miss Hewarth suggested my mother take me to the doctors, as I was always tired, so off we went. The Doctor prescribed Dexedrine tablets for me, which made me keep blinking. I found out when I was older that these tablets give you lots of energy but are very bad for your nerves, and should never be prescribed for children.

Many years later, whilst visiting my aunty, I discovered Miss Hewarth, who had now retired, and had just moved into the house next door. She was out doing her garden. I had my new car, a Corsair, parked outside, and my lovely new son in my arms. I always went out wearing nice clothes make up and jewelry. My aunty re introduced me to Miss Hewarth, who said, "you have come on well haven't you? I would not have recognized you." I then took the opportunity to tell her I had never lied when I was at her school, and all those strappings were not warranted. I told her how things really were and she looked very upset, then she told me, "You are a credit to yourself, and you should be very proud of yourself."

I felt reborn and became a much more confidant person, now that I had put right some of the injustices.

As a child, the only time I was happy was when I was in hospital. I went to have my tonsils out at Wythenshawe hospital; I loved being in hospital, as everyone was so kind. When I came home, I caught pneumonia. Doctor Alexandra was sent for, and when he arrived my mother was at the shop across the road, as I was too ill to go. I told the doctor "I don't mind if I have to go into hospital again" so he said he would send an ambulance for me to go into Pendlebury Children's Hospital. I was really excited at the thought of returning to hospital, and felt as if I had organized it myself My father came to the children's ward to see me a few times on his way to work, as Agecroft Colliery Coal Mine was also in Pendlebury and not far from the hospital. I remember the secure feeling I had that he couldn't hit me in there. When I told him I am having nine injections a day, I remember thinking it is worth the nine injections just to be here and feel so safe.

After I had my tonsils out I gained weight as lots of people do and felt very self-conscious about it. My father then started to call me a 'big fat cow'. I have never been able to tell anyone all this, but now that I am putting it down on paper I hope the horrible memory will leave me.

For getting home from school late one evening, as a punishment my mother locked me in the cellar. I knew we had rats in the cellar, as my dad had put the cat down to catch them, but in the morning the cat had been eaten away where its legs joined its body, so needless to say I was terrified. Sometimes I would have to go down there to bring up the coal or to put money in the gas meter, but then I would have a candle and leave the door open ready to run up the steps, but this was different. I was now locked in the cellar in the dark, this was sheer terror.

I was also remembering that every time one of our cats had kittens or the dog would have pups, my father would drown them in a bucket in the cellar, he would then throw them into the dustbin. I used to find this dreadfully upsetting, and would later cry myself to sleep.

In 1955 one Saturday evening just before Christmas, I was arranging the Christmas cards on the mantelpiece in the kitchen. I was wearing a pink flared skirt and whilst reaching up with the cards, my skirt went into the fire and set alight. I ran out to the scullery and tried to put the flames out with cups of water but to no avail, so I started shouting up to my mother, who was upstairs in bed. I had a pin in my skirt instead of a button but could not open the pin to get the skirt off.

My father was in bed downstairs as he had been on nights. My mother, thanks to her Red Cross training, knew exactly what to do. She kept shouting instructions to my father to put his heavy overcoat around me, and roll me on the floor. This caused the flames to burn into me, but did put the fire out. An ambulance was called and I went off on my own to the Manchester Royal Infirmary, which was only a few streets away.

My mother later came down to the MRI and was told that I had severe burns and was being transferred to the burns unit at Booth Hall hospital where skin grafts would have to be done.

Each patient in the severe burns unit was in a cubicle of their own. A day or two later, my mother came to visit me, and told me that the girl in the next room, Joan Wright, was also from The Holy Name School, which was the school I attended. Joan was three years younger than me, so was in a different class. Her nightgown had caught fire on Christmas morning whilst she was opening her presents, and the poor girl was burnt from head to foot.

I eventually had the skin grafts on my stomach, which was severely burnt, by cutting skin from my arms, the front of my legs and my thighs. I had nineteen stitches above my knee where the skin was cut off my right thigh. I felt so proud later when a nurse told me, that we had all donated skin towards Joan's grafts, as she had virtually none of her own left unburnt.

One morning a cleaner was washing my cubicle floor and I asked her how Joan was but she told me that Joan had died.

I became very ill and thought it was due to the shock of Joan dying. My mothers brother Tom came over from Ireland to see me, as he had been told I had been anointed. I knew this only happens when you are dying, so was frightened that that was going to happen to me too. Anyway I did not die and am still here to tell the tale as they say.

About a week later as I started to slightly recover I saw it said STRICTLY ISOLATED on my room door. I could of course only see this when the door was left open. I also had a cage over me on my bed to stop the blankets pressing on my burns and skin grafts. I still have dreadful scars on my stomach, which I was warned would never disappear, as the burns were so severe.

When my mother came to visit me she told me I had caught Scarlet Fever possibly from the blankets in the ambulance, and that is why I had been so very ill. She also told me I would probably lose all my hair.

Some weeks later I was transferred to an upstairs ward, so then had some company. I made a good and close friend of a girl called Dallas Tomlinson who lived in Bacup. I had to learn to walk again and Dallas used to help me with the aid of a food trolley.

When I finally went home, Dallas used to write to me. All my letters were first read by my mother, until one day a letter arrived, where Dallas told me she had a boy friend. From then on, all the letters were burnt before I could read them, in case I got any ideas of having boy friends, so that was the end of Dallas.

After leaving the hospital, I had to wear thick stockings, so as no one would see the scars where the skin was removed from the front of my legs for the skin grafts.

One day my mother had been out to the shop and when she came home I was standing at the front door without my stockings. My mother saw me, chased me into the kitchen and went berserk at my father for letting me stand at the front door, where everyone could see my scarred legs. I was shocked to hear she was so ashamed of me, or was it she did not want to let the neighbours see what they had let happen to me? That was an end to my feeling of being glad to be home.

A few months earlier whilst at a cookery lesson, the cookery teacher's watch had gone missing. This was the day before I got burnt and went into hospital and apparently when the loss of the watch was discovered I got the blame, and my bedroom was searched, as I was a easy target as I was not there to defend myself. I could not forgive my parents for believing it was me. We never did find out who the girl was who took the watch, but I remember thinking that if I had died, everyone would have thought that it had been me.

I had to wear a knitted hat as due to the scarlet fever, I had gone bald. My hair seemed to refuse to grow, and they said that was due to the stress.

I was sent back to school in the summertime, stockings, hat and all, which I found very embarrassing. The only good thing was that I would soon be leaving school, so there was some hope on the horizon.

When my hair did eventually re-grow, it grew lovely and thick and curly, so that was a little bonus for all my embarrassment. Another bonus was that every Saturday evening we had our hair washed with Derbark soap, and my father used to go through our hair with a nit comb, as we had long hair so as to be able to wear ringlets for the Irish dancing.

The nit comb used to really hurt and he hated the job so would be none too gentle. By going bald I used to avoid this, and don't think I ever had to have the nit comb again.

I apologize if this has been depressing to the reader, but it was my life as it was, and often even worse, as there is a lot I have left out. It truly was often a living hell.

I can only write the truth as this is my autobiography, but I must point out that I have long ago forgiven my parents for everything they did to me.

We did have a few nice days in my childhood, like when Posy would come to visit. I would make the tea, and go across the road to Patterson's shop for a cake and would always hope a nice big chunk would be left over for me.

We never went on holidays like other families. I only remember a very few times visiting relatives apart from the aunties who lived near by. My uncle Paddy, who was my mothers brother, lived in Urmston, so one Sunday we went to visit him, his wife Mary and their children, Joseph, who is three years older than me, and Patricia, three months older than me. (Patricia now lives in New Zealand.) We went for a walk in a meadow and collected daisies and my cousins showed us how to make daisy chains. This was delightful and a lovely day.

Another outing was to visit my mother's aunty Molly and Uncle Jack. Molly had quite a large house with a pantry; I had never seen a pantry before.

At teatime we had the biggest fresh cream cakes I had ever seen, they were really delicious, so much later when everyone was engrossed in conversation, I went into the pantry, closed the door, and ate another cream cake without being discovered. I can still remember the joy of this, as our shop, Patterson's, did not sell cakes like these.

We had a family day out in Southport, where my mother fell in love with a pearl necklace. My father gave her the money to go inside the shop and purchase the pearls, so peace reigned for the rest of that day.

A different year we had a day out at Blackpool. We all sat on the sands with a buckets and spade and my father went and bought a jug of tea which we had with our sandwiches, brought from home. Anne and I took a bucket full of sand with us on the train, so as we could play with it in our back yard when we got home.

Only a few times did I go on school trips, once to a place called Castletown where we went down the Blue John Mines, which was a fascinating place. The other trip was to Southport, where me and a few of the girls went on a boat on the lake. We accidentally overturned the boat but the water was only knee deep as it was a manmade lake, so there was no problem and our teacher sent us to the swimming baths to dry our clothes off. When I got home I told my mother what had happened, and was told I would never again be allowed on a school trip, and I never was.

I and a few girls from school went to the swimming baths. I was practising my Irish dancing and I slipped. The girls thought I was swimming but I was actually drowning. When I got home I told my parents what had happened and they then told me I could not go swimming again incase I drowned. I had the same problem with riding a bike. We did not have a bike, but I would not be allowed to ride a friend's bike in case I fell off it. So cannot now ride a bike or swim.

I especially loved our weekly school trips to the Manchester Museum every Thursday morning. We used to see and discuss lots of interesting subjects, including the Egyptian Mummies on display in a glass case. There was an art room on the top floor of the Museum, where we would then sit and draw the chosen subject.

One summer afternoon, the schoolteachers took all the pupils on several school buses to the Free trade hall. This was considered as educational, so we did not need permission from the parents. The Halle Orchestra was playing classical music, which I had never heard before; one of the tunes was Green Sleeves. I thought this was quite heavenly, and still enjoy the lovely memory.

That night after the school trip I stayed up most of the night with my mother. When I was going to bed it was just becoming daylight. I opened my bedroom window and could smell smoke. I ran down the street to the unused shop on our corner as I knew there were people living upstairs above the shop, and I could see that the shop was on fire. I banged on the door and woke the family up. The story was printed in The Manchester Evening News, which said I had saved these peoples lives.

This was the first of three occasions when I have been told that I have saved people's lives.

Jacqueline my baby sister was always very quiet and was my dad's pet. At weekends she would walk to the end of the street to meet him coming home from the pub. He would usually pick her up and carry her home; on an odd occasion he would give her a three-penny piece. Yet when my mother ordered a Dandy comic for me and a Beano comic for Anne, my Father insisted my mother cancel these comics, "Because they are not worth it".

I have always worked hard sometimes being employed by two or even three different companies at any one time, I have demonstrated makeup, sold vitamins, jewellry, held clothes parties or whatever to make money, as well as doing my full time day job.

I have always bought nice things for myself when I could afford them and often wonder if it is because of my fathers words, "BECAUSE THEY ARE NOT WORTH IT'. I believe that what keeps me well balanced is not harboring any hatred or bad thoughts. I have always been the eternal optimist; I look for the good in others, and always focus good and positive energy on the people in my surroundings.

Uncle Tom, one of my mother's brothers, used to work at Fords of Dagenham. His hobby was ballroom dancing. He would come to visit us for a few days, and his beautiful dance partner would stay in a guesthouse. My mother bought Anne and myself two floral dresses with white bibs, and frills around the bibs, Elizabeth and Jacqueline also got a new dress each, and we were all very excited. When Tom arrived I told him we had got these dresses especially for him coming, so I was told off again and told "you do not tell anyone anything, and if anyone asks you anything, you must always say, I don't know", so for the remainder of the visit I kept as quiet as possible, so much so, that whilst uncle Tom was out doing his dancing that evening my mother went to bed early and she told me to tell Tom that she had 'gone fishing'. So determined not to say the wrong thing, I wrote it on a piece of paper and put it on the kitchen table, Tom thought my mother had written it, he thought it was very funny and laughed a lot, so I had done the right thing for once.

Elizabeth was a beautiful looking girl, with lovely rich red hair and a lovely personality, I used to dress her up in a long skirt and anything nice I could find and she would dance and twirl around the kitchen. We always called her 'the doll', as that is what the nurse called her when she was born.

Elizabeth and I were great friends. If my mother was out on one of her First Aid courses, I would send Elizabeth to Patterson's to buy two cream cakes and a bottle of lemonade. We had a book so items of food would be put on the book and paid for every Friday. I would then pray that my mother would not check the book and see what we had bought, but if it was discovered, I knew Elizabeth would not get hit anyway.

Anne had a completely different nature from Elizabeth and Jacqueline. She had a more confident and mischievous personality and would sometimes become very angry. She had a squint in one eye and she wore glasses with a plaster patch on her good eye; our mother explained that this was to make the lazy eye work.

My mother's friend Mary McDermott tried to explain to our mother that, it was because Anne did not like what she saw in the mirror that made her angry. My mother said that maybe that was true as Anne became even worse when she caught impetigo and had to wear the Venetian Violet dye around her mouth. I used to feel really sorry for her. My father started to call her 'the witch', which she did not seem to object to. She used to pull really funny faces behind his back, and say " which witch? - which witch?" and she later admitted that she quite enjoyed the scenario; at least she looked for the positive in the situation. Chatting about it years later Anne and I had a good laugh about all of this.

On a few occasions I came home from school and asked my father if I could go to the cinema with one of my friends. He would say, "When the washing up is done, the kitchen floor brushed and mopped, and the front room floor polished."

I would very enthusiastically do these jobs, then to be told, "It is too late now". On one of these evenings, my friend called for me but he told her I had gone to bed, when I was actually sitting in the kitchen. I soon learnt I would never be allowed out in the evenings, so I gave up that idea.

If my parents had to go shopping on a Saturday, I would be told that I must not let any of my sisters go out to play in the street. I would be given the stairs, hall and landing to clean, the kitchen and scullery floor to wash, then polish the red tiles on the kitchen floor. Every second tile was red and black, so I only had to polish the red ones.

Anne would park herself behind an armchair, next to the shoe cupboard in the kitchen. There were two arm chairs in the kitchen; one was my mother's the other my father's.

In those days everyone lived in their kitchen. As I would be trying to wash or polish the kitchen floor, Anne would hurl shoes at me. Even though she was three years younger than me, I was nervous, knowing her misbehaviour would get me blamed, as I being the eldest, was always left in charge, and got blamed for what ever went wrong, as something always did if Anne was left at home.

To protect myself, I would then get behind the other arm chair, my mother's chair and throw the shoes back at her, which as well as me being hit with the shoes also meant I could not continue with my jobs. I used to beg my parents to take Anne with them, and leave the other two at home instead, as I found it a pleasure looking after the other two, and there certainly would never be any shoe throwing, or fighting.

But those were the days when children were seen and not heard, old enough to do the work and to be left in charge but not old enough to be listened to.

On one of these occasions after the shoe throwing, Anne decided she was going out to play in the street, which she knew was strictly against the rules, but she also knew it would be me who would be in trouble for allowing her to go out, so I ran to the front door to stop her, I pushed my hand flat on the door to close it, and my hand went straight through the glass, cutting my wrist. I took myself down to the Manchester Royal casualty department and had six stitches in my wrist. Later when my parents came home, even with the six stitches and my arm in a sling, I got beaten for breaking the glass in the door.

Our mother used to use Anne as a spy. One Saturday evening when I was going to confession, as we did every Saturday, Anne was told to follow me and see if I really did go to church.
Fully knowing the trouble she would cause, she went home and said she saw me get on the back of a motorbike. How I ever survived that beating I will never know. I did not know anyone with a motorbike, and even now, I have still never been on a motorbike.

On a different occasion Anne was sent to follow my father, then mischievously went home and told my mother that he had gone into a building with a green door, next door to a pub on Upper Brook Street. The next week my mother went to visit a clothes shop in that area, owned by a Jewish lady called Madam Rose. My mother enquired about the building with the green door, to be informed it is a nightclub, where prostitutes sometimes hang out.
There was almost murder committed in our house, due to these stories, which Anne later finally gave in and admitted she had made up. But of course she knew she could not be hit because of the fractured scull. The effects of this went on for years, when every time a Frankie Vaughan record called 'Green Door' was played on the radio.
Some of the words were, 'I wonder what goes on behind the green door?' and another line was, 'green door what's that secret you're keeping?' My mother used to go mad every time this song came on the radio.
Recently at a family funeral when Anne, me and some of our cousins were reminiscing about all of this, Anne's comments were, "if you are going to make up a story and tell a lie, you may as well make it a good one."

Occasionally we would have a visit from a nun called Sister Augustine and she would of course be put into the front room, which my mother kept as the best room, the room only used for visitors. I would be sent to the kitchen to make tea, and my mother would be doing her usual thing, saying how hard she works keeping the house clean and how naughty the children were. She would never tell the nun the truth, that I was the only one who had to do the cleaning. I would come back into the room with the cups of tea and get a good telling off from the nun for not helping my mother with the housework. If only she knew, if only anyone knew.

My mother had an aunty who was a nun; she was my grandmother's sister, so my mother had decided years ago that she wanted her four daughters to become nuns. She had decided that I would become a white sister, which was a nun who wore a white habit instead of a black one. Once the white sisters enter the convent they would never visit the outside world again. Occasionally on a Saturday my mother would take me to the Good Shepherd Convent in Blackley to visit to the nuns and I was informed that when I am old enough to become a nun, this is the convent my mother had chosen for me. My other sisters, she said, would be black nuns, so would be placed in a different convent, with the Sisters of Charity.

On our way home from school, me and one or two of my friends, usually Ellen Lynch who lived on Grafton Street, and Rene Davis who lived near the Dental Hospital, would sometimes call into the Holy Name Church. We would sit in the church and I would recite some of the ghost stories I had heard as a child in Ireland; my friends loved the stories and often asked me to repeat them. One evening after school me and one of my friends called into the church. On the right hand side of the church was a small chapel called the Strata Chapel, we walked straight in, and there laid out in a coffin was Father Dudley. We had not been told that one of the priest had died, so were horrible shaken, and stood there paralyzed to so unexpectedly see a dead body, but it cured me of telling my ghost stories in church, so that was the end of that bit of relaxation.

Uncle Paddy my mother's brother called to see us, to tell us that his father in law had drowned himself in the Manchester Ship Canal, and would be laid out in their house the next evening. They were now living in Norwood Road Stretford.

I had never met this man, but the next evening much against my wishes, I was sent with my father to the wake, as my mother was in bed and had not wished to attend; I had not recovered from the father Dudley shock, and the last thing I wanted to see was another dead body. When we arrived, the coffin was in the front room and thankfully the room was almost full of mourners. My father, who was standing in the hall behind me, raised his knee up high and kicked me into the room. I almost died of fright, but at least I was not to close to the coffin.

Later, when I told my mother what had happened, she said he had always been frightened of dead bodies, so would not have wanted to go into the room himself.

This sad event had given my mother new ideas, as for years she had been saying, "I wish I was dead" so now she started saying that she was going to throw herself in the canal. On the rare occasion she would go out, she would sometimes come home and say " I was going to throw myself in the canal, I don't know what stopped me". I used to feel so extremely upset at this, as I did love my mum, and used to think how does she think we would feel if she did something like that, and we would be left behind with all the grief.

I knew she had lost her twins, but she still had us, even though we were girls and not boys, as both of my parents had always wanted boys.

Every one or two hours my mother used to ask me for a cup of tea and two Aspros which were for her headache, and I made myself a promise, that when I grow up I will never get headaches. I have now been grown up for a lot of years and I do believe in mind over matter, whether that is the reason or not, I never get headaches.

When my father would be out in the pub, my mother would sometimes send me for ten Craven A cigarettes, but on this occasion they only had Woodbines, which were stronger. My mother took two then told me to hide the rest in the sewing machine drawer, as they would do for if she was ever desperate.

One night my father came home from the pub and found the cigarettes in the drawer. He asked my mother had she smoked two of them, to which she replied. "No I am too ill to smoke".

I was upstairs in bed asleep, two of us slept at the top of the bed, and two at the bottom. I was at the bottom of the bed, which had been purchased for us from Fahey's second hand shop. My father started battering my head and accusing me of smoking the cigarettes.

My mother thought he was going to kill me or had already done so. She started screaming and he went down stairs, got a milk bottle and threw it at the window next to the bed where she was lying in her room, smashing the window. She later said she thought he had already killed me and was then going to kill her for screaming.

The next day my father, for the first time in his life, sent me for headache tablets and I was only too pleased to get out of the house. I remember it was a lovely sunny day and my father was singing and replacing the broken panes of glass. I remember thinking why can't he sound so happy more often. I used to think maybe he is always in a bad mood as he is frightened of being killed down the coal mine, like so many other miners, or was it because my mother's tongue sometimes used to know no boundaries. She would try to embarrass him in front of us; if he was looking at the Manchester Evening News paper, my mother would say to us "don't think he is reading the paper because he cannot read or write, he is only looking at the pictures," on other occasions when he would come home drunk, my mother would cruelly say, " Thanks god the twins were taken, as they would probably also have come home drunk like their crooked footed father".

One Friday night my mother was upset and could not sleep and my father was on the night shift so she called me downstairs, and told me she had dreamt of Our Lady standing with flowers at her feet. Being a telepathic person, she knew something was terribly wrong, so she wanted me to stay up with her, which I did for quite a few hours.

At nine o'clock on the Saturday morning, the police knocked on our front door to inform my mother that her sister Kate's husband, Paddy Mannion had been seriously hurt down the coalmine, when the ceiling, only three feet high, had collapsed on top of him.

Four days later, Mannion died, leaving his wife and six children. I always remember Mannion as being a devoted father. Usually he would be sitting in a armchair, a child on each knee and a child on each arm of the chair, they all adored him. I used to wish I had a kind daddy like that. Mannion had planned, that when he came home from work on Saturday morning, he was going to look after the children, as whilst waiting in the city centre for a bus to go to work, he had spotted a black coat in Lewis's shop window, which he said would really suit his wife Kate, so Friday night before going to work, he gave her the money for the coat, and said she could go to town on Saturday morning, when he got home from work. Of course he never returned. Kate went and bought the coat the next week as this had been Mannion's wish, and wore the coat to her husband's funeral in Moston cemetery.

Tricia Rooney used to visit us occasionally; she was my mother's cousin. I was always delighted to see her, and she was one of the few people who seemed to know a lot of what I went through.

Tricia worked at Kellogg's cornflakes and earned good money, she always seemed to wear nice clothes and have her hair set, which I admired. We got on well and I liked her sense of humour.

On one of Tricia's visits, it was Christmas Eve and I was about to make a trifle for the Christmas dinner. Aunty Liz in Ireland had sent us a nice turkey, which was roasting in the oven.

Because the atmosphere felt so nice, I went into the front room, and brought out our best and only crystal bowl. I placed the jelly into the bowl, put the bowl on my left arm, went out into the scullery and as there was no table out there, picked up the kettle of boiling water and poured it into the bowl. The bowl of course smashed and I was left pouring boiling water on to my arm, so scalded myself.

Tricia took me to the Manchester Royal Infirmary and when I was all bandaged up she said to me " do you know, if it was not for your regular visits, the MRI would probably close down". She was laughing as it was only one week earlier, when going to the shop for my mother I had climbed over a fence, ripped the inside of my knee on a nail and had to have it stitched, and only a few months earlier, on my way to school, ran into a spike in a wall, where the iron railings had been removed to help the fight during the war, so of course down to the infirmary, to have the side of my forehead stitched. So Tricia was right I was a really good customer at the MRI and still have all the scars to prove it.

Tricia a few years later helped me to leave home, as she said I had put up with enough.

Another person who understood some of the suffering I endured through my father, was my cousin Joe Martin, whose family lived next door; his mother Tess and my mother were sisters. Joe used to also get severe beatings from his father, and used to tell me that his family knew when I was about to get beaten, as they would hear the radio turned up loud.

Joe and I are still good friends, maybe because we had such a lot of suffering in common.

Joe has two lovely sisters Ellen and Mary and three brothers.

My mother always favoured Ellen and used to invite her into our house when she should have been at school.

She would tell Ellen she must not tell anyone, or they would both be in trouble and they would both then enjoy tea and biscuits together, my mother loved to talk and would have enjoyed telling Ellen all her stories.

Tess, my mother's sister, who had always lived next door to us, later moved to a house in Fallowfield, as the houses in Norwood Street where we had been brought up were due to be demolished within the next few years. I knew my mother would miss Ellen's company but all the neighbours were gradually being re-housed.

In years to come, Tess was a person I enjoyed visiting when I was married, as we both then lived in Fallowfield. She was a most amusing and entertaining person and with the funny way she looked at life, she was extremely good company.

Tess and her husband Joe later on in life decided to run a pub in Salford. As I was married by then I would not be allowed in a pub, but used to hear a lot of very amusing stories of after hours drinking, and people falling asleep on the pool table. Different members of the family used to say it was the best laugh in Salford, and all had a great time.

I sometimes used to wish I could be there to share in the laughter and the fun.

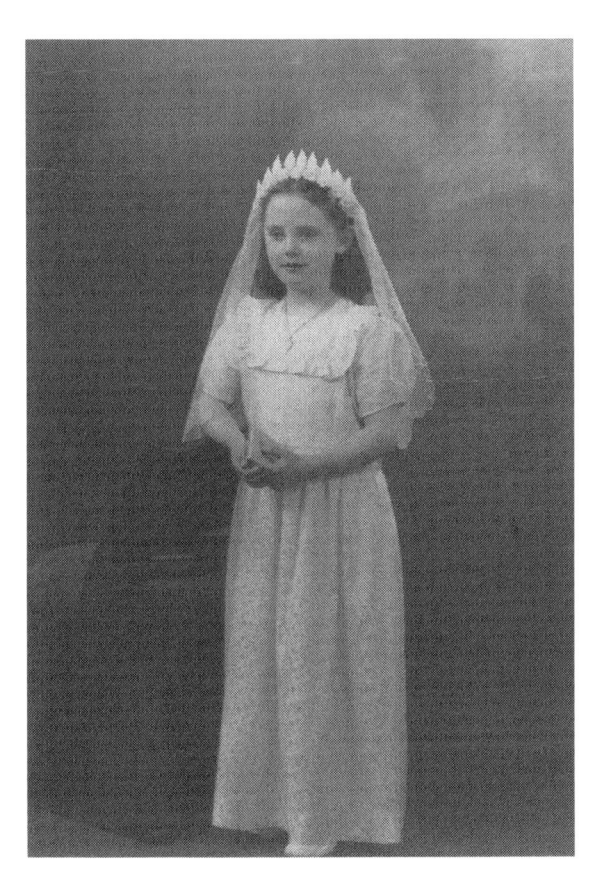

First Communion

Chapter Three

After leaving school I found my first job at Red Rose Works in Longsight as a machinist, making children's designer clothes; this company gave training to girls like myself who had just left school. The wages were three pounds five shillings a week, which today would only buy ten cigarettes. My parents told me that I had to pay three pounds for my keep, so was left with five shilling for bus fares, dinner money, stockings, and lipstick (which of course I was not allowed to wear, so would wait until I was out of the house every morning before applying it). Most days I would walk the four or five bus stops to work as the bus fare money would run out and on the last one or two days of the week sometimes my dinner money would run out too, so on those days I would walk over to the police station on Stockport road and watch the dog handlers train the police Alsatians dogs, as a way of taking my mind off the food, I also found this pastime very interesting.

I was obviously not in a position to buy clothes, so one day I borrowed my mother's aqua green cardigan to wear to work so it looked as if I had something new. This was her good cardigan she saved for when she might go to the Irish dance hall and would wear it with her white blouse and black skirt.

One of the girls I worked with, Ann Gest, asked me if she could borrow the cardigan as she was going out that night. I did not have the guts to say NO, and could not tell her it was my mother's. Ann had promised to bring the cardigan back the next morning, but she came into work and said she had forgotten it.

On Sunday morning my mother said she might go to the Savoy that night if she felt up to it. I was desperately worried, so instead of going to mass, I got a bus up to Levenshulm as Ann Gest had told me she lived at number 11 Anson Estate. But I found that Anson Estate was a large council estate, with lots of streets and roads, so lots of number elevens. I walked around and knocked on as many number elevens as I could, as I had only one hour, and still had to get a bus home to make it appear that I had been to mass. No one knew of a girl called Ann Gest, so my mother of course discovered the loss of the cardigan.

I told my mother I had worn it to work, as I had nothing else to wear, and would bring it home on Monday. Monday evening as promised I arrived home with the precious cardigan, but my mother in her nightgown got out of bed, came into the kitchen and put the cardigan in the fire. She said, "That will teach you to borrow my clothes." This was the only time I had ever worn anything of hers. I can still remember the beautiful cardigan burning, and thought she is spiting herself to spite me. She could just have let me keep it, since I really did not have much to wear to my first job, and when I could see all the other girls of my age had been bought new clothes. This incident did make me realize, now that I was working I needed more clothes so needed to earn more money with which to buy them, as five shillings a week was no good.

When I had been at the police station watching the dog training, I had noticed a very large building called Pownalls pyjamas factory, so one lunchtime I went in and applied for a job. They explained that it was section work so I would not be making the whole article; you were paid according to the amount you produced, and as I was a experienced machinist, they offered me a job. I was quite happy to be able to earn decent money, so worked away like a little beaver for a few months. I also applied at the police station to become a policewoman, and had three interviews. I was told I would be placed in D Division and I would get one pound ten shillings per week 'shoe money' on top of my wages, but at the moment I was five foot four and a half inches tall and needed to be five foot five. I was told to come back when I had grown half an inch, which he said he was sure I would do. I did have every intention of going back, as I would love to have become a policewoman, but never quite got around to it.

I then saw a advert for Linda Gays Ladies Fashions near Manchester city centre, so I decided as I was experienced in children's wear and pyjamas, I could now learn to make ladies dresses, so could make my own clothes. A Jewish family of four brothers owned the company. I was interviewed by Mr David, one of the brothers, and just knew I was going to be very happy working for them.

At home we bought a second hand Jones sewing machine, and I got 'stuck in', as they say. First of all I made my sister Jacqueline a beautiful dressing gown to wear when she went into hospital, I remember being excited, and very proud of my creation and when Jacqueline came home from the hospital she said everyone had admired it.

At lunch time I used to go to Goldberg's, the fire salvage shop next door to the Regal cinema, which was only around the corner from Linda Gay's. There I would buy good material which would have been salvaged from factory fires, at very little cost. I would copy some of the designer dresses we made at Linda Gays and take them to work to be over-locked, and to have any buttons put on professionally by a button machine operator. I was very proud of my dresses. We were allowed music all day to speed up production and I bought the record "O please stay by me Diana", which we played most of the day for nearly a week as everyone loved it so much; most of the girls would sing along which made a nice happy working environment.

My cousin, Winifred McHugh, came to live with us for six months. Winifred had been working and living in, at the County Hotel in Stretford, so when she left the job she had nowhere to live, as she was not getting on with her mother at the time. Winifred was three months older than me. She used to save all her old lipsticks, melt them down and make new colours, which I found to be quite amusing, and we were both interested in fashion, like most girls are at that age. I had the back room, a very small box room with a single bed, which Winifred and I shared, one of us at the top and the other at the bottom. .

I then went to see my boss, Mr David, to see if he would give Winifred a job. He said they had no vacancies for a machinist, but could use a girl to pack dresses in the showroom.

The company later put an advert in the Manchester Evening News, advertising Linda Gays dresses and they photographed Winifred wearing one of their dresses for the paper. She looked great and I felt very proud of her, especially as I had got her the job in the first place. That night Winifred's dad Paddy came and took us both to a Irish club in High Lane Chorlton; he said he was proud of his beautiful stylish young ladies.

Winifred and I were crossing Stretford Road when a motorbike ran over her foot and broke her big toe. I took her to the hospital, the casualty department was crowded as there had been a explosion at the Petra Chemical plant, and lots of suffering people were sitting around burnt, and suffering from shock.

Around about this time my mother made a major blunder. A young Irishman called Paraic O'Toole came to live in our spare room. He was a real charmer. Paraic used to sometimes sit on the stool in my mother's bedroom and chat to her and tell her stories of Ireland. They spent hours discussing Irish politics; she seemed to really enjoy his company, and would spend much more time in the kitchen in the evenings.

Paraic would put on the music called' Wheels' and teach my mum to dance the Cha Cha. Paraic also had a record called 'Sorter on the boarder' which my mum and I both loved. Mum went out and bought some stick-on paper to put onto the kitchen window fan light so as the people next door could not look in and see her dancing. She did on these occasions look very happy. Paraic seemed to take over the running of the house, and used to boss me and Winifred about, telling us what jobs we had to do, and that we could not go out until everything was done. The strange thing was my parents did not interfere. My father had said things like this to me in the past so I wondered if he had given Paraic the idea. If Paraic saw either me or Winifred wearing lipstick he would say in a stern voice, remove it or I will wash your faces with the floor cloth. Winifred finally got out of this by saying her father had always allowed her to wear lipstick and she intended to ask him to come and tell Paraic this, so Paraic backed down for the first and only time, but not with me.

41

Eventually Winifred left us and she went back to her family home and to her parents.

As for Paraic he worked at the same coalmine as my father, and told my mother in one of their chats, that he did not need to work as a miner, as he was only down the pit to steal the explosives, which he had hidden under his bed in a suitcase until he could take them over to Ireland. I remember my parents seemed to be very nervous of asking him to leave, but somehow it finally happened and he was gone. My mother told us all a few times "we could have been blown sky high" but it never seemed to dawn on her, that she was the only person who had wanted him in the house in the first place.

Linda Gay's eventually closed down, so Winifred and myself found new jobs. She was now living back in Stretford, so found a job closer to home. She met a really nice man called Eddie and she brought him to Manchester to meet me. The three of us went to see the latest new film South Pacific and then out for a meal. Winifred and Eddie appeared to be very happy together, and she confided to me, that she hoped he might ask her to get engaged. Only a few months later, however Winifred's dreams were shattered.

Eddie and his two brothers were out in a car one Saturday evening, when the car skidded and crashed into a chemist shop window in Chorlton and all three brothers were killed. Their poor mother was completely devastated. She had only recently been diagnosed with cancer but a very strange thing happened after she buried her three sons, her cancer went away. A few years later, Winifred decided she would visit her aunty in New Zealand and she stayed there for a few months. As she was about to return to England, a young man friend called Roy, who was giving her a lift to the boat, decided he did not want to lose her and proposed marriage. Winifred accepted the proposal, and she and Roy later had two handsome sons. She has remained in New Zealand ever since, apart from two holidays home to see the family in England. I went over and spent some time with her in her beautiful split level beach side house in November 2002, we had a incredible amount to talk about, it was a wonderful and sentimental holiday, she made me promise to go back and stay again soon, as she is sadly no longer able to fly due to ill health.

After Linda Gay's closed down, I went to a company called John England's and enquired about a office job, as I thought I would meet a nicer type of people in a office. The man who did the interview said that as I had no office experience, I would have to start as a filling clerk. I quite soon graduated to become a credit sanction clerk having control of customers accounts, and really enjoyed this. I made a lovely friend, a Irish girl called Bridie Duffy. Bridie and I had lots of laughs together and became very close. At Christmas I bought her a Max Factor set with perfume and cologne. She was overjoyed and said I should not have spent so much on her but she bought me a long beautiful umbrella with a hooked handle and a frill around the top, I had never seen a umbrella like it so glamorous and sophisticated, so we had both been very generous with each other. On Christmas Eve, some of the ladies had brought alcohol in to work and Bridie and I were given a few drinks of something. We had never had alcohol before so it went to our heads and I came up with the idea that we had better get a bus into town and sit in a cinema until this strange feeling wore off. We went to the Odeon and giggled our way through the film, until we felt fit to go home and I remember thinking that what ever happens I must not lose my beautiful umbrella, or leave it in the cinema. Bridie and I remained friends for a lot of years, even after we had both married and had children, she worked as a wages clerk in Lewis's in Manchester so I would go and have lunch with her in the staff canteen.

I was happy working in John England's and loved having my own desk, but the wages were not as much as I had been earning in the factories, so I got myself a great part-time job as a receptionist at the Essex Hotel on Oxford Road, working evenings and weekends. I was interviewed by an elderly couple with grey hair, Miss Goodier the proprietor and Mr Charles the manager. They told me I was very suitable and they looked forward to me joining their team. My uniform was a plain black jumper a straight black skirt and a stiff starched white collar fastened at the front with a brooch. I was extremely happy working in this environment. The Russian Cossack dancers were putting on a show at Belle View and stayed at our hotel for about a week; they gave all the staff complimentary tickets for the show, which was the first live show I had ever seen and really enjoyed.

One day my mother decided to call into the Essex Hotel to enquire how I was doing. The daytime receptionist told her that Miss Goodier and Mr Charles had gone to The Midland Hotel for lunch. My mother, as usual thinking the worst, assumed that the pair had gone to the Midland and booked a room for the afternoon. She promptly told the receptionist that she would not have her daughter working with such people, and that I would not be coming into work again. When I got home that evening my father told me I was not to put my nose in the door of that hotel again, and that he would collect my wages and tell the bosses what he thought of them. I tried to reason with my parents that the bosses were an elderly couple, and with a hotel of their own, why would they book into another hotel, but to no avail.

So I then found a job as an usherette in the Rivoly cinema, locally known as the (flea pit) to earn some extra money. This also kept me out of the house, as I was not allowed to go out at night, so I was quite happy to work the extra hours. It was the first time I had ever seen the beautiful film star Kim Novak in a film. I stayed for quite a few months until again I got the idea, now that I was experienced, to try to get further up the ladder.

A new company was opening opposite Granada studios called Bollin House, and they were looking for experienced credit sanction clerks to work in their legal department.
Brand new offices, new desks, all new Dictaphones and typewriters, this was a fabulous opportunity and I felt very lucky to have it.
Our office manager was a handsome smart young man in his twenties called Peter Wright and Mr Bailey, a well-spoken man in his forties, was our legal advisor.
The girls in our office were Iris, aged thirty-six, Kathy my age, who had worked as a secretary at Palmolive, plus we had two girls who were our typists. We were held in high esteem by the staff in all the other offices. With a great job like this, I left the flea pit and went to the Odeon Cinema in town for an evening job, a much nicer place to work and closer to Bollin House.
Mr Saunders, the Odeon manager, employed me and gave me a smart burgundy and gold braid uniform. All the part time girls used to

stand on parade in our uniforms each evening, as Mr Saunders checked that we each looked totally smart; no chipped nail polish or laddered stockings would be tolerated. He often told us he was proud of his smart evening girls.

Now at seventeen I felt as if my life was improving. Since buying the sewing machine, I was building up a collection of dresses and I was now in a position to be able to afford to make a purchase from a designer shop in Oxford Street. My first designer purchase was a black fitted suit with a large collar and a beautiful black and white rose on the front. This cost me over a month's salary, but it felt worth every penny.

With my smart clothes, high heels, and even a very smart uniform at my evening job, I decided it was not appropriate to continue to wear my long hair up in a bun because it made me look like a schoolteacher. I made an appointment and went to a top hair stylist in St Anne's Square, Deansgate, Manchester, to have my hair cut and remodeled. It was great, as in both my jobs, I was working in the city, so good shops, good hairdressers, everything new and exciting was to hand. After my new hairstyle, everyone said they could not believe how different I looked and how sophisticated, all that is except Mr Sander (Odeon manager), who said, "Miss Connor, I am shocked you have had your beautiful hair cut off." I highly respected Mr Saunders, who was a very handsome middle-aged man with white hair. He always wore a evening suit with a white bowtie, and black patent shoes, his wife was a smart and beautiful woman, I always thought they both looked perfect and imagined they lived a perfect life in a big posh house.

I decided with my new hairstyle, to put on my fabulous new suit and have a portrait taken, which I still have.

My working hours at the Odeon were four evenings a week, six o'clock until ten thirty, and Saturday and Sunday from two until nine o'clock. We were given two free passes per week for friends, which made us very popular, as everyone wanted a free pass, especially for the live shows, for example when Cliff Richard was on stage and I got his autograph on a ice cream carton. I was now enjoying all the latest films. Some of my favorites were Doris Day in Pillow Talk and Some Like it Hot with Marilyn Munroe, Tony Curtis and Jack Lemon.

I made a close friendship with an Irish girl called Bernie Murphy. Another nice friend was a girl called Silvia. Silvia had a very bossy older sister called Gloria, who was in charge of ice cream sales, and not very popular with any of the other girls, but that was OK as the ice cream staff did not use our glamorous dressing room, so we only saw her in small doses in the intermissions. My friend Bernie got reported by Gloria one Sunday; she was singing "You scream, I scream, we all scream for ice cream," only being her usual cheerful self, but she got reported for singing on duty.

I would finish work in the office in Bollin House at five o'clock and would then have a ten-minute walk to the Odeon. Most of the part-timers would meet up in Nicky's coffee bar, next door to the cinema. We would usually have hot dogs and coffee.
The part timers all had full time office jobs during the day, so would have lots to chat about when we met up. We would then all go up to the Odeon dressing room, which in the past had been a showbiz dressing room, with all the mirrors, and lights across each mirror. There we would do our makeup and hair, and don our smart uniforms, then go on parade for our inspection by Mr Sanders.
Most of the part timers were working in the extra job to save up for holidays in Spain, but all spent lots of money on clothes, shoes, handbags, and of course the latest in make up and perfume. This all interested me greatly as I felt as though I had lots to learn, most of these girls being between one and five years older than me, and worth watching and listening to, as I had come from a old fashioned background, and had no experience of these things. Of course I never confided this to anyone, I just quietly took it all in, and learnt as much as I could.

The day staff at the Odeon worked until we came in at six o'clock, so we did not really get to know them very well, only to say hello.
On the nights we finished at nine o'clock, was my first chance of experiencing a little bit of social life, when we would sometimes go across the road to the Prego coffee bar, to enjoy a coffee, a chat and a cigarette.

Now with my newfound confidence, I would sometimes join a group of the girls and go to The Continental Club above the Prego. They then introduced me to The Club De Parie, Dino's Club, and Mr Smiths Club even to The Ritz Ballroom.

When my mother was nursing she had used to go to the Ritz, and had told me about the glass ball, which reflected stars around the floor and on to the dancers. Going into these places at nine thirty or ten o'clock, was too early as only a few people would be in, the clubs would not get busy until much later, but it was still nice to see. The only trouble was I always had to leave at ten thirty, whilst all the other girls could stay there and enjoy them selves. If my father found out I was out in the town, he would make me give up the night job and I did not want that to happen again.

One night I was just about to leave the Odeon at ten thirty, when a Jewish couple came back all upset. The lady had been chewing a toffee, and had lost her gold filling, so we had to go through the ash trays on the Mezzanine floor, which was the most expensive floor, and the floor I usually worked on. The lady could not quite remember where she had been sitting, so even though we found the filling in the end, I missed my bus, so had to wait for the next one. When I got near home I saw my father waiting at the end of our street. He got me by the hair on my head and kept banging my head on the wall of the end house; even at seventeen he was still hitting me.

The next time I was late, remembering what had happened the last time, I got a taxi, but this time I got hit for getting a taxi. I was told that only prostitutes get taxis, and was warned not to go near one again. This was information I was not aware of, as I remembered my mother and myself getting a taxi late one night when we had missed our bus after visiting her brother, but of course I dared not mention this as it would have been considered as answering back. It never seemed to dawn on my father that I was in a completely no win situation, but that was how strict he was about me being home on time.

On night my mother and I had gone to Sharrocks an Irish dance hall on Brunswick Street, as there was a wonderful Irish band playing called The Melody Aces. This band was living in Ireland but spent much time touring around Ireland, England and America, as they were very popular. The lead singer Patrick MaGonagle known as Pat, offered to walk me home from the dance. Fortunately, that night my father was away in Ireland with my sister Jacqueline to see his mother, so my mother invited Pat into the house and they chatted and sang lots of old Irish songs. She sang her favorite song for him, The Close of an Irish Day. I was far too shy to sing and would not have known the words.

From then on, every few months when The Melody Aces were in Manchester my mother would make sure I went to Sharrocks, so as I would get walked home by Pat. She would make sure that my father was in bed so as she and Pat could chat about Ireland.

Even though it was only a platonic relationship, Pat and I wrote to each other for a long time. My mother then wrote to her family in Ireland to boast to them that Patrick MaGonagle from The Melody Aces was walking her daughter home after the dances.

One of my mother's sisters wrote back and said that Pat had been seen out in Cookstown in Northern Ireland with a girl. I knew he probably did have a girl in every town, but this story was unlikely, as Cookstown was four hours drive away, in Northern Ireland. My family were in the south of Ireland and this was 1958, so no one in the family had a car or a telephone and would never dream of visiting Northern Ireland in those troubled times.

All of a sudden I was told that Pat was banned from the house and I was never to go near Sharrocks again. From then on all of his letters were burnt before I could read them.

I had not fancied him as a potential boy friend as I thought he was too old for me, so this was no hardship for me and maybe a relief, as at least I would not now have to keep thinking, what can I write about in my letters to him, so this was maybe more my mother's loss than mine.

My mother had always said she did not want any of us girls to marry Irish men, as they drink too much beer. Yet when I went to the Irish dances with her, only because she had no one else to go with, she always seemed to encourage the Irish men around to talk to us, which gave me very confused signals, as I had even brain-washed myself, that

I did not want to end up with a Irish man, but then I used to think, maybe it is because she likes to talk to them about Ireland.

On one of our Sunday night visits to the Savoy, a man called Bernard McKernan asked me to dance. Most Irish men consider it an insult if you refuse to dance with them, so my mother kept insisting, "get out there and dance". Bernard offered to walk me home and of course my mother said yes. I kept telling her I didn't really like him, plus he had told me he was thirty-six, twice my age. But regardless of what I might say, he was brought into the house. My father was in bed asleep, and my mother again had someone from Ireland to talk to. I eventually went to bed and left them chatting and reminiscing. Had my father woken up, this would be fine as he was never a jealous man. He even used to tell my mother to dance with other men when he would pop into the dance hall after the pub had closed.

My mother and Bernard had arranged that he would meet me outside the Odeon, and see me safely home and of course my mother would be waiting to greet him when we got back. I was not a bit pleased to see him standing there, as I did not want the girls to see him, even though he was smart and good looking, I still thought he was too old for me and not my type. (If anyone had asked me what my type was? I would have said, "I do not know, but he was not it anyway.")

This went on for quite a few months and I can honestly say that I never once went out on a date with him, not for a meal, not for a drink, not even once, yet he asked my mother could we get engaged, to which she said yes, so Bernard turned up with a surprise for me, an engagement ring, which he told me cost £36, which was a lot of money then. I refused to wear the ring, so after a few weeks he changed it for a better one, which he said, cost £45.

I did wear this one to work so everyone could see it, as it was lovely, but I would not tell anyone where I got it from, so they all thought I was having a secret love affair.

Kathy, my colleague at Bollin House, even went and asked our boss Peter Wright were he and I secretly engaged and she then told him she would understand if we had to keep it a secret.

After all the fuss this ring had caused, I gave it back to Bernard, and told him I did not want to be engaged to anyone. He took it back and bought me a record player and a gold watch with the money, which he said, was for my birthday.

On two occasions when I had done overtime on Saturday mornings at Bollin House, Bernard had come to meet me after work and said, if you would like to go shopping, we can go to Lewis's and you can have anything you want. Both times I told him I had to go home and get ready for the Odeon, so he stopped after that. Some girls would have taken advantage of his kind and generous nature, but it would not be in my nature to do that.

I loved working Saturday mornings, as I would have the office to myself. I would sing Eartha Kitt songs into the Dictaphone and then listen to them back; a favourite one was 'Proceed with caution," and Johnny Rays' Blue Moon'.

Quite soon after all this, one night when I came home from the Odeon, Bernard was waiting for me in the house with my mother. He went down on his knees on the kitchen tiles and begged me to marry him. I now have to smile when I remember the proposal. He said, "I like a drink, I will always like a drink, but I like you better". When I said "I am too young, and do not want to get married" he started to cry and told me that if I did not accept him, he would join the arm. I had still never gone out on a date with him and never let him kiss me, no matter how hard he tried.

A few weeks later Bernard came to the house and told us all that he had sold his motorbike (which I had never been on and never seen as he did not bring it to our house) and enrolled for the army. My mother had given this poor man hopes of being part of our family, as he had no family of his own in England. I had always thought he is just lonely so never encouraged him. When I would come home from work after a very long day doing two jobs and he would be sitting in the kitchen, I would say I was tired and go to bed. He would then stay for hours and talk to my mother.

Bernard was stationed in Osnabrook in Germany. About one year later, on his first army leave near Christmas he came back for a visit. He arrived with presents galore. He had bought a pink satin dressing gown and matching pyjamas for me and a cigarette box, that when you pressed a button a cigarette came out of a dog's mouth. I had six presents and all of my sisters received presents, my mum and even my dad received presents and they were all displayed on the table in the front room. He had got six portraits done of himself, and told me I could keep all six. I did not want one, never mind six.

The thing he kept until last was a very beautiful diamond solitaire ring, which he told me had cost £75, as he still wanted us to be engaged.

He said he thought that with him being in the army, I might have missed him and he seemed to think that as he was away at a distance, I might consider becoming engaged to him. He told me he would not rush me into marriage, even though he knew I was not old enough. I felt sorry for him and realized the poor man just wanted someone of his own, but that someone was not going to be me.

Bernard then told me this was the third ring and that if I did not like it I would not get another.

The pressure was on from him now, and from all the family, who were over the moon with their presents but I was certainly not going to marry him, just because he had bought all these presents. Even though he was very kind, I think I would have had a very boring life with him.

My mother kept telling me "a man chases a girl until she catches him." I had no intentions of either catching him or of being caught myself. I do hope Bernard went on to find himself a wife and found the happiness he deserved. If he is still alive he will be now be about eighty-six.

I got my sister Anne a job in Bollin House, in one of the offices; she is the sister who used to throw the shoes at me. One morning I was passing the office she worked in and saw the jacket belonging to my new royal blue suit on the back of her chair. I had not even worn the suit myself yet, so I went into the office and took my jacket back with me to my own office. She later came to my office in a temper and I then saw that she was not only wearing my suit but she was also wearing the blouse I had bought to go with it. She kept demanding the jacket back, and when some people came into the office she had the cheek to say the suit was hers and I had taken her jacket. I had intended to give the jacket back to her, I was just letting her know that I knew she had been in my room and helped herself again. If she had been polite or had apologized, I would have let her wear it, as I remembered what it was like when I borrowed my mother's cardigan. But under the circumstances I kept the jacket, and took it home with me.

Anne in her temper told me some-thing she had read in my five-year lockable diary, which of course I always kept locked and in my bedroom.

When I went home and told my mother, she said that Anne had taken the diary downstairs, unlocked it with a fork and read it to her. She even recited some of the entries; and told me they now knew how much I had paid for my clothes and shoes, which she thought was far too much.

Years later, Anne admitted to me that she had made up a lot of the things she had read out to my mother, she was only making it more colourful.

I went and bought a new padlock and from then on kept my room locked, and the keys with me. However a few months later, I came home from work unexpectedly, and found Anne had been in my room again. I could not understand how she had got in, until my mother told me that Anne climbed onto the shed in the back yard and in through the window bringing the diary down to read to her, and any clothes she wanted to borrow." So from then on I kept my diary in my office desk.

Most of the coffee bars in town were Greek employing only Greek men. These men would often ask me and the other girls for dates but I always refused these, all that is except one man who owned his own coffee bar and he was called Andrew. Andrew had asked me to go out with him several times. I was not very experienced in dates but had listened to the girls talk, and felt as though I had learnt enough to be cautious. We went to the Gaumount cinema, then on for a coffee and he started to tell me that I had beautiful eyes and that he would marry me one day. He kept telling me he loved me in Greek, saying "sagapoor". I of course did not speak Greek but he explained what it meant, a bit strong I thought on a first date. All the girls in the Odeon had kept saying he was gorgeous and how lucky I was, but I think the marriage statement must have frightened me, as I did not want another Bernard situation, and I was still living in my mother's nightmare marriage at home. So after a few dates I decided I would not go out with the gorgeous Andrew again.

A German lady called Frieda, who worked in one of the offices, offered to rent me a room in her bungalow. I arranged a week off work as my annual holiday. My mother's cousin, Tricia Rooney, came to the house on Sunday evening whilst my parents were out, and she helped me pack my clothes and walked me to the bus stop. I had finally left home. I went to live in Denton, which was a long way from Manchester city centre. I remember the song 'Never on a Sunday' was on the radio when I got there, this was a very popular song at that time, and was top of the charts.

My mother kept going down to the Odeon to try to find me, and caused a lot of trouble with Mr Saunders. When he said I was off work for a week's holiday she accused him of hiding me in his office and when he showed her his office, she then accused him of hiding me behind the curtain in the cloakroom. When I found all this out, it was highly embarrassing, as Mr Saunders was a very dignified man and would not be used to people behaving like this, and the fact that he held me in high regard made it even more embarrassing, so very much to my regret, I gave my notice in and left the Odeon. This was a very difficult thing to do as I was extremely happy there, but I knew my mother would not give in. I then had to give my notice in at Bollin House for the same reason.

Our solicitors for Bollin House were John Benthams. Mr Bentham, on hearing I was leaving, asked me why, so I explained my position to him. He immediately offered me a job in his office on Whitworth Street as a clerk/typist. I should have been happy, as it would be another step up the ladder working for a solicitor, but in fact I was quite heart-broken and lonely at leaving the other two jobs, and all my friends.

I then found two evening jobs in two high class coffee bars / restaurants, in the city, three nights a week in each, The Sherazade and The Mogambo, both owned by a Jewish couple, Mr and Mrs Norton. Mrs Norton drove a very impressive sports car, a purple STAG with a black soft top. I remember thinking, I will work hard and have a car like that one day.

The only trouble with these new part-time jobs was that quite a few nights I would not finish work until twelve o'clock midnight, then have to get a bus to Denton, and a bus all the way back to the city in the morning,

My mother eventually found out where I lived and came there causing trouble, so I agreed to go back and live at home, as I knew she would send my father there after me, and he would bring me home, so I had left Bollin House and the Odeon for no reason.

My parents made me very uncomfortable, and embarrassed me a lot. My mother kept coming to the Sherazade and offering to wash up. She told them she did not want any wages, as she liked the atmosphere, and could keep a eye on me at the same time. On some of the nights when she stayed in bed and did not feel like coming to wash up, then occasionally my father would be waiting outside and would walk me to the bus stop in Piccadilly, then he would get on the bus and travel home with me.

I got really sick of all this, so I applied for a job to work in America. An office had opened in St Anne's Square and a man called John Smith was the manager. He dressed like a really old-fashioned city gentleman, with a hat and a walking cane, even though he only looked to be in his late twenties, he was very interested in a invented language called Esperanto, and he loaned me a book on it, and recommended that I learn it.

I told Mr Smith I could not have any mail delivered to my home, so each week I used to call into the office, then finally Mr Smith said he had found me a job on Long Island, not to far from New York. He explained they were a religious Jewish family called Rosenberg. He said they keep all dairy product pots pans and cutlery washed and stored separately from anything to do with meat. My job would be to look

54

after their three children. As I was the eldest of my sisters in my family, he felt sure I would be suitable; he said they wanted a smart polite girl. I agreed to the job, and applied for a passport.

Then the crunch came. Mr Smith informed me that I would need a visa. This was applied for, but when the forms arrived, they stated that I needed my father's signature. My father also had my birth certificate locked away in his wardrobe, where he kept everything considered to be important. I explained to my father what I wanted to do.

I knew he could not read or write but as I was old enough I did not think he could stop me, or at least I hoped he would not. My father took the forms out of my hand and ripped them into small pieces. He then took me with him to show him where Mr Smith's office was situated. We got the bus down to St Anne's Square, and walked into the office. He told Mr Smith that if he ever heard his name mentioned again he would break every bone in his body and would then put the windows in, and then he would not be capable of sending any more girls to America in the future. Imagine my shame. I was also highly annoyed with myself, as I thought I should have just signed the form myself and said nothing, but too late for that now. I now thought it was time I left home again. There was a girl I had worked with in the Odeon called Brenda, who had her own house in Rusholm, so I had a chat with her. She offered to share her house with me and I would have my own bedroom. I grabbed the opportunity.

A gay man called Terry worked at the Sherazade, (in those days they were called 'Queers.') Terry always talked of a Persian man he fancied. He used to tell me the Persian had beautiful eyes and drank Russian tea. One evening Terry and I were working together, he had just borrowed my eyeliner and made up his eyes and we were repeatedly playing the latest record called 'Sway'! which went 'When calypso rhythm starts to play, make me dance, make me sway.' A customer came in and Terry literally flew across the restaurant floor to meet the man. He took the man's coat and hung it up, he then came back to the bar and ordered Russian tea, and said to me "it is a good job I had my eyeliner on", so I guessed this was the special customer he had talked of.

A few nights later the Persian came back and had his usual lemon tea. He introduced himself as Parviz and he was very good looking and charming. I had glitter in my hair as it was almost Christmas and he said it looked very nice. He then asked me what perfume I was wearing, and I said it is called 'Christmas in July' and told him I bought it because it was almost Christmas and my birthday was in July. He asked me if I would like to go out with him, but I said No! I am sorry but I never go out with customers.

He started to come in on a more regular basis and after a few more visits asked me if I would like to go to the Wimpy bar which was only a few minutes walk away. This seemed innocent enough so I agreed. When we arrived in the wimpy bar, we went down stairs, and there were twelve Persians sitting around a group of tables they had pushed together.

I did not find out until months later that because a few of them had been into the Sherazade at different times and had tried to chat with me and I had ignored them they thought I was big headed, and so I became a challenge to them. They then had a bet with Parviz that he would not be able to get me. No wonder he had persevered; if I had known this at the time I would have walked out and gone home. We had our coffee then Parviz ordered a taxi and saw me home to Brenda's house. When we got there, he followed me into the sitting room but I told him we did not allow men in here, so thinking it was my house he left. The next evening when I went into work I found that Terry was not speaking to me, as I had stolen his dream man.

We were closed for Christmas, so after Christmas Parviz came to the Mogambo and asked me to go out with him on my night off. I went home from the office the next day quite excited, and got ready for my date. I wore a very expensive green velvet dress, as I wanted to give a good impression. I met him in town and we went to the Odeon in the best seats in the mezzanine. After the film, we went to a coffee bar where the Greek waiter told him "you are very lucky to have this beautiful lady on your arm." Parviz got annoyed, and asked me how I knew this Greek. When I got to know Parviz a bit better, he told me he had that night, gone back to the coffee bar and asked the Greek did he know me, apparently he had replied, he only wished he did. Parviz told me if the Greek had known me, I would never have seen him (Parviz) again.

Meanwhile once again my parents found out where I was living, so I found a one-roomed flat in Didsbury, and Brenda helped me to move my belongings in. The landlord gave us free tickets to go and watch the Pete Murray show being televised at the BBC studios.

At the end of the show, Pete Murray came up to me and told me that my landlord was his friend and had asked him to make me welcome. He then asked if I would like to go to a club for a drink with him, and even though I knew he was famous, I declined, as I thought he was probably married.

On my next date with Parviz we went to Guys and Dolls. He liked to dance the Cha-Cha and I had watched Poraic teach my mother how to dance it, so I was glad I knew the steps. When Parviz asked me who had I danced it with, I told him I had never danced it before, but he was reluctant to believe that, and wanted to know who the man was, which of course I denied. I did explain to him that as I had always worked in a day job and a night job, I had not had time to go out with men.

The next time we went out he took me to a club called The House of Bamboo, on Canal Street, which was owned by a fellow Persian student, a young man called George.

On Saturday nights in the House of Bamboo they used to hold dancing contests for the cha-cha and Parviz wanted us to enter the contests. I refused as I felt far too shy and did not think I would be good enough, so he danced it with one of his friends girlfriend, a girl called Wendy. They did not win and he became in a foul mood, and blamed me, saying that if I had danced with him, he would have won.

The House of Bamboo and Guys and Dolls did not serve alcohol and both clubs seemed to be very popular places where the Persians liked to take their girlfriends

I did not invite Parviz to my new flat, as I was very virginally minded. A girl at the Odeon called Wendy had told me she had become pregnant a few months earlier, and had, had an abortion. She said it was horrible and painful, so I did not fancy going down that road, as I considered I had had enough pain in my life already and was determined to keep myself to myself. I also feared my father would kill me if I became pregnant.

The flat was in a big old house, converted into several one-roomed flats, with one communal kitchen. All the other tenants were students but I did not mix with them, as I had my meals out or at work, and only needed the flat as somewhere to sleep and keep my belongings.

I had lived at the flat for about two weeks, when my father once again came to where I worked and insisted on coming back to the flat with me, as he said he was taking me home. He ordered me to pack my belongings, and off we went home again.

When we got there it must have been about two o'clock in the morning. My mother was up and sitting in the kitchen and she seemed pleased to see me. I was wearing a gold ring with a big green semi precious stone belonging to Parviz. I had always admired the ring so he had let me borrow it. My mother spotted the ring immediately and wanted to know where it came from. I kept telling her it belonged to a friend but she would not drop the subject so in the end I told her I had met a man from Iran, but he and his friends preferred to call it by its old name of Persia. My mother like myself had only heard of cats and carpets coming from Persia, not people.

On Valentines Day, Parviz's best friend Shahpoor called at our house with a card for me.

I was very surprised, as I would not have expected he knew about Valentines Day, but I was also impressed. My mother had told me to invite Parviz in to meet her when he saw me home, which I did. She seemed to really like him. But when she went into the kitchen to make the tea she sent my sister Jacqueline in to the sitting room to keep a eye on us. Jacqueline was told not to come out until my mother goes back in, I do not know what she thought we would get up, in that few minuets.

Parviz was then given tea and biscuits in our best china tea set. He was a Iranian Muslim sitting in the best room. My sister Anne at this time was standing outside the front door on the coal grid with her boy friend Eddie.

Anne had only recently met Eddie, so poor Eddie was not allowed into the house as he was a protestant. My mother and father both being of strict Irish Catholic families, were brought up to hate Protestants, which to me was a dreadful state of affairs.

I felt so sorry for Anne, as with my parents, you could be any religion so long as you were not protestant.

Parviz invited me to his flat, which consisted of one room and a kitchen in Oak Avenue. Iranian students occupied all the flats in Oak Avenue, as it was close to the college.

I could see he was not a very house proud person, as he had lots of suitcases all across one side of the room but he said they all belonged to the Persian boys who had not yet got flats of their own.

Parviz had explained to me that he and his friends all received allowances from their parents in Iran every three months to support themselves. This would be for rent, food and all living expenses. From what he told me, usually the boys seemed to live it up when the allowances arrived, but then in the last few weeks they would live on rice and eggs and would not go out, but would congregate in each other's flats and listen to Iranian music from home.

When I visited his flat we would spend the evening listening to records. Not many people had a TV in those days but all the students seemed to have record players. Some of our favorite records were Frankie Laine's Western songs, also 'O'Carroll', and 'One Way Ticket to The Blues,' but the real favourite was Ben E King's LP, Spanish Harlem.

There was also a lovely song called Nature Boy, about a man who had wandered very far over land and sea.

Parviz had two very good friends called Mike Bakhshayesh and Peter Poluticof. They used to visit his flat and we would all eat the rice and listen to the music. The only bad thing was that they all insisted on speaking Farsi, which was the Iranian language, so I never had a clue what they were talking about. Their excuse was that their English was not good enough, and yet in every other way they were polite and well mannered.

Each time I went to the flat, I would stay until it was time for the last bus, then Parviz would walk me to the bus stop. When the bus arrived, he would not want to leave me, so he would hop on the bus with me in his slippers and we would go upstairs so as the other passengers could not see his feet, (the stairs being at the back of the bus in those days). After a few stops, he would get off and walk back to his flat. Each time I was due to go home, we would say he was not going get on the bus that night, but each night when the bus arrived, the same thing would happen.

When his allowance arrived, we would go to Guys and Dolls on a Saturday night and usually when Parviz had seen me home he would then go back to the club, and continue to dance the night away, but now that my mother had met him, one night she waited and invited him in, someone new to stay up all night and talk to. He was too polite to say no, so at about three or four o'clock I went to bed, and they were still there when I got up at seven thirty. My mother then informed me that she had taken him to six o'clock mass, and as he was far too nice to get married, she thought he would make a good priest. She said she also wanted everyone to see how nice he was, but I did not think most people we knew would be at mass at six o'clock in the morning. Later he told me he never understood what she was talking about, he just kept saying yes, so went along with everything.

After a few months he asked me to get engaged to him, so we set a date for Saturday September 2nd. I was quite surprised at this proposal, as he had already told me that his parents had planned for him to get a university degree, then go back to Iran and marry his cousin, whose photo he had already shown me. So I was surprised and flattered. He then told me I must give up my night jobs, as he would not be engaged to a waitress. I had become very settled at The Mogambo and The Sherazade and had enjoyed the people I worked with and now I was having to give this up, all over again.

I finally gave the jobs up to please him. I had found out he was becoming very controlling, but of course when you love someone you do things to please them.

I was feeling the pinch financially, as I now only had one wage with which to pay my mother for my keep and to support myself, as I had to pay my bus fares to the city every day, as well as my bus fares to and from Parviz's flat. We rarely seemed to go out anymore, as he was always saying he could not afford it.

One Saturday afternoon he had invited me to his flat and very unusually I had got a taxi. It was a two-bus journey, so I got one bus then picked up a cab as I had just missed the second bus, plus I could not wait to see him.

Parviz must have been watching me from his window and had seen me get out of the car, somehow not realizing it was a cab, as it was not the usual black cab. When I got inside the flat, he went completely mental, asking me who the man was, who had given me the lift, as he knew no one in our family had a car at the time. I could not prove it was a cab as I had picked it up on the road. To my horror, he thumped me in the face. I was wearing a purple dress and he snatched the matching belt off the dress, threw it around my neck and tried to strangle me, telling me he did not want anyone else looking at me or touching me. I remember falling on the edge of the bed and thinking that if he killed me my parents would say it was my fault for being in his flat. I had already begun to realize that the more I was seeing of him, the more unreasonably possessive he was becoming; I was finding this a very confusing and difficult relationship, but I had fallen in love with him.

Parviz's landlady was called Mrs Simpson and she was in her mid forties. His friends always joked about her and said she obviously fancied him. She would often find excuses to come around to his flat and I could see the strange look in her eyes when she would arrive and find me there.

One evening I went to the flat unexpectedly when he was getting ready to go out and he said that Mrs Simpson had been around and had invited him out for a drink, so I could either stay there and let myself out later, or I could go home. I decided to stay, as I had only just got there, and it was a long journey home. I spring cleaned all the flat, all the kitchen cupboards, everything in sight, I even did all his ironing, but as it got close to the time of my last bus, he was not back, so I walked to the bus stop and went home.

The next time I saw him, he told me they had not gone out, but stayed at Mrs Simpson flat and she had sent a taxi to the wine shop for a bottle of gin she had got him tipsy and they had finally gone to bed together.

I was quite devastated by this news, as we had planned to get engaged in September and was supposed to love each other. I was shocked that first of all he had done this, and with an older woman, I was also shocked that he would even tell me what they had been up to, after he had always been so jealous and possessive with me. Could he not have just kept it to himself instead of hurting me like this? The most unbelievable thing was that he did not even seem to be sorry. But I also remember him telling me that his mother had fixed him up with one of her friends to break his virginity, so maybe he liked older women. What a mess.

After hearing all this, my mind was in a whirl, should I finish with him for good and go home, or should I try to find out why it happened. So I tried to find out why but all he would tell me was "men are men." In my confusion I was now also thinking that if this was true, it means I would never be able to trust him or any man ever again. I asked Parviz for some headache tablets, as this was something I would never normally use, so would not carry in my handbag.

I took two tablets, then a while later I took another two, and as the pain would not go away, I thought they were not working, so I took two more. I did not mention this to him, as I had not thought of it as being considered harmful, and my head was in turmoil.

Finally, feeling heartbroken, I got the bus home. When I got in, my mother was in bed, she wanted me to stay up and talk to her but I told her I was exceptionally tired, I did not feel well, and as the pain was still there, I then took another two tablets.

She kept asking me what was wrong but of course I could not tell her what Parviz had done, so I told her I had taken all these tablets as I did not feel well and was very tired. She would not let me go to bed, instead she insisted I go to the Manchester Royal and she sent one of my sisters with me to tell the doctors what I had done.

When we got there they put me in a cubicle, put some thick tubes down my throat into my stomach and I then had a stomach pump. They kept me in all night and early the next morning a doctor came to my bed and gave me a severe telling off saying that if I ever did anything like that again I would be sent to a psychiatrist.

I tried to tell the doctor that I had been very upset and had not realized how many tablets I had taken, and that I had not tried to kill myself, but he would not listen.

I was then discharged and I went home, still not able to decide whether to finish with Parviz or not. My head kept telling me to do it, but my heart would not let me. I had even left my two night jobs to please him, but he was still not pleased, so I was feeling confused and very isolated. But I had to keep my self-respect at all cost.

When I got home my mother said she had phoned Parviz tell him I had taken an overdose, and to ask him if he knew why. She then told me that Parviz had told her he had not seen me and knew nothing about it. He was lying of course, but she told him I must have been at Nicky's Snack bar (which I had not been in since I had left the Odeon).

She then told him she had never liked me going in there anyway, with all those Greek men. She had forgotten to tell him she had met Nicky and his Irish wife and had told me what a good family man he was, as he employed some of his nephews, and how much she liked going to his coffee bar.

I asked my mother how she had got Parviz's phone number and she said they found it in my room, (obviously rooting in my belongings again). I went out to Nelson Street to the public phone and phoned Parviz, I told him I had been in the hospital all night but he need not worry as I was now out and was all right. His reply was "I am not interested, do not to tell me, go and tell your boyfriend Nicky"!!!!

So my mother had once again managed to put the poison in and to cause more damage and destruction in my life.

This was my first real relationship; it had become a very claustrophobic overpowering one. Sometimes I was very happy, but I spent a lot of time being very unhappy.

Parviz seem to get great pleasure from accusing me of things I had not done and carrying on until he made me cry (even though I had never before been a crier). After he had achieved this, he would seem to become happy again, and then of course I would forgive him. I had started to walk with my head down looking at the pavement whenever we were out together, as if a man looked at me I was accused of having been out with him, and then more arguments would follow. I had until now felt powerless to do anything about it, but now for some reason I also felt frightened.

I decided not to see Parviz again. I prayed very hard for the strength to carry out my decision, and to stick to it. I finally got the nerve to end the relationship, even though it broke my heart.

At age 17

Chapter Four

Finally free, feeling very poor but very wise, I knew I would have to get a second job again, whilst keeping my full time job at John Benthams. So I went to work as a part time usherette in the Deansgate Cinema in Deansgate, three evenings a week plus Saturday and Sunday afternoons. I made friends with two girls in particular, Joan and Julie, both of whom had had Iranian boy friends, and had been badly treated by them. I remember Julie telling me that her heart had been scarred by her experience. I used to think Julie's heart was scarred but mine was completely broken, as I had really given my heart to him (my ex.). I was of course too proud to tell anyone this, so I struggled on in my own very sad world.

The film Tequila was showing in the Deansgate, which had some great music and this sometimes cheered me up. I lost quite a lot of weight and seemed to shrink, even though I was not overweight at the time, my measurements being 36-28-38. But now people I met used to say they hardly recognized me and asked had I been ill.

The Deansgate was harder to get to from my day job, also further to travel home at night, and I cannot say that I enjoyed working there, at least not in comparison to the Odeon, so after a few months I decided to look for a different night job.

I went to reception at the Midland Hotel and they sent me to the catering restaurant to see the headwaiter. He was French, elderly and looked like Dracula but he offered me a job as a silver service waitress one or two evenings a week. I was employed to work when they had functions booked from some of the big companies. On one of these evenings we had eight hundred guests for dinner, when a company had their yearly conference and dinner dance. I asked my sister Anne if she would like to help out just for that one evening, she agreed and seemed to quite enjoy the experience, but they were not taking on any more staff so I could not get her a more permanent job.

All nationalities worked at the Midland Hotel, Greeks, Italians, French, Polish and more. There were dozens of chefs and hundreds of waiters. Some of the waiters would steal bottles of wine and lots of cigars, they would hide them in their lockers and share them out amongst themselves at the end of the evening, but never offered any to us girls. As the new girl, I got lots of offers from all nationalities of men working there to go out on dates, but coolly turned all advances down, as no one was going to get the chance to hurt me again.

As there was not much evening work available at the Midland Hotel, I went to The Golden Star Chinese Restaurant, as I had heard the owner had a vacancy and he employed me on the spot. I worked a few evenings a week and agreed to do an occasional Saturday afternoon. The great thing about this job was that every evening I would finish work at the office at 5pm. then it was only two minuets walk to the restaurant. Before each shift you were allowed a Chinese meal free of charge, which I really enjoyed, then a cup of tea and a cigarette with a nice Irish girl called Frankie who was working there full time. It was Frankie who had told me about the job in the first place. After our lovely meal and a chat with Frankie, I would start work at 6pm in a nice happy environment.

The wages were £5 per week, which was average in those days; the tips usually amounted to about £15, which was excellent.

Another bonus was that the restaurant was almost next door to the Odeon, so I could go and have an occasional coffee with my lovely friends who were still working there and whom I had missed so much.

I felt so much better working in the city centre again instead of at the Deansgate and it also gave me more time to myself between jobs and less time spent traveling.

I did not go out to socialize at night, but sometimes if I had an evening to spare, I would go and sit in the Odeon to watch the latest film and have a chat with everyone. On one such evening I took my little sister Jacqueline to see Hayley Mills in Whistle Down The Wind. Jacqueline really enjoyed the film and the ice cream. She had not been to many cinemas, since she was still at school and she talked about the film at great length afterwards all the way home on the bus, which gave me great pleasure to see her so happy.

I was still living at home with my parents. Each week I would buy my mother a present, something nice, makeup, perfume, or whatever I thought she might enjoy. I bought a wooden table for the hall and would every week buy her the Woman magazine and an Irish magazine called Irelands Own, I would leave these on the table with what ever else I would buy for her. One week I bought a china cup and saucer with Mother written on it but she said it was too nice to drink out of and was only for looking at. I used to get great pleasure out of 'doing her up', as she called it. I would pluck her eyebrows then put make up, eye shadow and rouge on her to cheer her up, then when I had finished she used to say to us girls, "If any of you turn out to be as good looking as your mother, you will do" so of course I was pleased she was feeling nice.

If she was in bed and depressed I would make welsh rarebit for her, which is egg and cheese mixed together and grilled on toast. I had seen this being made in the cafes and I would then take it into the bedroom to her, as I knew she always enjoyed that. I also started to buy Sanatogen Tonic wine for her. Even though she was not a drinker she would enjoy a glass of it and would then sit and wait for it to start taking effect (bless her).

Life carried on as normal for several months, until one evening just before Christmas. Parviz arrived into the restaurant. My heart skipped several beats, and even though he sat on one of my tables I asked Frankie to serve him. He sat after his meal and waited until I had finished work, he kept telling me he had missed me and wanted to see me again.

I felt a strange mixture of excitement and fear, fear of not being able to cope with his jealousy, and fear of myself not being able to say NO!

The next day was a Saturday; he arrived in the afternoon I had just been paid, so I was going out on my break to do some Christmas shopping. I was going to H Samuels to buy a set of coloured tumblers in a gold coloured stand, which I knew my mother, would like. I thought she could put them on the sideboard in the front room in case we had any visitors over Christmas.

Parviz walked with me to H Samuels then came inside the shop and insisted on paying for the glasses. He then came with me to the record shop where I wanted to purchase the latest Elvis record called Little Sister, the words started "Little sister don't you do what your big sister done".

I was wearing a very smart Astrakhan coat with a fur collar, which I had bought a few weeks earlier. Parviz admired my coat and asked me if I would help him choose a winter coat for himself, as the weather was very cold and he was used to a much warmer climate. We choose a really good coat for him. Somehow or other, even though I had not really consented to it, he acted as if we were back together again.

Parviz then told me he wanted us to get married. I felt complimented and truly terrified at the same time, even though I now find this hard to explain.

His next move, which should have been no surprise to me was when he said that he can not be seen to be going out with a waitress and "he did not want me to go back to the Chinese restaurant ever again, and in fact he had never liked me working in the town centre in the first place so without giving my notice, I simply never went back to the job in the restaurant or the Midland Hotel.

I wish now I had put my foot down with him, but I cared too much for him so I did everything he said, just to keep him happy. So I was back to going to his flat in the evenings, listening to records, and eating rice, sometimes with an egg on it.

Now after a lot of years of loyalty to John Benthams, I decided to change my job.

I applied for a position as wages clerk at Dunlop's on Upper Brook Street, which is the street I was born on. I quite liked this job, working out all the piecework, over time, holiday pay, tax and insurance for all the factory workers, then on Friday mornings all the cash would be delivered and we would make up the wage packets. My mother had also worked at Dunlops during the war.

On March 17th 1962, on Saint Patrick's Day, Parviz and I became engaged.

Around about the month of May, I kept feeling sick at work so went to visit the nurse who examined on me and told me I might be about two months pregnant. She told me I should go and see my doctor, which I knew I could not do as he was friendly with my mother and I was frightened that he might inform her of my condition. I do not think I had quite realized that at the age of twenty, I would not now be beaten; the beatings had actually stopped quite a few years ago, but the fear remained.

When I was about six months pregnant the nurse sent me to the hospital for a check up. When I asked for the morning off, Stuart, the wages manager, asked me where I was going and said that If I did not tell him then I could not go. When I repeated this to the nurse she told Stuart off and said it was a private and personal matter, and nothing to do with him.

As the nurse was still the only person who knew I was pregnant, apart from Parvis, I felt very privileged to have her support and she seemed to respect me and did not look down on me for being in the condition I was in.

My mother had once asked me, was I pregnant and I said no. When I was over seven months pregnant, one Saturday morning my father's sister Mamie came to visit us from Birmingham. Mamie had four daughters of her own, Maureen, Anne, Bernadette and Margaret, all about a year younger than each of us. Mamie, who was a nurse, after some time in our house, said to my mother "of course you know she is pregnant don't you?"

I just wished I had been a piece of snow and could have melted on the spot. My mother understandably got annoyed, and as she said later, I had made her look stupid, her being a nurse herself and Mamie having to inform her that her daughter was pregnant.

The cat was well and truly out of the bag now, as they say.

My mother headed down to the Holy Name Church to see the priest and tell him her troubles. The priest put her in touch with Sister Augustine who used to visit us.

St Augustine was responsible for the placing of unmarried mothers into unmarried mother and baby homes. After the telling off I knew I would get and had been dreading, St Augustine said that when the time came she would arrange for me to go into Knowsley House in Handforth, about six weeks before the birth.

This felt like a big weight taken off my shoulders, as I now realized I was not the one and only girl to get pregnant, since there was a home for such people.

Parviz had absolutely no involvement in this arrangement as he had already told me "to get rid of it or have it adopted."

One day Parviz was going to a college in Leeds to try to get accepted there as a student.

I asked him could I go with him on the train, as I was bored being at home with nothing to do. He said yes, so we arrived in Leeds in the morning but Parviz told me I could not go the rest of the journey with him, as he was also going to visit some of the Persian students whose names he had been given and he did not want the Persians to know I was pregnant. He told me I had to wait on the corner of the street in the city centre until he returned in a few hours. I asked him if I could go and sit in a cinema or a café, as being pregnant my feet were swollen but he said NO! I had to wait where he told me to, as he would not want anyone talking to me. So there I stood like a fool all day until nightfall, then we finally caught the train back to Manchester.

My father had already told my mother and me that because of the shame I had brought on the family, he would now have to go a shilling bus ride to a pub where no one would know him.

With my last weeks wages and my holiday pay from Dunlop's, I bought one blanket for my baby, a dozen nappies and some white and lemon knitting wool and knitting needles. I bought lemon as I was not sure if I was going to have a boy or a girl.

I prayed every night that I would have a boy, as I had found out that Muslims always favour sons and do not place much value on daughters, so I thought if I had a boy Parviz might change his mind and accept him.

I arrived at Knowsley House at the beginning of October 1962. There was accommodation for twelve girls and cots for their twelve babies. Knowsley House was a very big grand old country house set in beautiful big gardens, about two miles down a country lane in Handforth. The house had a very wide staircase as you would expect to see in a stately home and a large nicely furnished sitting room with a television set. We did not yet have a television at home so this was a nice novelty. There were three large bedrooms with four beds and four cots in each room. The girls were all nice girls easy to get along with, and very supportive of each other.

Every day we had a list of household chores to do and this list would change every week. The house was run by a nice matron, with one nurse on duty all day, a lady cook and a gardener, and we girls would do all the cleaning. This was no trouble to me as I was used to that. We worked well together, most of us smoked, as most people did in those days, so in the evenings we would watch TV in the large lounge and have a cigarette if we had any.

Some of the girls had already had their babies, but babies were never allowed in the lounge. A lot of discussion used to take place regarding the birth of the babies; some of the girls said they had had a hard time others said it was not too bad. Some of the girls were having their babies adopted and my heart would go out to these girls, as I could never give up my baby for adoption. My baby would be the closest thing in the world to me, and after the way I had been brought up, I would make sure I showered it with love and kindness. I knew I had a lot of love to give and this would be the person I could trust to give it to.

Most of the other girls said they lived with their families and would be taking their babies home with them. On listening to all this discussion, I decided to phone my mother to see if I could take my baby home when it was born but the short sharp answer was, "No your father would not allow it."

What was to become of me? Apart from my future being so insecure, I felt quite at home at Knowsley House but knew I could not stay here indefinitely. I often helped the other girls look after their babies and knew it would be great practice for when my own arrived.

None of my family ever came to visit me. Anne was now eighteen, Elizabeth was sixteen and Jacqueline fourteen and still at school. My mother did not ever visit, but a few times she wrote letters to me. I still have one of the letters with that address on the envelope.

The girls at Knowsley House hardly ever seemed to go out, as it was a two mile walk, up the lane to the village, then most of us would not have the bus fare to go anywhere further. I spent a great deal of my spare time knitting. I had already bought plenty of wool, so I knitted matinee coats, pram sets, hats, bootees and mittens. I intended to make sure that my baby was going to be well dressed and want for nothing.

We were all told to sew some sort of marking on each of the nappies so that when they were washed we would each recognize our own. I have no idea why I chose to, but I made a black cross with a needle and thread on the corner of each of my nappies.

November came and we all watched the Royal Command performance; every year since then when I have seen this programme, I always remember us girls all sitting watching it together, and I wonder what became of them all.

Most of the girls had had their babies; some of the girls had gone home. I was still sitting there waiting, and now three weeks overdue, the visiting doctor decided to send me to Stretford Memorial Hospital to be induced. This was a very small hospital with only four wards. I was told I had high blood pressure, so was told not to eat ham, bacon, or salt. After a few days they transferred me in an ambulance to Park Hospital, which was a very big hospital, but they did not tell me why I was being transferred, I presumed they thought it was going to be a difficult birth.

I remember finally being in labour then on December 5th 1962. During the night, I was taken into the delivery room, my legs were put up on stirrups and strapped in. There were a lot of people around the operating bed, at least one doctor, and a lot of student doctors also some nurses; they had told me this was a training school. Then without any anesthetic I was cut open for the delivery of my baby. I was in chronic pain, and kept wondering if they had done this because I was not married, or was it because it was two thirty in the morning and they were annoyed at being got out of bed. I was told I had had a boy. They did not give me my baby to hold, as other people said they had done, but got on with stitching me up still without an anesthetic. I have often read since that things like that mostly happened to unmarried mothers, as if life is not tough enough for them!

The next morning I phoned Parviz to tell him that I had had a baby boy weighing seven and a half pounds; since I had prayed so often for a boy, I felt a good chance now that Parviz, being a Muslim, would want me to keep him.

I then phoned my mother to tell her my news. My parents had always wanted a son of their own, but I was not pinning any hopes in that direction.

Later that morning, Parviz came to visit me, but he did not even look at the baby. The only thing he said to me several times was, "IT IS HIM OR ME, HIM OR ME, HIM OR ME", then he turned around and walked out. I was completely devastated and heartbroken, as I had at least thought he would be a little bit proud that he had a son. What a terrible ultimatum to be given, to choose between the two people you love most in your life.

There were babies been born in the hospital at that time that were badly deformed, some born without arms or legs! These babies were called thalidomide babies, which was the name of the sleeping tablets the mothers had been prescribed by their doctors to help them sleep.

Here was I with a perfectly healthy baby, being told by his father to get rid of him, and grandparents who did not want him either.

I admit I was in pieces when later on that day my mother came to visit me. I told her what Parviz had said and I also told her I could not have him adopted. I begged her to look after him for me until I could find a live-in job or somewhere to live. She told me once again that my father would not agree, so she could do nothing about it.

Later on that day, they transferred me back to Stretford Memorial Hospital. I am ashamed to admit that I just cried and cried all day and all night. The nurse told me "lots of mums get upset, it is just post-natal depression." Little did she know what I was going through, but I would not tell her, and as usual kept every thing to myself.

I phoned Parviz and asked him to come and see me, so as we could talk it through but he just put the phone down on me; I have never felt so desperate and isolated in all of my life.

After about ten days I was transferred back to Knowsley House where I was told that six weeks after the birth is the maximum length anyone can stay, you then go home, or get a live-in job. The place had completely changed in the two weeks I had been in hospital. most of the girls I had befriended had now gone home, and new pregnant girls were coming in; even this now felt a lonely place, where I had felt reasonably happy and secure in the past. Here we were, me and my beautiful baby boy, whom no one wanted apart from me but none of the girls I had befriended were here to discuss things with. The new girls were not experienced enough to understand my problems. No visits from my parents, my sisters, and certainly not from Parviz.

Most babies when they are born get welcome cards and a present, usually of clothes.

All my baby and I got was one card from my mother; it was as if he did not exist.

I did have one visit from a girl who had worked with me at the Odeon, Bernie and her boy friend Roy; thank God they brought their camera, as that is the only photo I have of Kevin and me.

I phoned my mother again in a desperate attempt to get her to let me go home but she again said daddy would not allow it. I asked her to have my baby whilst I found somewhere to live, as there was no way on earth I would have him adopted again she said No! I was the only girl not to have either an adoption or a home coming arranged.

After a few weeks, I told Matron I was going out, and asked if she would she look after my baby Kevin for me. I then got the train to Leeds and went to see Parviz. I begged and begged him to change his mind. I did not want to keep Kevin against Parviz wishes but I certainly was not going to let him go. I just wanted Parviz to accept him, but of course he would not. The next morning I caught the train back to the home.

The Matron had phoned the police, and reported me missing, as I had stayed away over- night, due to there not being a train. Matron asked me why I had not told her where I was going, and I explained that if I had told her, she would have been compelled to stop me, to which she agreed. I explained why I had gone and she kindly said that she understood, but had already called the police to report me missing. I had not been back long when the policeman arrived and interviewed me. He told me off, and then he said, "Initially when they first phoned, I thought you need a good spanking but now that you have explained I see it differently." I was quite shocked when he said "Well God love you, you will be heartbroken one way or the other, and that foreigner does not deserve you, he would not be worth you giving your baby up for, because if you did do it, he would probably then give you up, as that is what they usually do." I did explain to the policeman that I had no intentions of doing any such thing.

After the policeman had left, the Matron told me she was supposed to call in a doctor to examine me after my night away, in case I would become pregnant again. I must have convinced her I would not be so stupid, as she said she would trust me and not call a doctor. All these humiliations, when the only important thing was that I could find us a home together.

I eventually went and had a long chat with Matron, who said that since my family would not have me home, I would need to look for a live-in job, but these were very limited with a new baby. She said she would get in touch with Sister Augustine, who was the nun who arranged for me to come into the home in the first place. She was also the nun who used to tell me off for not helping my mother to keep the dust down. Well the truth finally came out, Matron told Sister Augustine, that I was a excellent mother and I also excelled at my household duties in the home. She told the nun I had given some of the girls excellent advice, I could hardly believe it when she told me all this, then she said "I cannot speak highly enough of you".

I realized this was the first home I had been appreciated in, and I would be sorry to leave.

Before I left the home, I asked my mother to arrange a christening for Kevin in The Holy Name Church, as that is where I had been christened. I made my Holy Communion dress into a christening robe for him. I still have his christening robe and intend to have it buried with me. I took Kevin down to my parents home on the bus and thought when they saw how beautiful he was with his beautiful long eye lashes, they would want us to come back and live at home. My father was called John Connor, so hoping to please him I christened my baby John Kevin Connor and both of my parents were godparents. After the christening in the Holy Name Church we went back to my parents house for tea and cakes, and then I had hoped they might let us stay at home for just one night, but we were sent back to the Knowsley House in a taxi.

At the end of the six weeks, St Augustine had arranged for me to go and work for a lady doctor in Southport. When the day came I took Kevin went and caught the train, and arrived with all our belongings at the doctor's house. The doctor greeted me with, "the baby must be kept in the bedroom at all times" and told me that I would do all the housework, bring in the buckets of coal and the buckets must be full, and not half full, then light her fire and have her meal ready in the evenings, when she returned from work

She then said, "The other girls only lasted a week, and I don't suppose you will be any different". When the food order was delivered, she had ordered butter for her and margarine for me; at home we had always had butter, but not here.

The second day in Southport, Kevin started to be sick. The doctor phoned the matron in Knowsley House, who informed her that a few of the babies had got gastroenteritis, so Kevin must have caught it before he left. The doctor then had him sent into hospital.

On the Saturday I went to visit Kevin and whilst I was at the hospital, my sister Jacqueline came all the way to Southport to see us, as my mother had wanted to check who I was living with. The doctor was at home and told Jacqueline that her sister could not even cook peas. She did not bother to tell Jacqueline that I had cooked all her meals and I had even made Seville marmalade for her and stored it in jars, as we had been shown at school. She did not let Jacqueline wait for me to come back, and sent her home, after her travelling all that way from Manchester on the train. I decided I was not staying here to be treated so badly and to be insulted again, I had had plenty of that from my parents whilst at home. I packed up our stuff and told the Doctor I was leaving, hoping I would now be able to find us a home of our own whilst Kevin was in hospital.

I had a friend in Goole, near Garforth, who had worked with me in the cinema, so I went to visit her. She had now moved into a caravan with her partner and she said she would see the landlady and try to get us a caravan.

Our van was tiny and old, I lit a fire but the smoke kept coming back into the van, instead of going out of the chimney. It was now early 1963, one of the worst winters in history, with very deep snow everywhere. I was dreading Kevin coming out of hospital into this caravan, as it was bitterly cold. I bought a newspaper and looked for a flat; my friends drove me around, as I did not know the area. But no landlord would give me a flat when they found out I had a baby, so poor Kevin came home to the caravan and sleeping in a drawer.

Parviz came over to visit once and kept asking me when I was having him adopted.

I finally found a job in Selby, living in with a lovely Irish family, who were carpet fitters and had three children. The house was really big and very nice, the family seemed to be very kind, and I just knew we were finally going to be happy here. They said they had a cot and a pram we could use, in fact everything we could need. There was even a big garden that Kevin would be able to play in when he was a bit older.

That night I fed Kevin at ten o'clock and I put him down in his drawer to go to sleep, propped on two chairs. He kept lifting his head up to me, and I was so excited as this was a sign of him being a bit older, he was now almost three months old. Our new life was about to begin in the morning, in our first ever proper home together.

February 28th 1963. That night my baby Kevin died in his sleep.

I phoned the ambulance, and then I phoned the Irish family to explain why I would not be accepting the job. The ambulance took us to the hospital where Kevin was pronounced dead. My baby had been taken out of my arms and out of my life without any warning.

I left Yorkshire and went home to my family's house. I sat on the stool in my mother's bedroom for a long time listening to her talking. She never once asked me where Kevin was, and I could not bring myself to say the words.

Kevin had only once been in this house, which was the day of his christening, and even though it is now hard to believe, that was also the only time my father or sisters had seen him, my mother had seen him twice. It must have been over an hour later when I managed to tell my mother that Kevin had died.

Anne and Elizabeth had just come home from work, and when she told them, one of them said all right and they just carried on making the tea.

No sympathy, no hug, no emotion from anyone. I had expected some sympathy from my mother as she had after all lost her own twins. She just said, 'There are not meant to be any boys in this family."

A few days later after the postmortem, the undertaker said to me " we will be bringing the baby back to Manchester tomorrow from Leeds Infirmary, he will arrive at 6pm."

I went to the chapel of rest to see Kevin for the last time. I asked Parviz to please come with me, as I could not do it on my own. I stood and looked down into the coffin at my son, whom I had loved so much and been so proud of in the three months we had spent together. My heart felt ripped into little shreds, yet every one around me was so cool and unaffected. It all became too much, and I just turned around and ran out of the building,

Parviz said I ran across all the traffic on Upper brook Street, he does not know how I was not killed. He reminded me later, of what I had said, "I would not have minded if I had been run over as it could not be any more painful than the incredible pain I am feeling.

When I got home I was sitting in my father's chair near the cellar door in the kitchen, I asked my mother to please let me have one of her sleeping tablets but she said no! because I might become addicted. I ended up begging her, I kept telling her I only wanted one but she still said no and she then told me she had seen a little angel over my head which she explained was Kevin giving me comfort, and he was now on his way to heaven. She then said, "You will be alright now."

At the funeral on March 6th, Parviz, and my family attended, and some aunties and cousins; none of these people had ever even met Kevin.

I had purchased a grave for him in Moston Cemetery and I will never as long as I live, forget the sight of that little white coffin being lowered into the ground.

After the funeral we all went to a café on Oxford Road for the funeral breakfast arranged by my mother. I have no memory of that.

The pain of losing a child never ever goes away; you simply learn to live with it.

My son Mark and myself are the only people who ever go to visit the grave; we go every Christmas and on Kevin's birthday.

Since I have been in Ireland, I have not always managed to get there, but Mark never misses, which proves what a kind, thoughtful person he is, especially since he is three years younger than Kevin, so never knew his brother. And yet has such a great love for him.

Chapter Five

My world felt as though it had come crashing down, so I was going to have to recover and pick up all the pieces. Where does a person begin, when starting to rebuild their life?

I stayed at home with my parents, I did not ask could I stay, I just stayed. I now had to start all over again. I found a job with an engineering company called Francis Shaw in Ashton near Clayton. I was employed to work in the cost office, and my job was to cost all the parts that go into the making of an aeroplane.

Our office manager was a very arrogant Irish man, who often offered me a lift home in his car, but my instincts told me to keep away from him. He became so persistent that I asked for a transfer to a different office. The new office was in a new extension of the building and much more pleasant, so I settled down and liked the job and the people in the office.

One Tuesday in June 1963, Parviz and I were walking down a street in Manchester, when he suddenly said, "we can get married on Saturday" but he then told me I must not tell anyone. I went down to the registry office at All Saints to book the wedding. The registrar did his very best to talk me out of the marriage, and explained to me how very differently these foreign men treat their wives and especially when they get them back to their own country. I then went to the florist and ordered three orchids to wear on my coat lapel.

My parents did not know I was getting married, so I stayed at a girl's flat the night before the wedding. A girl called Pauline lived in a flat in the same house as Parviz's friend Peter. Peter was having a party for all the Iranian students and their girl friends, so Parviz and I went along. I was under strict instruction that no one must know that we are getting married; this would have been a wonderful opportunity for a wedding party. Peter who was to be our best man told me he had held the party to tell everyone about the impending wedding, but Parviz had told him not to tell anyone, and would not even now change his mind. After about an hour I left the party, went back to Pauline's flat and went to bed very upset. I kept thinking, this is supposed to be the happiest day of a girl's life. Parviz of course stayed at the party.

Even at this late stage I knew I should call the marriage off, but could not bring myself to do it, as I cared so much for him.

The next morning me, Parviz, Peter the best man, and Pauline's sister Jan, (even though I did not know her, Parviz had asked her to be our witness), all got on a bus to the registry office. A photographer was outside the registry office; Peter offered to pay for the photos as a wedding present. On our wedding photo's, Parviz is standing with his arm around Jan, the girl he had asked to be our witness, with me, his new bride, standing on his other side. Much too late to call it off now!!!

After the wedding, we all went to Central library, which was like Parviz's second home as he spent a lot of his time in there; all the Iranians went there to study and socialize. I still do not know the reason why but, Parviz told me and Peter to wait for him outside, which we did for over an hour, then we all went to a coffee bar and had lemon tea;

This was my wedding breakfast. I later asked one of my friends was I in love or was I insane; she informed me that there is not much difference between the two.

I then got a bus to Moston cemetery on my own to put my orchids on Kevin's grave. Whilst travelling I kept pondering, had Parviz married me just to get a passport, so as he could stay in England, otherwise why all the secrecy?

After that, I got a bus home to my parents house and put my wedding ring on a long chain around my neck, so as no one would see it. I continued to live there, and kept my marriage a secret.

A few months later, Parviz said he had ulcers and was going back to Iran to see his own doctor. He said would be staying with his parents for six weeks and he told me when I wrote to him I must pretend to be John Connor, and must be careful what I wrote as some people in his family could read English, and he was not telling his parents he was married.

I left home once again and got a one room flat in Whalley Range. I decided to rent a television set, and I gave my married name, with my mother's name and address as guarantor. I did not realize that the TV company would check this out with my mother.

She and Jacqueline arrived at my flat. Parviz had asked me to look after some of his belongings, so as he could give up his flat and would not have to pay the rent.

While my mother was interrogating me, Jacqueline found Parviz's shoes and a few of his clothes in my wardrobe. My mother immediately thought I was living with Parviz, and would not believe I was married. I showed her my marriage certificate but she took me and the certificate home to show my father, who instantly ripped it up and said it did not count, as I was not married in a church. Needless to say I did not get the television!

I promised my parents I would see the priest about getting married in the church, as I knew this would be important to them. When I went to see the priest to arrange this, he said I would have to apply for dispensation, from the Bishop. The priest applied for the dispensation for me, and told me the Bishop's reply had said that we could only have a church blessing and would have to come in one evening at 7.30pm when it was dark, and he would provide the blessing for us.

Now that my family knew we were married, I decided to get a bigger flat for when Parviz came back from Iran. I found a great unfurnished flat in Hart Road Fallowfield, which had a large sitting room, bedroom, kitchen, and bathroom.

Lots of people turned up to view the flat, but the landlord Mr Turner chose me, as he said he had a house full of nice people, and I would be very suitable.

Mr Turner wanted one month's rent in advance, which I did not have. The only thing I could do to get the money was, to give my notice in at Francis Shaw's, so as I would get my two weeks holiday pay, which would pay the required deposit.

I also bought some wallpaper and paste and every evening after work I would go and decorate the very large sitting room. I had always helped my mother to decorate so was a 'dab hand' at it.

I had a bell fitted at the front door and very proudly put our name on it.

My aunty Mary gave me a piano, a old-fashioned double bed with a wooden head board and footboard, a kitchen cabinet which I painted, and a really old chest of drawers with all the corners knocked off. I discovered plastic wood and managed to make new corners on the chest of drawers, I also filled in all the keyholes. I then painted it, the first coat in a cream colour; when that was dry, I painted it with varnish, then with a rubber comb I made squiggly lines on it to make it look like good wood, as me and my mother used to do on the kitchen doors. I then bought and fitted new handles. I was really proud of the end results, and it became well admired by my visitors. Even Aunty Mary was amazed at how good it looked; she said she would never have recognized it.

My father actually came and helped me move all my belonging in to the flat, which seemed like a sign of approval; he admired the flat and said it was very nice which it was.

My mother bought us a round glass coffee table with a picture inside the glass for our wedding present, Mrs O'Hare, one of the neighbours in my parent's street, bought us a candlewick bedspread, for which I was incredibly grateful. The bedspread was pale blue, so I dyed it deep pink to match the wallpaper which I had put on the bedroom walls. Thank goodness the last people had left us a gas stove, one less thing to buy.

I painted the surrounds of the wooden floor in the sitting room with black paint. All the jobs completed, I then went to Wades furniture shop in town and bought a three-piece suite and a large square carpet, all on hire purchase. The flat looked fabulous, and took on an extra cozy glow when I lit the coal fire.

I had just completed the flat when my friend Bernie from the Odeon called to see me, with some very upsetting news. One of our friends, Silvia who had also worked at the Odeon with us, had been sick and had died in her sleep; Silvia had been a very beautiful looking girl, for quite a few nights I kept having nightmares about this, and said lots of prayers for her.

I was now working in an office at Lovell and Christmas, just off Brunswick Street.

The company made butter and cheese for Marks and Spencer's, British Home Stores and lots of other big companies, they just put different wrapping papers on and changed the recipe, depending on which company the order was for. Frank, the factory manager, showed me crawly cheese under a magnifying glass; I was astounded that people would choose to eat it, but he did explain that the crawly things were removed in the factory, after the cheese had matured.

Every lunch time I would walk to my mother's house, which was only a few minutes away and we would have something to eat together, then Beauty the dog would walk with me back to the office and would then find her way home again across the busy main road.

One evening I was at my mother's house after work when we heard someone banging on the front door. We opened the door to find Parviz there in a rage; he had been to my old flat, and the landlady told him I had moved.

I tried to tell him about the new flat, which I had not been able to write to him about in case someone might read it, so I had hoped it was going to be a big surprise, but he was so angry he would not listen. He had not written to tell me he was coming home so how was I to know?

Now living together for the first time and in our marital home, I was cooking my first ever proper home cooked meal for us. I bought a leg of lamb to roast, I made roast potatoes, veg and all the trimmings;

we did not have a table to eat off, but I wanted this meal to be special as it was the beginning of our new life together.

He waited until I had plated up the meal, then told me he did not like meat, and only liked mashed potatoes, and refused to eat the meal. I then had to get the bus to the shop on Oxford Road to buy a chicken and start all over again, by the time this meal was ready, he said he had a headache through waiting too long, so he went to bed and left the food. This was the beginning of many such occasions.

After work in the evenings I would catch two buses back to the flat, bring the coal up from the cellar and light a fire. Parviz would stay in Central library and come home about nine pm. He explained he had to wait until the flat was warm enough for him,

So of course he would arrive home to a nice big fire and his evening meal. I always made sure the housework was done, and everything was perfect for when he would eventually arrive home.

The people at Lovell and Christmas were great and I liked working there. I had a friend called Dorothy Chapman who had been brought up in our street, so I knew her mother and sisters very well. In our coffee breaks in the canteen, we all used to do the cross word in the daily paper together. I always worked Saturday mornings as overtime, also one Sunday morning each month we would all work for stocktaking. Each week I would give Parviz money for his bus fares, dinner money, and cigarettes.

Early on in 1965, I found out I was pregnant again. I was hoping and praying that Parviz would be acceptable about it this time but in fact he once again went mental and told me to get rid of it.

He was so annoyed, that he went to a shop in town and bought some tablets called Penny Royal. I had lit a fire in the bedroom because I was afraid of how the tablets would affect me, and was worried that they could make me very ill, when he would force me to take them. He had left the tablets on the mantelpiece in the bedroom, and told me I would be taking them on Saturday afternoon when he came home from the library.

I still regularly thank God for my mother paying a rare and unexpected visit. When I told her what the tablets were for, she took

85

them and threw them on the fire. She waited for Parviz to come home and she told him I was not to take any such thing, as I could still have a baby, and it could be born deformed.

One Saturday after working overtime well into the pregnancy with my big bump, one of my work colleagues Irene, offered me a lift part of the way home, when her husband came to collect her in their car, as she said I looked really tired. When I got home and told Parviz how kind they had been, he immediately started to throw things around the flat, breaking some of them, saying that was what he would do to me, if I ever took a lift off anyone again, even married couples.

The last time he had smashed things in the flat was after my sister Anne's wedding, which was April 4th 1964. After the church wedding service, Anne and Eddie went to the hotel where the reception was to take place. The newly married couple stood at the door, to welcome all their guests. I do not remember how many guests there were, but it would be well over a hundred as we are a large family. We had all lined up in a queue to congratulate the happy couple, and shake hands with them. Parviz and I then went to sit on a table with my cousin Joseph Mc Hugh and his wife Judy, who was a schoolteacher.

I could see Parviz was throwing nasty looks at me, but I had no idea why. I knew a lot of people had complemented me on my outfit, but surly that could not be the reason. I had worked overtime that Saturday morning, and had met Parviz at my mother's house, so really could not be sure what had set him off on this occasion.

Much later on in the day I went to the ladies and when I came out, Parviz was waiting outside for me. He took my handbag from me and slung it across the landing of the hotel, spilling out all the contents. He kept hissing at me so as not to be overheard, that Eddie our new brother in law, had shaken my hand harder than he had shaken anyone else's; this was completely untrue, as we had been standing in a queue where he could not possibly see how hard Eddie had shaken the other peoples hands.

He then demanded that we go home and when we got home he smashed several ornaments, and my portable radio. We had so little, it seemed a shame to smash the few things we had, and since I had worked so hard to make a home for us, to now watch it being ruined.

Thankfully I was working that Sunday morning for the stocktaking, so managed to escape, because these moods when they set in, usually lasted for two or three days.

Anne later told me what a great time everyone had had and what we had missed, but I could not tell her why we had gone home early or what it was all about; in fact I never used to confide in anyone, as I was too embarrassed to let people know that I loved a man who treated me so badly.

I bought a great big black and cream pram called a Royal; it was top of the range for my new baby. I knitted lots and lots of clothes and had bought every thing ready.

On one of my visits to my mother, I noticed in Gordon's shop, which Gordon had now bought from the Patterson family, a nice weekend case for sale, which would be perfect for the items of clothing I would take to the hospital to bring my baby home in. He also had a painting in a gold frame that I had fallen for; it was a copy of a John Constable painting, of a man and a dog on a horse and cart in front of an old cottage. This was exactly as I remembered my grandfather in Leitrim. I still have the painting in my study. Every Friday when I got paid, I would visit the shop and pay five shillings off the price of the case, which was three pounds, and five shillings off the painting, which was three pounds and ten shillings. When they were paid for, I took them home and could not wait to pack my case just in case the baby arrived early. If my baby was a boy I wanted to call him Mark; if it was a girl, I had decided on Anna Marie. Now with everything ready, I was very excited and could not wait.

About three or four weeks before the baby was due, Mary and Bob, the couple in the top floor flat, bought a house of their own and moved out. I thought it would be warmer up there for the new baby, so I phoned the landlord and asked could we move upstairs and he agreed. I had to start to decorate the whole flat, again by myself. I had asked Parviz to help me, but he just said it did not need doing. I went to Woolworth's as paint was cheaper there; what a mistake, because it was cheaper I had to give everywhere three coats. I have never bought cheap paint since that experience. My Aunty Mary called to visit and told me I should not be reaching up and painting ceilings when I was pregnant, but there was no one else to do it as Parviz had refused, and I was limited for time before my baby was born. When it was all finished, my sister Elizabeth came to visit and said "there is only you who could make a palace out of a pigsty," I took this as a great compliment.

On July 15th I went into labour, and twenty-four hours later in Stretford Memorial Hospital, I gave birth to a beautiful baby boy, eight and a half pounds in weight. This was my dream come true, as I had kept dreaming I was going to have a boy. I was so very excited. I had already made up the cot in the bedroom weeks ago, and put a shelf on the wall for his toys and his lovely pram was in the hall waiting to take him for walks in Platt Fields Park which was close to where we lived.

Every day I walked around the duck pond in Platt Fields Park, the proudest mum in the world, with my baby in his pram; he was the most precious thing in the world to me and I could not wait for him to sit up and enjoy seeing the swans.

We had Mark christened at St Kentigans Church on Hart Road by Father Connor. I had asked Anne to be his godmother and Elizabeth was delighted to carry him. All my sisters, and their partners, some cousins and aunties came back to the house later for the christening party, it was a very happy family occasion. Mark whom I adored was my first son to survive, and became even more precious because of that.

I had read about a new product on the market called Bonny Bouncers, which was for babies over three months old. On the morning Mark was three months old, I had him in his pram at nine am, and I walked all the way to the baby shop in Withington.

What a brilliant investment, Mark absolutely loved it and he used to happily bounce about for hours, giggling and enjoying himself. It was also supposed to be good for strengthening children's legs.

This was a nice happy time in my life; I used to take Mark in his pram around all my Avon customers. A lot of very wealthy Jewish people lived in the houses on Wilbraham Road in those days. They spent a lot of money on cosmetics and perfume; they also used to enjoy seeing Mark. My sister used to visit, and loved to play with Mark, as he was such a sociable child, he loved everyone and everyone loved him, he certainly got lots of attention.

Father Connor the priest who had christened Mark, called to visit us a quite often, he became a nice friend and said he would teach Parviz how to play the guitar.

Anne's husband Eddie and Elizabeth's husband to be, John, had gone out a few evenings to socialize with Father Connor, Parviz would not go, as he did not like going out to pubs.

They later reported back that father Connor was a good laugh and they had all had a good time, they also said Father Connor had gone out in civvy clothes, not his priest's clothes.

Once Parviz heard this he dropped the guitar lessons, and the priest; he said the priest was only giving him guitar lessons as an excuse to see me, as he must fancy me.

A few weeks later, Father Connor called to see us, but Parviz was out.

I was at home feeding Mark his lunch. The priest explained he had come to say goodbye, as he was being moved to another parish. His eyes filled up with tears when he said, "that is a beautiful picture, a mother and son so happily enjoying each other's company." He then told me that his greatest wish would have been to get married and have children, but his mother had wanted him to be a priest.

One evening our doorbell rang and being on the top floor, I looked out of the window to see who was there. I saw Farad, an Iranian man, standing with a fabulous very long two-tone green car parked in our garden. When he came upstairs, he told me the car belonged to an Iranian man who was leaving England and going back to Iran. He had left the almost new Corsair automatic-drive car with Farad to sell. Farad told me the car was to be sold for three hundred pounds. As I had fallen in love with the car at first sight, I told Farad to keep the car for me, as I was having it. I raised every penny possible, from every direction possible; I claimed all the commission from the household catalogues I used to run. I even sold all my samples of Avon, which I used to buy, then carry around to show my customers. I finally managed to collect the three hundred pounds, which was a considerable amount of money in those days. So I now became the proud owner of the Corsair, one of the biggest and nicest cars on the road at that time. I had often gone on buses with Mark and his push chair, to look at houses which were for rent, now we could drive in our smart car and look for houses. I had also planned to start giving Parviz driving lessons.

Mr Turner our landlord told me he would be selling the house we lived in, as he wanted to retire. The house had six self-contained three-roomed flats. I asked the price and he said three and a quarter thousand pounds, so off I went to the bank to see about a mortgage. The bank manager said he could give me a mortgage, as the flats would make a good income but not my husband as he was a student. I was so thrilled I still have my letter of acceptance. Parviz became very angry and said the Bank manager can keep his mortgage. I tried to reason with him telling him it did not matter whose name the mortgage was in, the house would be in both of our names and owned equally by both of us but this did not suit him as he said that only a man's name should be on a property.

I now took a part time evening job at a driving school called Goodfellows, on Oxford Road working for Mr Williams, and his son. I would work five evenings and Sunday afternoons. Some evenings my cousin would look after Mark, other evenings Parviz's brother Combiz, who now lived in one of our flats, would come and stay with him. I knew it would only be for a few months as I was pregnant again, and Parviz had not objected this time.

One evening I went to pick Parviz up from the library, he kept insisting on driving home even though he had not yet passed his driving test, so he got into the driving seat and off we went. It was pouring rain and as we drove into Hart Road, Parviz ran into two girls who were crossing the road and were sharing an umbrella. One of the girls was lying on the road unconscious. Parviz and the other girl lifted her onto the back seat and I drove to the Manchester Royal. When we got there, Parviz told the staff that I had been driving, which was completely untrue. The girl was still unconscious, and the other girl kept screaming at him that he was a liar, and asked him what sort of a man would blame his pregnant wife, and what if her friend died. The girl eventually recovered and I had to pay all the hospital costs.

I got in touch with a housing association, who told me they were building new houses in Macclesfield, so one afternoon I took Mark and drove to have a look around. I spotted a lorry on the road loaded with bricks, so I followed it to a new housing estate. On enquiring, I found out that Manchester City County Council were building the houses. I excitedly told Parviz about them when he came home from college that evening. I remember I could not sleep that night with excitement, determined we were going to have one of these houses. The next day I went down to the council for an interview and the lady there said she could offer us a flat. I drove all the way back to Macclesfield to look at the flats and decided they were not for me, especially when I had already seen the great houses. I telephoned the town hall and said no I did not want a flat; as I was pregnant again I would prefer a house. A few weeks later we were given the address of a brand new really great house, with front and back gardens, upstairs and downstairs toilets, which were just finishing being built.

About this time, Parviz was getting off the bus coming from college, when he got a sharp pain in his eye. I drove him down to the eye hospital; after seeing the doctor; they said he would have to stay in for an operation, as he had a detached retina.

I got a letter from the town hall to say the house was complete and I could pick up the keys. My next baby was due in three weeks, so every day I went first to the Eye hospital to see Parviz, and then drove 20 miles to Macclesfield to get the house ready. I bought some flat pak children's wardrobes, put these together and painted them white; I later put some children's transfers on them, one for Marks room and one for the baby's room. I then emulsioned our bedroom blue. I was putting up curtain rails in the kitchen when my next-door neighbour Betty came and introduced herself. She said "in your state, you should not be doing jobs like that" but I told her there was no one else to do them. We would then drive back to Manchester, and I would go to work at the driving school.

Every night before he went to bed, Mark used to kiss his brother or sister in my tummy Goodnight. When Parviz finally came out of hospital, I drove him up to Macclesfield to show him what I had done with the house, but as usual, him not being a home maker, he did not appreciate what I had done. I should have been getting used to this by now, as this was the third home I had made for us since we had been married.

A few days later I went into labour. Parviz went to bed and left me on my own, he said he must have his sleep, so I sat all night hoping I could wait until morning before giving birth.

About six o'clock in the morning I woke him up and told him I could not wait any longer, and must go to the hospital.

I had been teaching Parviz to drive so even though he had not yet passed his test, we took Mark to my aunties, then he drove me to the hospital.

The nurse asked Parviz if he would like to stay or come back in a hour or two to witness the birth; my own general practitioner Doctor Alexandra was called and he delivered my beautiful baby daughter, nine and a half pounds in weight.

Parviz arrived several hours later and said he had been busy. I now had what I considered the perfect family, one boy and one girl, Mark and Deborah. I had considered calling the baby Lara, after the girl in Doctor Zhivago, but settled on Deborah.

While I was in hospital Parviz came to visit us and brought me in a speeding fine.

I thought this is quite amusing, and knew my new baby would grow up to become a fast driver, as she had been speeding even before she was born.

I had continued to work at the driving school until the day before Debbie was born, so would now give that job up.

When Debbie was three weeks old, we moved into our lovely new house. I remember sitting on the settee in the sitting room nursing my new baby, with Mark standing in front of me with his arms around her.

I remember tears running down my face with joy and thinking life can never get any better than this.

Our first week in our new home, a friend called John and his Iranian wife invited us to their house for a meal to celebrate the birth of our daughter and our new house.

They had wanted to see the new baby but they did not have a car so it was arranged we would visit them. They lived in North Manchester, so it would be about one hour's drive.

I got the children ready, put Debbie in her carrycot on the back seat of the car and I was just about to get into the driver's seat, when I had a strange feeling, I told Parviz we were going to have a car crash. When I told him this, he would not let me drive and decided he would drive instead, as he had now passed his driving test.

We had driven through Stockport and were heading down the A6 on the outside lane, when all of a sudden a car careered across the road in front of us; we crashed into it, which was unavoidable. I jumped out, saw Mark was OK, looked to the back seat but the carry cot had disappeared, and was jammed down the back of the seats. My heart felt as though it had stopped, I seemed to be frozen to the spot, and I kept thinking please God not again, please let her be all right. I was terrified of pulling the carrycot up in case of what I might find. I was telling Parviz to go and get witnesses' names and addresses while I saw to the baby. When with my heart in my mouth I did move the seats and get the carrycot up, there was my beautiful baby fast asleep and unharmed.

I then also got some of the witnesses' names and addresses, before they disappeared.

Parviz was very shocked and very angry and kept telling me it was my entire fault, as I had unnerved him by saying we were going to be in a car crash.

When the police arrived, they sent us to the hospital in Stockport for a check up as I had banged my head, even though I kept telling them I was OK. Whilst we were waiting in the hospital, a policeman came and interviewed us; he said we were lucky to be in such a big car, as it probably saved our lives. Then he told us the other driver had had a heart attack. A few weeks later, a court case had been arranged but at the last minute it was called off as the other man accepted liability, when it had been discovered he had had the heart attack before he crashed the car, and in fact that is why the crash happened. The court case was cancelled! And Parviz never did apologize for blaming me for the accident.

Chapter Six

During the summer of 1968, I had seen lots of advertisements looking for people to emigrate to Australia. I discussed this at length with Parviz, and finally got him to come to Australia House, which was situated on the Piccadilly approach to Piccadilly station.

The advertisers had said they were looking for young families and it would only cost ten pounds to emigrate to a superior life, in a new young country Australia. We filled in all the forms but were turned down, as Parviz is of Iranian nationality we were told we would not qualify, as they were only looking for British people with a British passport.

I was a bit disappointed. I then talked to Parviz, telling him I would like us to go and live on a farm in Ireland. He sounded agreeable but nothing happened, as I could not even get him to visit Ireland for a holiday, his excuse being that he did not like holidays.

I heard an announcement on the radio that Doctor Alexandra's wife had been attacked by one of his ex patients who had called to his home then stabbed his wife as she opened the front door. I was now living in Macclesfield, but Dr Alexandra had agreed to keep me on in his Manchester practice, which I really appreciated, as I had been his patient since being a child. I phoned the doctor and told him if he wanted any help to look after his two boys I would under the circumstances be happy to do whatever I could. Dr Alexandra said he appreciated the kind gesture, but his mother was already there helping. When I told Parviz what I had done he flew into one of his usual rages and accused me of fancying the doctor, and told me that he insisted that I change doctors, which I did, as I had no choice.

I decided to go for my advanced driving test, as I had already had the lessons, I was delighted when I passed the test the first time. This considerably reduced my car insurance to almost half the usual price, and I now sported a triangle badge on my car as a sign of being an advanced driver. It had been a tough test with lots of running commentary and driving at high speeds around Manchester Airport, but that did not matter, as I was now an advanced driver.

When Debbie was about eighteen months old, 1969 a man called James Heath gave me a job at ELS, selling furniture and carpets on a commission only basis. This was a Sunday only job, so Parviz looked after the children. On my first Sunday, I earned the equivalent of a full week's wages.

After a few months with my newfound experience, I then decided to run a furniture shop on Regent Road Salford just at the time the high-rise flats in Salford were being built.

I had a lovely lady called Edna Fairbanks who looked after the children for me, and cleaned my house a few days a week, which was a wonderful help. This gave me more time to do the shopping and cooking. I always did the washing and ironing in the evenings, and spent as much time as possible with Parviz and my children.

Each morning I would drive twenty-two miles from Macclesfield to the shop. I used to put rolls of carpet outside the shop, also items of furniture to attract the customers. I decorated the shop in a lovely gold coloured emulsion, I nailed carpets and rugs to some of the walls and it started to look really nice. A fourteen-year-old schoolboy called Albert called in to see if there were any odd jobs he could do after school. Albert was a very nice and agreeable boy, he was a great help as he would go and do some small items of shopping for me, and at closing time he would help me to bring in the unsold furniture and carpets.

Sometimes on my way home from Salford to Macclesfield, when I would be near home, I would pull into a lay by, where there were lots of trees and flowers, I would take deep breaths and sit there for a few moments and look at all the beauty around me and thank God for the love of my two beautiful children whom I was rushing home to, I used to think that putting up with their father was the price I had to pay for their love, then I would say a little prayer that Parviz would not be in a bad mood, as me working always seemed to make him.

One Saturday lunchtime, the phone rang in the shop. It was Parviz, and he said he was just going to have his shower, he wanted to wear his blue underwear, but it was in the airing cupboard, and not in his drawer, where it should be. I did explain it was ironed and ready for him to wear and was in the airing cupboard so as to be nice and warm for him. He told me to shut that bloody shop and come home and put his clothes in his drawer, where they should be. I took all the furniture and carpets inside, closed the shop, drove twenty-two miles to Macclesfield, to take his underwear out of the cupboard and put it in his drawer, he then went off in a foul mood to the students union, and I stayed at home with Mark and Debbie.

Another Saturday Parviz came down to my shop, and started causing trouble again, as an Iranian Jewish man called Amiel Josephs, who owned a carpet company called Magic Carpets, had called into the shop to see how well the carpets were selling.

Parviz said Mr Josephs was only there because he fancied me. This man was happily married with a very beautiful wife and a gorgeous daughter called Jasmine, both of whom I had been introduced to at ELS. James Heath and my sister called over to the shop at closing time, they saw the foul temper Parviz was in, and took us both to the pub for a drink, hoping to change his mood. This would be mission impossible, as when he went into these moods, no one could get him out of them.

After the drink we each in our own cars drove home to Macclesfield, but when we got home he was uncontrollable, because people had again seen the other side to him, and once again saw his temper. So I told him I could not take much more of this unreasonable behaviour, so I was leaving the children with Mrs Fairbanks for one night, and going to spend the night with my cousin Patricia in Altrincham, until he cooled down.

I was travelling on the road to Knutsford, when all of a sudden a car coming from the opposite direction was travelling down my side of the road. To try to save myself, I pulled to the left, then hit a high verge and my car went out of control. It crossed the grass verge, careered through a hedge and ended upside down on its roof in a field.

The police, fire brigade, and ambulance all arrived, I remember a policeman saying to me "we will have to get you out in case the car goes on fire". This really frightened me as the doors were all damaged and jammed closed; finally I was cut free from the car, and amazingly not injured, I had only banged my head. I was glad I was not wearing a seat belt, as I would have been tied in upside down. (seat belts were not compulsory in those days).

The police had phoned Parviz to come and pick me up. When he saw the car upside down in the field, and realized what I had survived from, he was shocked. He really apologized for his earlier behaviour and said he would try to be less possessive in the future. This statement made me think the accident was almost worth it.

There was no problem with the insurance, as the skid marks left on the road by the other car showed what had happened, and that I was in no way to blame.

I had only bought this car, a top of the range Aquatic Jade coloured Cortina; brand new in February and now in July the Insurance Company said they were writing it off.

The next day I drove Parviz's car, which he called his 'old lady', so I did not lose my nerve to drive.

On Friday evenings, after I had closed the shop, I used to go across the road to Christine's the hairdresser. I used to wear a hairpiece made into curls on the top of my head as this was the latest fashion, Christine could do this style in a way that it would last all week.

The year is now 2009, some thirty-nine years later and Christine and her husband Derek are still close friends of mine. Christine and I spent ten days in Florida together, when my friend Margaret got married on a yacht. Then only a few weeks ago I spent three glorious days and nights with them both at their lovely home, staying up all night chatting and having fun and we have planned to spend some time together this summer at their holiday home in Benidorm.

Anyway back to the past. I had a friend called Irene Smith whose husband was a policeman and told me that Strangways prison in Salford was looking for prison wardens. He said the salary and holidays were excellent and I should apply.

I went to Strangways prison had a interview and was offered a job. They did explain that the prison first opened in 1868, which I remember thinking was one hundred years before Debbie was born so felt as if this was going to be a good career move for me. They also explained that this was a men only prison and that they no longer took women prisoners.

I had arranged to pick up my uniform and start to do the prison training, but the night before this was to happen, Parviz suddenly said, "You are not going to do that job". He kept going on at me about, what sort of a person was I, that wanted to do such a job?

We had a dreadful argument, which became so bad that poor Mark made a placard and walked into Macclesfield protesting about his father hitting his mother, and why wouldn't anyone do anything to stop it.

The police picked Mark up and brought him home in the police car, they then witnessed what Mark was protesting about. The police asked Parviz what the trouble was all about. When Parviz told them his wife wanted to work in the prison, one of the policemen told him," you are bloody lucky, I wish my wife wanted to go to work." They then asked me if I wanted to charge Parviz with assault, to which I replied No.

This only infuriated Parviz all the more, so when the police left he then smashed our beautiful antique oil lamp, which we had bought at an antique shop in Wales. He had already told me I had to choose, it was either the furniture shop or him, I had because of my children chosen him, now he would not let me work in the prison, and we desperately needed my wages to live on, so what was I to do?

I bought the Manchester Evening News, as I had decided to find a job with a company car and I left home the next morning, telling Parviz what type of job I was looking for, hoping he would not disapprove.

When I got home that evening, I told him I had found a fulltime job as a representative with a company car. I felt as though I had achieved what I had set out to do. I was employed to work for Masters Stores as a traveller, covering the town of Macclesfield, Whally Bridge, and Disley, which was near Buxton.

My boss Joes Syer, had interviewed me, and after explaining that this was a tremendous sized area and had only ever been worked by a man, and he was worried it was to large an area to be worked by a woman. I told him you do not know this woman. He gave me the job.

(Joe his wife Irene and daughter Judith since remained friends of mine until he passed away in August 2006.)

I would drive twenty miles from Macclesfield to the office in Manchester every morning and then twenty miles back a few hours later, before I even started work on my rounds. There were one hundred travellers working for the company and we would cash in our takings for the previous day, do our office work, collect our stock, and have various area meetings, which would take about two hours. Then we would drive out to our various areas, and sell furniture, carpets, ladies fashions, and all electrical goods such as TV's, washing machines and so on.

Twice a year, Masters Stores would have fashion shows; all customers would be encouraged down to the showrooms. As I lived and worked in the farthest out area, on the Saturday, the company would put on two coaches for my customers, which I would always manage to fill. I was the only traveller to have this privilege because of the distance involved. My wages at Masters were excellent, and would be even greater after all my commission from the fashion shows. Joe Syer used to use me as an example at the general meetings, where he used to tell the other travellers, "If Mrs Farazian can do such brilliant sales all the way out in Macclesfield, then there is no excuse for some of you who are working on the doorstep and selling very little."

I got my sister Elizabeth a job with a company car and she worked part of the Stockport area. I also got my cousin Patricia a job working on the area she lived in. We were all three on the same section; they called us the Cheshire group. Mr Harold Hulme was our section leader; he was in charge of the seven areas in his group.

Mr Hulme did not have a sense of humour, but the rest of us used to have lots of laughs.

My sister used to wind up Mr Hulme; she once asked him in February could she please have a week off work in September to go to Ireland to attend a funeral. He looked at her in amazement and asked her how did she know she was going to a funeral in September, Elizabeth replied she had been to see a fortune teller.

In the meantime Parviz's brother Combiz and his son Steven had come to live with us, as Combiz's wife Josephine had died of stomach cancer. Combiz was a very quiet and inoffensive kind of person. Parviz being the older brother always bossed him about; he used to get very angry with Combiz, and said he crept around the house and you could never hear where he was, but I put this down to good manners and consideration. Combiz coming to live with us was a blessing in disguise as I noticed now that Parviz had Combiz to fall out with he was leaving me alone, and was OK about my job.

I used to make lots of cockaleekie soup for Steven, by putting baking flour into a plastic bag then adding pieces of chicken and shaking it all together then putting it into the pan with chopped up leeks to boil. This was one of Stevens's favorite meals. Combiz and Steven stayed for a few months then found a flat of their own in Manchester.

A few months afterwards Parviz's other, much younger brother Changeese was sent to us from Iran by his parents. Parviz had always talked fondly of his baby brother, but now they were living in the same house, they simply did not get on. They really did not know each other because of the age difference. Changeese had been very young when Parviz had left Iran, he was a very nervous and very insecure person, and did not show Parviz any respect. Eventually, after a few months, Parviz told him to find a flat as far away from him as possible, which

Changeese did; sadly they have never seen each other or been in touch since, and I believe Changeese now lives in the South of England.

Parviz is neither in touch with his other brother Combiz, who still lives in Manchester, nor with his father, who lives in Iran.

I made friends with a girl at Masters called Christine Skidmore, who lived in Mosley near Ashton Under Lyne. Chris often came over to Macclesfield with her children. She also had a boy and a girl. The drive would be over fifty miles each way, but that did not deter her and we also occasionally went over to her house. Chris introduced me to two of her friends, Margaret and Eva. Margaret lived in Henrietta Street in Ashton and is still one of my very closest and most longstanding friends, even though she now lives in Florida in America, I go over to stay with her every two or three years. Eva lived in Stallybridge and the last time I heard from her was four year ago.

At Masters I earned excellent wages, commission and bonuses, which I needed to, support the family. One month I also won a freezer and stereo player for having the most new customers. Yet Parviz once again told me to give up the job, becoming resentful of my achievement and my success. (As he was still a student) I told him we could not survive without the income but he told me to send back the telephone and the coloured television and to stay at home. I was earning all our income, not just the TV and the telephone, since I was the one who had to manage everything, so I said I could not do that. He then told me, "It is the job or me." He had given me ultimatums like this before, so this time I told him "I will choose the job." He went off to Manchester and found himself a flat, as he was still a student at the university there. After some time I went to visit him one night to give him his mail; he had a girl in his room and they were both drunk. I told him I was divorcing him, so he tried to push me out of the window of the second floor flat.

My sister Elizabeth and her daughter Lavinia were not getting on too well at this time. Lavinia had told Elizabeth she wished she could live with Maureen. I had always been very fond of Lavinia, she used to sit in my mother's house with her knees crossed as I always did, and be pretending to smoke a cigarette and she used to say to my mother "do not call me Lavinia, call me Maureen." I always took this as a lovely sweet compliment. I told Elizabeth that Lavinia could come and live with us if she really wanted to and Elizabeth and Lavinia both readily agreed.

The house felt lovely and happy, with no arguments. I now had three children to look after. During the school summer holidays, all three of them would come to work with me, and play or draw pictures in the back of my company estate car. In the mornings whilst I was in the office, all three of them would stay at my mother's, which was only a few minutes away, from the office. About two hours later I would pick them up and take them on my rounds with me, until one day my mother got in touch with Parviz and told him I kept dumping the children on her, to which he replied, "They are not my problem".

I was incredibly upset about this as it had been her idea to have them in the first place, and why had she not mentioned it to me, if she had changed her mind.

So I then arranged for Mrs Fairbanks to look after the three children in the mornings.

Every Thursday night when I had been paid I would bring home an Indian take away curry, which we all really looked forward to and enjoyed. Life was very simple and very calm, no arguments, and as a family we were very happy together, the sort of peaceful happiness a family should be sharing.

We used to sit and happily chat away in the evenings. I often talked to the children about how to be kind and considerate to other people, and how to respect people's feelings.

I used to explain to them that people will always remember you by how you make them feel. Because of my strong protective love for my children, I had always tried to build a strong solid foundation for them, giving them plenty of confidence, unlike the way I was brought up. I knew I would never say anything cruel or unkind to my children or call them an unkind name, and I never have, as I know how bad it feels, having suffered it from my own father. I then used to feel sorry for my father that he had not experienced the joy that I was feeling at these precious times.

I had always been interested in of psychology, so I would explain things to the children, like "you do not love the people that you love because they are perfect, you love them because they are what they are." Lavinia loved our chats and in her enthusiasm used to say to Mark and Debbie "your mum is right you know, yes your mum is right."

A lot of these chats would take place by candlelight, as at this time the miners' strike was on, and as I drove home from work there would be no street lighting and no traffic lights, then when I got home, there would be no electricity or heating for about three hours, so I often had to do my accounts for that day by candle light, but I did not mind that, as life was nice and peaceful and happy.

About six months or more later, Parviz phoned me and told me he had managed to get a job in Iran, but would not leave for three weeks, so could he stay with us until he left England as he had to give notice on his flat. He arrived with all his belongings, and then acted as though we had never been apart but he seemed much more relaxed, maybe because of his new job, and we were getting on OK together.

My sister Elizabeth always said we were like Elizabeth Taylor and Richard Burton in a sometimes fiery and other times very loving relationship. She said she would move in for a few days and look after the children if we would like to take a holiday together and talk things through. We had in our entire marriage only ever been on one holiday together to Butlin's. My family had not taken holidays, so I had not been brought up to expect them, and Parviz did not like holidays, so I was hoping that this time spent on our own might be a good idea.

We decided to tour Scotland; I drove as far as Inverness, and we arrived about teatime, and found a hotel. Parviz decided he had a headache and went to bed. About eight o'clock he woke up, saying he did not feel well and was staying in bed, I asked him if I could go into the dining room in the hotel and have a meal but he got annoyed that I would even suggest going on my own.

That was it, the beginning of another few days of bad moods.

He complained about absolutely everything; every time we stopped for a meal he would complain about the food, and he complained about every hotel we stayed in.

I did all the driving all over Scotland for the four days and the moods lasted until I drove into the motorway services near home, then all of a sudden he was nice and loving again. He said he did not like being away from home and could not help his moods, and as usual I felt sorry for him and forgave him. When we got back to Elizabeth and the children, I was completely worn out, and he was being pleasant to everybody, so if I said anything now, I would have looked like the bad one. I have since learnt that women who are abused whether physically or mentally by their husband or partner usually cover for the abuser.

The stress I felt under with this man was unmeasurable, and I find it all very difficult to explain. So I never did say anything to anyone, as I would never, and had never criticized my husband to anyone.

Parviz was now in Iran, and I was full of renewed hope. I thought that maybe his mercurial moods had been insecurities and now that he had found a proper job, maybe he would be easier to live with in the future. When he was working in Iran, he kept sending me lovely romantic letters. He would come home on leave every few months, we would go shopping, and he would have a shopping list of perfumes and items of clothing for his mother and his aunties, which I would choose for them. I would then happily see him off at the airport.

I applied for a job at Tobacco Kiosks Ltd, known as TKL. The interview took place in a café in Wilmslow with a very friendly lady called Merrial, who said she was a supervisor for the company. Merrial was accompanied by a German lady called Dagmar who introduced herself as the stock-taker for TKL

At the end of the interview Merrial said she would be in touch with me when all interviews were completed and a decision had been made, which would be in about a week. That same evening Merrial phoned me at home and told me I had the job, as they knew what they liked when they saw it.

I went to a hotel in Manchester on a training course and then worked in the Wilmslow branch, which was situated in a Tesco store, as this was a franchise business.

I had only been with TKL for a few weeks when Parviz's parents came to England. Parviz's mother had kidney failure and needed to go on a Dialyses machine.

I phoned my manager, Phyllis Weedall, and explained the situation and also told her that my husband and my in-laws did not know I had a job, so I would now have to leave the job, as my in-laws did not speak English and I would need to spend all of my time with them, and to find a private doctor for them.

Phyllis was incredibly understanding. I did explain that I was embarrassed at having to let her down, as it is not in my nature to do so but Phyllis told me to take a few weeks off and to get in touch with her when everything was sorted out. This was wonderful as I really enjoyed the job.

I found a private doctor for Mariam, (Parviz's mother), who said that she would have to go down to London on a dialyses machine three times a week for several weeks.

Sometimes I would drive Mariam down to London but other times when she felt up to it we would fly down. Combiz had offered to give his mother one of his kidneys. The doctors had explained that a kidney transplant would in this case only work in the short term, but that they would never take a kidney from the young to give to the old as the younger person had much longer to live and might be dependent on that kidney one day.

So after a month of dialyses Marian went home, after being told her condition was very serious, and she would have to continue with Dialyses treatment immediately upon her arrival back in Iran.

Parviz phoned me and said that when his mother got back to Iran, she told him he was very lucky to have a wife like me. She also told him that I could do any job a man could do. I was delighted to hear that she said I was very heartwarming, as I always sat with my arm around her which made her feel protected. But then of course I was especially fond of her, and I had enjoyed looking after her.

Parviz seemed happy enough with his job in Iran and after one of his visits home we bought a piece of farmland, which was for sale, belonging to Bluebell Farm in Tytherington. We eventually had a very nice four bedroomed house built on it, with lovely views of the countryside all around. We were surrounded by fields; in one field in front of the house there were sheep, on one side there were cows, across this field lay the village of Presbury, and on the other side two beautiful chestnut horses. I thought I might be able to have a horse in the field next to us then the children and I could have riding lessons.

Whilst the house was being built, we used to visit the site a few times a week and it became very exciting to watch the house progress.

We discovered that the land we had built on had been an Anglo Saxon graveyard, so I bought Parviz a metal detector, but he never found any treasure. My mother and I discussed names for the house and she liked Wyvern Height, so that is what it was named. I then could not wait to have my addressed notepaper printed, with our house title at the top.

My longing for a horse originated from when I was young in Ireland, my grandfather had two horses one called Dandy and one called Neddy and he told me that Neddy was my horse. A few years later, when we were back in England, my mother received a letter telling us that Neddy had fallen in the river and had drowned.

The dream of me having a horse in the field next to our house fell through, when a piece of spare land which had not previously been for sale, was purchased by a young Scottish couple who got planning permission and built a house on it, so we were no longer next to the field. But never mind, it was just not meant to be, and I would probably never have got around to learning to ride anyway.

At the end of June 1976, Parviz came home on leave. The next day my mother went into hospital. I went to see her in the afternoon, and then my sisters went to see her in the evening whilst I stayed at Anne's and looked after everyone's children. The Doctor informed the family that my mother had cancer in at least four places, and gave her about one year to live. Elizabeth said she would move into our mother's house and look after her.

That same night in the early hours of the morning, on July 1st 1976, the ward sister from the hospital phoned to say that my mother had passed away. This had been my mothers wish since1949, which had been The Holy Year, but it still came as a dreadful shock.

I remember thinking god must have sent Parviz home on leave, as I was so devastated, I do not know how I would have coped without him.

The grave had been dug for the funeral, when all of a sudden a letter was found stating that my mother wanted to be cremated. She had said this for years, as she had always said she did not want to be buried with my father in case they might continue to fight after they were dead. This was a very sad time for all the family.

Parviz returned to Iran on July 22nd full of plans for the future. He said that next year, when he could find a house for us over there, he would send for us. I did not relish that thought.

My grandmother in Galway died on July 26th 1976 at about 6pm; my dad and Jacqueline were in Ireland with her. Thank goodness my dad had Jacqueline with him, as this was a very sad month for him; first he had lost his wife, then three weeks later his mother.

Later that year, I took Mark and Debbie camping. We went to Chigwell with a friend of ours, Dora, and her children. It was just the change we needed. I slept really well in our tent. I had only rented the tent, but I decided I would buy one of our own, when we got home.
After the holiday, as soon as we got back to Macclesfield, we bought a great big tent with three bedrooms, three blow up beds, a gas stove and everything we could find to do with camping. This was a new way of life and very relaxing and we really enjoyed it. We travelled around a few weekends and explored new campsites, the favourite being in Solway Lido, in Sillioth, Cumbria.

I spent most of the next year sorting out our new house. I ordered a kitchen from Kitchen Queen but three months later, when it was due to be fitted, I found out that the order had been lost, and we had to wait another three months before the kitchen could be fitted. We had by now moved into the new house so thank goodness we had a camping stove and could survive very nicely. I had a stone fireplace built and bedroom furniture fitted, I bought all the carpets and furniture, I ordered a fabulous Youngers Toledo Range dining room suite from Anne and a beautiful Velda three-piece suite from a very expensive furniture shop in Wilmslow, I bought some super luxury curtains from Curtain King, and was determined to have it all finished by the time of Parviz's next visit, when-ever that would be.

I then started on the large garden; first I had a lawn laid then I planted evergreen trees down both sides, with an apple tree and a pear tree at the bottom, I then created a vegetable patch, growing potatoes, cabbage, carrots and so on. The only vegetable I had trouble growing was cauliflower as they always went to seed on me.

Every evening we would go out into the garden and pick our vegetables or salad and would only have to purchase the meat; everything tasted so healthy and so good.

I bought a few exotic trees one being a monkey tree which I thought was quite splendid, I finished it all off with a bird house and two white doves.

The house and gardens now completed, I started looking for the luxury items so I took Mark and Debbie to Lewis's department store in Manchester and I found some exceptionally good crystal glasses in the sale, and I decided to purchase six whiskey glasses, six white wine glasses, six red wine glasses, and six liqueur glasses. When I got home that evening, I decided that I really should have bought eight of each glass to allow for breakages, so I decided the next morning to drive all the way back to Manchester to purchase the extra glasses.

I had parked outside Lewis's and spent approximately thirty minutes in the store purchasing the glasses. When I came outside, to my horror I saw my car had disappeared, and a policeman was standing on the pavement informing people that that their cars had been taken to the compound, and that we would have to pay a fine of thirty pounds before we could reclaim them. So the glasses, with all the petrol and now the fine, were not such a bargain after all, but were very beautiful and I do still have them.

June 7th 1977 was the Queen's Royal Jubilee. We put the new big tent up in the back garden, and decorated everywhere with streamers. I invited family, friends and neighbours from our last house. My godmother Posy came, with her son and

daughter-in –law, also her sister who was on holiday from Canada.

Every one had to be totally dressed in red, white and blue and each family had to have a uniform way of using these colours. I spent days happily organizing the garden, the food and doing lots of baking and I then went out and stocked up on lots and lots of booze. The party was a great success and lasted three days.

Thank God Parviz never found out about the party, other-wise it would have caused more trouble, but nobody ever told him, as everyone knew what he was like from past experiences. I hid all the photographs, but am glad I still have them now, as they are a part of our happy memories.

Chapter Seven

JULY 26TH 1977, MY SON Mark and my daughter Debbie and I flew to Tehran, which was the capitol city of Iran. Mark was eleven years old and Debbie was eight. Parviz and his friend Resher were waiting at the airport when we arrived, at twelve o'clock midnight their time.

Parviz had booked us into a hotel. The next morning after breakfast we all went to visit Parviz's parents, Mariam and Mustafa. We walked a long way in the hot sun, and I am not sure what I expected but it was nothing like this, scruffy old buildings, and lots of peasants in the dusty streets guarding their fruit stalls, and all the fruit covered in flies. Debbie kept saying "can we go home?" and even though I was happy to see my husband, I must admit I felt the same. We finally got to Parviz's parent's flat. His mother gave Debbie and me a chador each to wear, which was a full length black cloak worn by females, covering your head, clothes and part of the face. She also gave me a cookery book called In a Persian Kitchen, written by an American. I was greatly surprised to see that Mariam had spread a tablecloth on the floor; she had made a nice meal for lunch and this was the first I knew that Iranians eat sitting on the floor. (They also sleep on the floor covered by their chadors.)

Parviz had told me nothing about Iran. Knowing it was supposed to be a wealthy country I thought it would be like London, but it was more like pictures I had seen of Iraq.

The traffic was terrifying; a two-way road often becoming one-way, then essential services like fire brigade could not get through and motorbikes would ride on the pavements.

One evening Reisher took us out to an open-air nightclub for a meal; it seemed strange and rather nice to be in a nightclub and be able to see the airplanes going overhead. Ladies were not allowed to drink in this club, Parviz pointed out to me, where men queue up for the prostitutes upstairs. I did not need that information, and would have preferred not to know.

In this country public toilets and private toilets are a hole in the ground and everyone including the women, just stands there and aims, so you do not sit down on the loo, plus they are usually disgusting and smelly.

After our few days in Tehran, we drove ten hours non-stop to a place called Sabzevah; four hours further on and we would have been at the Russian border. Parviz worked in Sabzevah, which is on the edge of the salt desert; he worked for an American company called Hunt International. We stayed in a hotel for about a week, as our house was not ready. Parviz said he did not want us to eat in the dining room; we must stay in our room. I ordered lamb chops for lunch and a plate arrived with at least forty tiny skinny chops with a thin layer of meat on them, as there is no grass for the sheep to eat. We ate about half the chops and put the remainder in a cupboard for later but a few hours later when we took the plate out, I could not see the chops for ants. I did not know that you could expect this in these hot dry countries as I had never been abroad before. What I did realize was that I had a lot to learn.

The company had provided a nice house for us, and a Chevrolet Blazer car; all we had to do was have furniture made. We also had to buy material for me to make sheets and blankets, as in the primitive areas you could not buy these items, since local people did not have beds. If Parviz had told me this, I would have bought some bedding in Tehran, it being a city.

Our house was next door to the chief of police, so I started off feeling quite safe. However that feeling did not last for long when I learnt, that in Iran, if a man beats his wife, it is assumed that she must have earned it, and a man can hit his wife as much as he wants so long as no serious injury occurs.

Every time I drove anywhere, people would stop in the middle of the road and stare at me. Parviz said it was the hair, as they had never seen a blonde before. He also told me that if I drive on my own, on the out of town roads, because I am a woman, the men drivers would probably run me off the road, as women should not be seen to be independent.

I decided to learn Farsi, which is the Iranian language, and I set myself a target to learn two sentences every day, from a book I had bought in Tehran. After about a week, I ventured out in the dust and heat for a walk with the children, Debbie and I wearing our chadors. When we got to the end of our street, a lovely young woman started to talk to me. In my limited Farsi, I told her I have come from England, my husband is Iranian and called Parviz, but known locally as Mr Engineer. I introduced my children to her, she told us she was called Nushka, and she then invited us into her home, where we sat on the floor and had a glass of tea. Tea in Iran is served in a small glass from a samovar, they do not put milk in their tea, and if you take sugar you chip the sugar from a big block, put a piece of the sugar into your mouth and sip the tea through the sugar.

Nushka told me they do not yet have children, as they have not long been married and she then showed me her sewing machine and very proudly showed me the diploma she had earned for her sewing.

I felt quite proud of myself being able to communicate with my newly learnt Farsi, and Nushka was excited as she was managing to learn a few words of English. She said she had never met an English person before, and I knew she would not be likely to in a small off the track place like Sabzevah. This felt like the beginning of what might become a nice friendship. Nushka's husband then came home for his lunch, and as was the custom of the Muslims, as a man enters the house, all the females in the house must put on their chadors, which we did. After our visit, I could not wait for Parviz to come home to tell him all about it.

When I did tell him however instead of him being pleased as I had expected, he went mental, and warned me I must never go into anyone's house again, no matter who invites me, as all the houses have men, either fathers or husbands, living in them.

I started to wonder was it the men he was worried about, or was he doing what he had done in England, segregating me from people, so as when he ill treated me, I had no one to go to. If this was the case, I could now see what a shock he must have got, that I was learning the language all on my own and willing to go out and make new friends, even in a country like this. When we were in England he had told me he did not need friends as I was his best friend, and he did not think I should need friends either.

A part of me had thought that when I came to live in his country he would be happy and everything would be all right, but he was still being very a aggressive man.

I had a very interesting visit from a Mullah one day, they are like a high priest, and held in high esteem. I did not know who had sent him, but he spoke excellent English. I told him Parviz would be home later, so asked him to come back then, but he insisted on staying and was definitely not the type of man you would argue with. He told me he had come to tell me of the 'Rules of Islam' and to explain the rules of the Mosque which is the Muslim Church, and the Koran, which is their equivalent of the Bible.

After he talked a lot, I asked him could I write it down, in case I forgot and he told me I would not be allowed to forget, but I wrote most of it down anyway. He said the Koran dictates: -

Allah gave man authority against women, as women are deficient.
The witness of two women is equal to the witness of one man.
Men are in charge of women.
Everywhere the husband goes the wife should follow.
A man can hit his wife though only lightly, they recommend prodding at first.
Adulterers and Drunks must get a Flogging
People must Discriminate against Homosexuality, as it is an abomination against Allah, they must be thrown off the top of a mountain.
The prophet Mohammed married a girl of nine years old, as it is quite permissible to marry a girl before puberty.
Jihad has a love of Martyrdom.
And he said that I must wear my Chador at all times.

When Parviz came home I showed him the list, and he said the Mullar will probably be back every week looking for money for the Mosque, I never opened the door to him again, as he had certainly put the fear of Allah into me.

After being warned that I must not go into anyone's house, I lost all enthusiasm for learning Farsi, and settled down to a very lonely and boring life, living in a part of the country where there was no English radio or TV, no books or newspapers. If Parviz had warned me about this, at least I could have brought some books over from England. I so wished I could go home.

About every six or eight weeks on a Sunday we would drive four hours to Mashad, which is the Holy City. That was the nearest place where I could purchase a newspaper, the only choice would be a two weeks old News of the World, but I was just glad of anything to read and any news of what was going on in England. It was two weeks after Elvis Presley had died that I found out he was dead. I thought of how I remembered seeing Strictly Isolated on my door in the burns unit when I was in hospital, but this was a more severe case of being, Severely Strictly Isolated!

On one of our visits to Mashad we went to visit a Mosque; Debbie and I had to wear our chadors. The domes on the top of the Mosque were painted in real gold; there was a service-taking place so like everyone else we left our shoes outside, which was compulsory. After the service everyone rushed outside like lunatics, you could so easily get trampled underfoot, as Parviz told me had often happened. There were lots of jewellry shops in Mashad; we bought Mark and Debbie each a gold chain with a gold medal of Allah. I already had a medal and chain so I started to collect bracelets instead. Parviz bought me a very beautiful big diamond and sapphire ring; he said this was my welcome to Iran ring.

Mark and Debbie had befriended a nice family across the road, which they used to visit then sometimes the daughters of the family would visit us. Debbie went over there one holy day when the ritual is to kill a sheep, which is supposed to bring good luck to the family. I was upset that Debbie wanted to witness this but would not stop her if it was so important to her, and a custom of the country.

Also if a wedding took place, a sheep would be killed and all the guests would step over the sheep for prosperity; this is not something I would be capable of doing.

Another custom strange to me was when anyone buys a new car; a dead animal's blood must be painted on it.

A few times Mark and Debbie played out with the local children, until the local hotel owner came to see Parviz and told him," you do not know what horrible things these boys are saying to your daughter in Farsi, and girls should not be allowed to play on the street." So Mark and Debbie were now grounded as well as me.

After that the boys used to play on a neighbour's flat roof and kept trying to look into our sitting room, so I used to have keep the blinds closed, making us really feel imprisoned.

We went to the bakery for some bread, to find it is only made in one very large slice, approximately 24 x 12 inches, and everyone then carries it home over their arm, much enjoyed by the flies, which keep alighting on it. After my first experience, I then started to wait in the bakery until the bread was cool, I would then wrap it in a tea towel, and put it in a carrier bag, to the great amusement of all the bakery workers and the customers.

The first time I wanted to buy a chicken I went to the butchers. There were three chickens hopping around the counter in the butchers shop and I thought this quite quaint until I found out I was supposed to choose one, then the butcher would kill it, for me to take home. I just could not do this, so chicken was off the menu that evening.

The eldest boy of the family across the road volunteered to go to the butcher's for me in the future. The first time he brought me a chicken, I put my hand inside to clean it out expecting to find the giblets, instead I pulled out something which turned out to be the chickens head; this made me feel sick so I still could not eat the chicken. I had also ordered some yogurt, which I had now found out they only sell by the bucketful, so the boy arrived with a bucketful of yogurt on the back of his motorbike, flies, dust and all, as no one over there would even think of putting a cover on it.

We could not buy fish as we were too far away from the Caspian Sea, and they did not sell frozen food in those small towns. The only tinned food that was available was tins of tomatoes. Eggs would have white yokes, and when you could find meat it would be incredibly thin pieces, as there was no grass for the cows or lambs to eat because of the baking hot sun. I used to dream about our butcher's shops windows, and think when I go back to England I will buy one of everything. We found an orchard, which had lovely fruit growing, so we bought plenty, but unfortunately it was about thirty or forty miles from where we lived, so too far to go to often on the dreadful roads. When we came out of the orchard, I was just about to step into the car when I saw a lizard on my seat, which I almost sat on. I yelled but Parviz told me to shut up and don't make a fool of myself as these people will think I am a idiot screaming at a lizard, but I had never seen a lizard before so did not know it would not bit me. I was sad to hear that what the strangers thought was more important than the shock I had just suffered.

It reminded me of when we had first met, when we were sitting in a restaurant, and I being very happy had laughed at something he had said but he immediately told me off and "said do not laugh out loud as people will look at you, and it is not ladylike."

Parviz found a local farmer and ordered some milk for us, though he himself does not drink milk. Every morning a metal bowl of dirty uncovered goat's milk would be left on our front doorstep, some times with flies or a wasp in it. We did not like to upset the farmer by canceling the milk, so we used to accept it each day and throw it down the drain.

Parviz's parents came to visit us for a week in Sabzevah. In Farsi the word father is Pedah, and so we called them mother and Pedah. Pedah worked as a barrister, and they were lovely down to earth people. We had a great relationship and even though neither of them spoke much English we made ourselves understood very well. Parviz used to be very surprised when he came home in the evenings to hear how much we had managed to communicate to each other, and the stories his mother had told me.

His parents also told me I must not let Parviz upset me too much, they told me he had always been jealous of his younger brothers Combiz and Changees, when they were babies and getting attention from his mother, he used to keep slamming the doors in temper, and was very possessive about his mother, so they seemed to know that I would be treated similarly, but I did not admit anything, because if they told Parviz off, then I would have been in trouble, so as usual I kept quiet.

Parviz's parents did not drink alcohol, but Parviz and the local men used to buy bottles of Vodka, and then drive out into the desert away from the women and children.

They would cut a cucumber in half, then scoop out the inside, and pour the vodka into the cucumber then drink from it, and proceed to get drunk.

Hunt International the company Parviz worked for gave him an allowance towards having a servant. I did not think that we needed one, but it was considered that anyone who was anyone should have one!

A man who worked on Parviz's site brought a woman to us but she was horrible and she was also a drug addict, which the man later admitted he knew about, when she stole my electric cigarette lighter. So I got rid of her. The man then brought a very nice woman called Fatima; she was much younger and a widow. The man spoke a little English so he acted as interpreter. In the interview, he told me Fatima has a boy and a girl, and Fatima showed me with her hand how tall her children were. One day when she came to work I gave her some of Mark and Debbie's old clothes for her children, and a black negligee of mine for herself. I never found much to laugh at in that country, but the next day was really funny. When Fatima turned up for work and took off her chador, she had worn the black negligee with a blouse of Debbie's on top, open as it was too small to button and she had then put Debbie's little short Scottish kilt on top of the negligee. We had a paddling pool in the back garden and every day Fatima would stand in the pool to clean it. I went out to the back garden and all I saw was her standing in the pool with all this regalia on, beaming happily as she thought she was dressed as a westerner. It turned out that she did not have a boy and a girl but two boys, so she had assumed the clothes were for her and were meant to be worn whilst she was in my company.

One day when I gave Fatima a lift home, she introduced me to her children. They had nothing in their flat, only one pan one mug and one plate and I felt sorry for them, so the next day I gave her two mugs, two plates and three pillows. When Parviz found out he went mad and told me, "no one should ever spoil the servants." He then told Fatima We would not need her in the future so she had to leave. I was very upset by this as I was very fond of her and she seemed happy whilst in my home, plus it was a bit of female company.

Mark and Debbie could not go to school, as they did not speak the language. I had hoped to learn it myself and then teach it to them, as Parviz certainly made no effort to teach them. But my hopes of wanting to learn were now fading, with my enthusiasm, as I was longing to be back in England. In sheer desperation, Mark Debbie and I sometimes dressed up as cowboys and cowgirls and painted our faces. We would then have a singing and dancing party pretending we were in a nightclub.

Mark and Debbie became very good at table top dancing; I still have the photos of these parties.

Parviz and the other men had a chef on the site at work, so he would have breakfast, lunch and occasionally an evening meal at work. One evening he came home boasting that he had made his chef cook twenty boiled eggs that morning, and he kept sending each one back until the chef managed to cook one to his satisfaction. The poor chef!

Occasionally we would drive out and have a picnic. We used to save unwashed jam jars and we would half fill the jars with water to drown the attracted bees and wasps, then we would put the lid on the jar when plenty of the pests had gone inside, and eat our picnic in relative peace. We would place our bottles of coke and seven-up, which were the only soft drinks on sale, in a crate then lower them into a stream to keep cool. On one of our drives, we found a dog and her pups under a bridge and we were busy making a fuss of them, when a young boy and his father came up. They told us the dog is not wild as is usually the case, and we could have a pup if we liked; we were delighted.

I learnt when I took our dog out for a walk that anyone we would meet on the street would cross the road, as dogs were considered as vermin, and should a dog touch them they would have to go home, bath and wash their clothes. I then found out from our neighbours that if you have a dog in your house, no one would want to visit.

Clever Parviz!

Dogs in Iran were usually out in the wild and hunt in packs; ours was the only one we came across that was a pet. Some nights we would go out in the car and throw food out of the window to the wild dogs, but they would be very dangerous if you approached them.

We spent a nice weekend when we went to the Shah's birthday party; we stayed at the Hyatt Hotel in Mashad, where we met another couple, a man called Parviz and his German wife called Miriam. Both the Parviz's worked for Hunt International.

On the second day Miriam was in a dreadful state; she told me that while she had been living in their marital home in Germany, and her husband had been working in Iran (his home country) he had met and married an Iranian girl, and they had a baby. Poor Miriam had found out years ago that she could not have children. Her husband Parviz had told Miriam that the girl's father had forced him to marry the girl, but Muslims are allowed four wives so no law was broken, and he would divorce her as soon as possible. But in fact he was telling my husband, that when Miriam goes back to Germany it was she that he was going to divorce, so that he could remain with his Iranian wife.

Some evenings in Sabzevah, just to pass the time, we would go out and walk around the shops, which were open until about ten pm. We would park on yellow lines; the first few evenings Parviz introduced himself to the police as Mr Engineer from Tehran, so the police, thinking he must be someone important in town, would guard our car on the yellow lines whist we looked around the shops.

On one such evening we visited the jewellers to buy another bracelet for my collection. On the wall was a beautiful picture of two open pages of the book of Koran; the picture was surrounded in a beautiful gold frame. When I admired the picture, the shop owner told me I could have it, and take it home. Parviz kept hissing at me under his breath to shut up, and not to take the picture. When we got outside I got a long lecture, that in this country, you do not admire anything, because if you do, the person owning the item is then compelled to give it to you, as the Iranians believe that if you admire something that you cannot have, that could lead to envy, and would be bad luck to them.

That is why they must offer it to you, and you must refuse.

I tried to explain that I was only admiring the picture and did nor want it, and was not aware of these rules, and that these things should have been explained to me in the first place, then I could deal with them correctly. More Restrictions!

One day we drove out to the desert to visit a man who was a labourer on Parviz's site. This man had six wives, even though Muslims are only allowed four wives. He was telling us that his wives ranged from sixteen to forty years old, and he treated them all equally; if he bought a rug for one, he bought a rug for each of them. He informed us that Allah will not frown upon him, as the more wives he has, the more children, and the more he is spreading the Muslim religion.

Later on that day we drove further in towards the desert and stopped in an area where in whichever direction I looked, there was nothing in sight, not even a tree. Parviz informed me it is his dream to build a bungalow here for us, where there is not a human being in sight; he did say we could have an Alsatian dog. I asked Parviz how did he think he would get electricity and water out here but he said he would see to that.

I was really panicking inside, but did not dare say anything. Parviz had often told me he did not like being in people's company, and he does not really like people, but this was in my estimation going much too far, I felt as if I would be approaching the gates of hell, if I were to spend the rest of my life in this isolated area.

Most of the people in Sabzevah lived in mud huts and in a lot of cases the front door of the mud hut would be a car door, taken from a broken down old car. I still have photographs of these. Quite a few of the mud huts seemed to have new TV aerials on the roof, so people were now seeing what was happening in other parts of the country.

Slowly the students of the universities were getting together and agreeing to revolt against the Shah. One day I walked up to the post office to post a letter to my sister and saw lots of tanks and soldiers lining the streets. I knew if a revolution was to start, this would be a very dangerous place for us to be, and my son could be held there to fight in the army, as thousand of young boys would have to.

I started to get extremely worried, as I was in Iran on a Iranian passport, and knew I did not have a great enough knowledge of just how serious the situation was, as the Shah was restricting news coverage, obviously his way of trying to keep control.

I then took seriously ill with food poisoning; I was delirious for a few days. Parviz later told me that the doctor had told him off for bringing us to such a dirty county. He had explained that westerners cannot cope with the conditions, he also told him he could not send me to hospital as they were also to filthy, and I would only deteriorate.

When I recovered, I kept telling Parviz that I wanted to go back to England, and we would return to Iran after the troubles were over but he kept telling me we would be OK. He said he would buy me a Paykan car, which was like a Hillman Hunter. He then rethought and changed his mind, but I did not want another car anyway, as I had nowhere to go in it.

After a dreadful argument, I started to pack one evening and said I was leaving him. He said he would not take us to the airport, I said that is OK I will hitch a lift but Parviz told me if I tried that I would get raped and then probably murdered. I did know that the Iranians always put obstacles in the way, that is how they keep control, but as it was ten hours' drive to the airport, I decided I was not going to risk it, and decided to stay.

I did not know at this stage that I would not have been allowed out of the country.

Then I tried telling Parviz we needed to go back to get school books for Mark and Debbie as they were not being educated, and I also needed to buy clothes or material for clothes for them, as they had grown out of most of what we had taken over with us.

We finally applied for air tickets to be told that I had to be vetted by the Sovak Police, which is Iran's secret police, as I was an Iranian citizen on an Iranian passport, and this procedure would take at least one month, so we all had to go to Mashad again to have several passport photos taken for the Sovak Police. I really do not want to write anymore about this, as I found it all very disturbing and frightening at the time.

Finally we got clearance to travel to England, so Parviz drove us the ten-hour drive to Tehran. On the way we hit a very bad part of the road and we all bounced off our seats, hitting the top of the car; poor Mark hurt his head. Later we nearly ended up in a jube, which is a very deep, very wide type of trench designed for the heavy rainwater to drain off the roads. I was extremely nervous and at this stage wondering if I would ever see England again, as this country was notorious for having the worst drivers in the world.

I did write a poem about driving in Tehran, I sent it up to a English written paper in Tehran and they published it and sent me a copy which I will print at the end of this chapter.

We went to stay in a hotel for two days, to spend some time with, and say goodbye to Parviz's parents before we left. We were driving in Tehran in the City centre in Parviz's usual erratic manner. It was now evening and dark and raining, we were waiting to turn right and a bus in front of us wanted to go straight but Parviz kept inching forward and would not let the bus go, so we ended up getting arrested.

A policeman got into our car and forced us to drive to the police station. Parviz demanded to see the officer in charge and told him he was living in England and only in Iran on holiday, which did not go down well.

He should have told the truth, as the officer turned out to be the chief of police in Tehran. He told Parviz, if you live in England you should know better, if you lived in Iran I would have made allowances. He then told us he had been to London several times and his one ambition was to have all the people in Tehran driving as well and controlled as they do in London.

He fined Parviz hundreds of tumons, which was the currency over there, and let us go with a warning that we could have all been locked up in jail!

Finally on December 5th 1978, on my late son Kevin's birthday, we flew out of Iran.

I was so happy to be up in the air and on my way home, with my children safe and sound.

On January 16th 1979, the Shah was exiled from his beloved Iran.

In 1980, the Shah died in Egypt. Ayatollah Khomeini took over the running of IRAN.

CODE TO ROAD CROSSING IN TEHRAN.

You stand there on the pavement, taking it nice and slow,
Wondering if you should turn around, or close your eyes and go.
The traffic now is tearing past, the bodywork ripped and torn,
Driven by men with staring eyes, and their elbows on the horn.

You now advance upon the road, and are sure you've made a boob,
You step back as a cycle shaves your feet, up to your knees in the jube.
Angry and wet you try again, the traffic roars its threat,
You dash along a line of cars, it's as far as you will get.

Now you're one-sixth over the road, cars to your front and back,
Quaking with fear you look around, and your nerve begins to crack.
You step aside for an army truck, feeling it's all your fault
That you're stuck here in this roadway hell, as a Paykan screams to a halt.

You make a dash, your eyes are closed, forget the Highway Code!
You've made it to (though God knows how) the middle of the road.
Your confidence is returning fast, it's really a piece of cake,
Then a taxicab runs o'er your toes, and your knees begin to shake.

With wild eyes you look around, at the traffic dashing past,
Become convinced that if you move, you will have breathed your last.
Then lady luck takes up your cause, a gap a hair's breath wide,
Opens and you, trembling, dash through; you've reached the other side!

The pavements beneath your feet again, you can go where you like,
When suddenly you find yourself, squashed by a motorbike.

Manchester to Galway and Leitrim via Iran

Iran

Chapter Eight

It was one of the happiest days for a long time, when we flew into Manchester airport. The excitement of being home was overwhelming, and I was delighted to see my family again. The next day my sister Jacqueline and I met up and went into Kendals in Manchester and I bought the biggest Christmas tree I could find to celebrate our freedom and homecoming.

I had read an article advertising the New Rover car, which stated that they had stringently tested it and should it overturn in an accident, the passengers would remain safe and unhurt. It was a very expensive car, in fact you could buy a small house for the price, but after my experience in overturning the Cortina, I considered the New Rover a good investment, not that that I intended to continue to overturn cars.

I ordered the top of the range Rover 3.5 with automatic drive. The colour I choose was Caribbean Blue, with Caviar coloured interior. The man in the garage said, "I envy you as this is really some car you are ordering and has exceptional luxury." A record came out at this time called Automatic Lover, so as my car was automatic and I loved it, I bought the record and used to play it as loudly as possible whilst out driving.

I had wondered what comments my father would make about the new car, as it had cost more than twice the price of the new kitchen I'd had fitted. My father's remarks about my beautiful luxury kitchen were"you could buy an awful lot of pints of beer for that amount of money." So I told him you can have the beer, but I prefer to have the kitchen.

My brother-in-law Herman offered to build my greenhouse for me. Herman had a great sense of humour, he was a happy and sociable person, and he was also a Manchester United supporter. I had my front door painted royal blue but Herman was adamant he would not walk through a blue door unless it was into a pub, as that is Manchester City colours, so he would always walk around to the back of the house and in the back door.

Herman usually smoked rollup cigarettes, but when he was coming to Macclesfield to build the greenhouse, he said, "you can not smoke rollups in a posh area like that," so he went and bought Benson and Hedges, and went on to make a great job of the greenhouse.

Once the greenhouse was up and running, this inspired me to be more adventurous in the outdoors. The next thing I did was to cultivate a herb garden near the kitchen door, and a rose garden; I then advanced to designing and building a rockery with a monkey tree in the middle, which I was very proud of.

I took a job with a company called Coprima, which entailed driving around to all the retail shops, showing them how easy it was to make and paint their own advertising posters for their shop windows, the idea of course being to get them to buy the paints, which I excelled at. As usual anything to do with selling was always a great challenge to me, which I really enjoyed.

Ken and Phyllis Weedall came over for a visit one evening, and Phyllis asked me would I consider going back to TKL, as she needed somebody mobile to drive around all areas of Cheshire and Stafford, including Macclesfield, where there were three outlets, Altrincham which had two outlets, also Wilmslow, Winsford, Fegg Heys, and many other areas. The job would involve the moving of stock from one area to another, the training of new staff, ordering stock and occasionally standing in for staff who might be off work due to illness. The Winsford kiosk used to sell £12.000, worth of cigarettes per week, which in the 1970's was a massive amount of sales.

Phyllis said I could claim all my petrol and car parks and would also get a mileage allowance for my car, so I happily agreed to the job, and since I had already worked for the company, I knew quite a lot of the staff, which made it even more pleasurable.

I really enjoyed the job going around to all the big stores and getting on well with all the store managers. The Wilmslow Tesco Store manager Tecwyn Williams and his wife Shirley had become friends a few years earlier. They came to look at my house in Tytherington, then tried to buy the house next door, I was extremely relieved when they found out there was already a sale in progress, as they had been very good and looked after my cat whilst I was in Iran, but I really did not want them in such close proximity to me.

Late one night Parviz phoned me from Iran. He told me that because of the revolution there was a curfew in place, and no one was allowed on the streets after ten pm at night. He then told me that he and some other men had decided to walk on the streets at ten thirty so as to get shot, as they wanted to give their lives for their country and become martyrs of Iran.

After I got over the shock, I asked him did he not think it much more sensible to save his life for his children, and how did he think they would feel for the rest of their lives if he did such a thing. The only promise I got from him was that he would think about it, as he had already promised the other men.

To get away from all this worry, I took Mark and Debbie and the tent and went to Cumbria, to a site called Solway Lido in Sillioth on Solway. My friend Dora and her twins joined us with their own tent but the weather was atrocious and we could not use our camping stoves, so we went to a town called Carlisle one day and Maryport town the next day to have our meals. On the second day, when we got back to the site, all the other tents had blown away over a hedge; only our tent and our friend's tent had remained standing. We had previously looked at some caravans which were for sale and I promised Mark and Debbie I would try to get us one, but knew I would have to have Parviz's approval. Any-way we packed up all of our belongings and our wet tent and went home to Macclesfield.

A few months later, Parviz came home on leave and we went for a day out and decided to drive to Sillioth on Solway to show him where we had been in the tent and to look at the caravans. We pointed out that we would feel a lot safer from the weather elements in a static caravan than we did in the tent. The caravans were very impressive, boasting of a sitting room, dining room, kitchen with plenty of cupboard space, two bedrooms, shower and separate toilet, with plenty of electrical plugs for TV and so on. We were very surprised when Parviz agreed that we could probably have one, but I must admit that Mr Mayes, the site manager, was a excellent salesman. He even said we could spend the night in one of the sites rented caravans free of charge, so as we could get a feel of the site which we did. The site was very family orientated with lots for the kids to do, and a very nice swimming pool, also only five minutes walk from the sea. So we all went off and chose a site, Mr Mayes said our new van would be ready and sited in about six weeks, and the next day we drove home very excited, and made a list of all the things we needed to set up our holiday home.

Things never stayed happy for long in our household, however. Once we were all happy Parviz would create some sort of drama, in his soul-destroying mood swings, so he then told me to phone Mr Mayes and to cancel the caravan as we did not really need it.

But the children finally talked him into letting us have the caravan for a few months to see how it went and Mark very wisely told him we could sell it when Parviz returned to England for good if he still wanted to, so we pretended to forget about it and did not discuss it again.

We had had a shower installed in the new house. Mark and Debbie and I had always used the bath, but Parviz said he wanted a shower, so a very nice unit was installed. However when it was fitted it must not have been sealed sufficiently. Since Parviz had come back, this was the first time the shower was used and we discovered that the shower was leaking into the sitting room and onto our beautiful new three-piece suite. Parviz got very angry said that he is not willing to have a bath and insisted on using the shower. The next bit is hard to believe, but I had to stand on the arm of the settee and catch the water coming through the ceiling in buckets while he continued to shower. I used to think this man would test the patience of any saint, with his extremely unreasonable behaviour, who else would treat a new house with new furniture and carpets in this manner? Parviz told me it was my job to make his life as easy and as comfortable as possible, and he told me, it was his job to expect it. I used to find this attitude disrespectful, and felt that it would eventually be quite destructive. I was very relived when we went to see him off at Manchester airport, as while he was at home, he would not allow me to go to work. Thank god Phyllis was very understanding but she and her husband had met him quite a few times so they really did understand. When he was at home the house would become a cage again, even though I must admit A Gilded Cage. As gilded cages go, this house would rate highly, but a cage of any metal is a cage nonetheless.

Mr Mayes phoned to say that the caravan had been sited and was all ready for us. I had worked all day at our Altrincham store, including the late night, so did not get back to Macclesfield until nine pm that evening. We could not wait until the next day so, with great excitement we loaded the car with a TV set, bedding cutlery, pots and pans a tea and dinner set which had a picture of a country scene on it, which Jacky and I had gone and chosen in Manchester. We packed lots of ornament and plenty of toys for the kids, not to forget stacks of food. We also took our lovely black and white cat called Whiskey whom we had adopted from the cats' home. Whiskey used to sit on the front ledge of the car and just loved travelling. After driving the one 165 miles, we finally got there at about one thirty in the morning. The site manager had already been in and lit the fire, put some flowers on the table, and soft lighting on as a nice welcome for us, how very thoughtful, which I really appreciated. My bedroom was big with lots of fitted wardrobes, Mark and Debbie's room had bunk beds and we all three of us fell in love with our new holiday home. Solway Lido was a very large site; there were about a hundred privately owned caravans, lots of caravans and chalets owned by the site for holidaymakers to rent, and a large area for tents with toilets, showers and washing facilities, which is where we had previously stayed in our tent. There was a hairdresser, café, indoor and outdoor swimming pool, a pub and a nightclub, a really great and very popular site. On our first morning,

Mark and Debbie went out to play and not long afterwards they came back and said they had already made a new friend whom they brought back with them, a boy called Glen, and they had been in Glen's caravan next door and met his mum. Glen, who was about Debbie's age, told me that his family lived in Maryport, which is only sixteen miles away, and that he and his mum Anne came to Solway Lido every weekend. He told me his father was a policeman and did not care for caravans, so he rarely visited the Lido. Glen was a real little chatterbox and very friendly. Mark told me that Glen's mum Anne had offered to have a set of steps made for us as an easier access to our caravan, which I thought, was very kind of her, as I had not even met her yet.

Mark also informed me that Anne worked as a traveller for the same company that I used to work for, but she worked for the Whitehaven branch, whereas I had worked for the Manchester branch. Anne, who was one year older than me, turned out to be one of the nicest people I had ever met. On our next visit to the caravan, she took us up to Maryport to meet her parents Elsie and Charlie, and then to meet her brothers Stuart and Thomas, and her sister Margaret.

We did not go to Cumbria every weekend as I often worked Saturdays, but went every few weeks, and on every visit Anne and Glen would be there, Anne and I hardly ever went out in the evenings. Sometimes I would have a brandy and babycham, and Anne would have vodka and yellow lemonade. I had never heard of yellow lemonade, but found out it is only sold in Cumbria. We would happily sit and chat until the early hours of the morning and both our families became really close friends. We arranged to have our summer holidays at the same time, so as we could all spend the time together at our caravans, even though Anne and Glen usually spent most of the time in mine.

We would take turns to cook; one day I would cook the dinner then the next day it would be Anne's turn. In the evenings, then, as we were on holiday we would have a drink, have a singsong, sometimes a dance or play party games. We used to call these our party nights, and we never invited anyone else. Anne had one other friend on the site, an Irish lady called Bridie. Bridie's caravan was about ten minutes walk away, on what was called the gas site, as they did not have electricity, but Bridie always said she did not feel at home in the new posh caravans, and was frightened she might spoil something as she was a heavy smoker, and she enjoyed a drink, so we always visited her caravan.

On the last day of October, the site would close for the winter, so during the winter, Anne, Glen and Anne's husband Ray would come down to Macclesfield to stay with us, and sometimes they would bring Anne's mum Elsie. Elsie was a lovely lady; she used to often say to me "I love you lass, like one of my own."

In the second year of our relationship, Anne's husband Ray decided to buy my Hillman Hunter car, which I did not use now since I had bought the Rover. I had been keeping it for when Parviz returned to England, but he had now informed me he was going to buy himself a Fiat on his return, and did not want the Hillman, so Anne and Ray came down to collect the car. When they were going home, they decided to take Mark and Debbie back to Maryport with them, and because Debbie said she did not want to leave the dog, they also ended up taking the dog.

A few days later, I received a phone call from Anne's sister, saying that Anne had been diagnosed as having a brain tumour. I left Macclesfield and at speeds over one hundred miles per hour drove to see my friend, and of course to take my children and the dog home. Anne was admitted in-to hospital in Newcastle, which was the other side of the country, so I would go to visit her as often as possible, then she was discharged from hospital with only a few months left to live but she still insisted on coming to her caravan, although was no longer able to drive. Anne's husband or brother would drop Anne and her mother off at her caravan, but only if I was going to be at mine. Anne now started wanting to go out, so I would drive her and her mum and we would go and sit in the Raffa Club, a club for RAF members.

Anne was extremely ill now and would regularly pass out, but was determined to enjoy herself while she could, even though she had not been told she was dying.

I gave Anne one of my reclining garden chairs, so as she could relax in our gardens and not fall to the ground and hurt herself if she did pass out. These were sad days, watching her so determined to carry on as normal. On her very last visit to her caravan, I had to phone her brother to come and take her home, as I could no longer lift her into my car when she would pass out, as this was now happening more regularly.

I phoned up the next day and her mother told me that the doctor had confined Anne to her bed. The next week, Parviz came home. I had intended to drive up with Mark and Debbie to visit Anne, as I knew she did not have much time left, so I asked him to come with us.

We went into Anne's bedroom and even though she could not open her eyes she said to me, "sit down lass, I've been waiting for you. I've got some vodka, so we can have a party". She then repeated what she had often told me, saying "I love you like a sister, even more than my own sister." That was the last thing I ever heard my lovely friend say. A few days later, On August 23rd 1980 Anne passed away.

My friend Dora, whom we used to go camping with, had borrowed my caravan for her and her two children, so I decided I would stay with them the night before the funeral.

I drove up to Cumbria on my own. When I got to my caravan, Dora and her two children were there, but unbeknown to me, she also had her other daughter from America and her two grandchildren staying there, so with six people already staying in the van, of course there was no room for me. I drove over to see Anne's friend Bridie to see if she was going to the funeral, and told her I must find a hotel. Bridie said, "go to the Queen's Hotel in Sillioth. Joe Hays will give you a room". She then said she would come with me and introduce me, it was only a few minutes drive away. Even though I had had my caravan in Sillioth for over two years, I had never been in to the Queens and hardly any other hotels or bars, as this would be forbidden territory according to Parviz, and I did not want him to tell me to sell the caravan.

We got to the Queens, which was crowded, people standing five deep at the bar, and Bridie introduced me to the proprietor Joe. I explained that I needed a room for two nights, but Joe told me they were fully booked as they were having a policeman's ball and Joe being a ex policeman they all came to him, but he said he would have a word with a few of the lads and see if he could move some of them around, to make room for me. About twenty minutes later, Joe retuned and said I could have a room. I replied that I had been waiting so long I thought he was building an extension. Joe then said I like cheeky lassies like you. I went back to the caravan but it was so noisy with all the kids that Dora, Carol and I decided to go to the club on the site, this was also my first visit to the club. When the show ended, the compere, Stan came over and introduced himself, and started chatting to Dora's daughter Carol, as I think Carol had been giving him the eye all night.

Carol then asked me could we have a party at my caravan and invite Stan. I agreed, so we went to the bar to buy some alcohol to take out, but they did not have any Brandy, so I drove back to the Queens to ask Joe if he would sell me a bottle. Joe asked me who was going to the party? I told him Stan, Joe said, "Stan is my best mate, can I come along.?"

I agreed. We all had a great night laughing and telling jokes until the early hours of the morning.

The next day was the day of the funeral, attended by over five hundred people, and all invited back to a hotel in Maryport for a buffet. Lots of these people were Anne's customers and all held her in such high esteem. I had met a lot of them before, as I had gone out on Anne's rounds with her. I used to do her paperwork while she sold to the customers.

I spent most of the day with poor Elsie; as Anne had always been so close to her mother, I knew she was grieving deeply. She kept saying, " I don't know what I am going to do without my lass."

I went out and bought two bottles of whiskey and some ribbon. I gave one bottle to Elsie and I then put a big bow on the other bottle and left it on Bride's caravan steps, as a surprise for her, for when she got home, as I knew she never had much money, and would be missing her friend Anne.

Much later that evening, I went back to the Queens Hotel, where there was some entertainment going on in the ballroom. Joe came over to me and asked me to join him and his wife. He introduced me to his wife Liz, and told her that I was the lady that had kept him out most of the previous night, to which she just laughed. Liz told me their life stories that Joe was born in September 1941 in Maryport and they had lived in Wigton where he was a policeman, he was originally trained as a builder and he had built them a bungalow when they had first come to live in Sillioth. Liz then told me she came from Workington where she was born in April 1944 and she told me that she and Joe had been together since she was sixteen. They now owned The Queens a 55-bed Hotel and lived in a large house in the next street. Liz showed me photos of her two daughters, Kris and Erica and told me she was now pregnant again. Liz and I become instant friends and she invited me around to her house the next day before I went back to Macclesfield. Mark on hearing all this, said "mum I think Anne has sent these new friends to you to make up to you, for you losing her." What a beautiful thought, from someone so young!

Liz used to come around and sit in my caravan with her girls. She always put herself out to be helpful. When I told her I would like some net curtains put up she said, "you just get your material and Joe will put them up for you, and any other odd jobs you need doing." On September 4th 1980, Liz had a beautiful baby girl whom they named Alana.

(Alana who is now twenty-eight years old and recently got engaged in South Africa is coming to Ireland to stay with me for a few weeks with her fiancée.)

Liz was delighted when I volunteered to give her driving lessons in their white Granada car. She was very enthusiastic and did very well. She said her and Joe usually fell out when he tried to teach her, but I told her this is usual with husbands and wives.

Liz was chatting about when Joe was a policeman; she told me he used to drive from Wigton to Sillioth to man the police station there, which was only open for one hour a day. I told her I remembered seeing him in his Police car, with a loud speaker chasing everyone off the no parking yellow lines, and looking as though he was enjoying the power of his uniform. One day Liz asked me to give Joe a lift to pick up his car so I got a great pleasure from parking on two yellow lines, and going into the chemist shop, leaving him sitting in the passenger seat on the yellow lines, for everyone to see, Joe was so embarrassed, but Liz thought this was hilarious.

Joe used to tell everyone that if he put all his police driving skills into force, he could not keep up with the speed I would drive at, but Liz used to laugh and say "that just goes to prove that Maureen is a better driver than you are."

About a year later, Liz called around one day and said that Joe's uncle in South Africa had offered him a job so she feared they would be emigrating, and would have to sell their hotel and house. The plan was for Joe to go to South Africa the next month, to start work and to find a home for them, then in a few months time and when the properties were sold, Liz and the girls would follow. Liz was not very enthusiastic, but agreed they would go, as this had always been Joe's dream. About a month later, I drove Liz, Joe and Alana to the bus station in Carlisle, and we waved Joe off to start a new life in South Africa.

Parviz came back from Iran for good and went to work in an office in Didsbury in Manchester, so he bought himself a small yellow Fiat car.

I was in Macclesfield Tesco, chatting to a work college called Kate Davis one day and I happened to say I was on my way to Boots the chemist to buy Ginseng tablets, and flu tablets as Parviz, Mark and Debbie were all in bed with flu. A lady was standing at the kiosk who had been talking to Kate called Norma Gay and she said you should buy Shaklee vitamins as they are excellent. Norma Gay came around to my house that evening and she told me all about the Shaklee products and managed to recruit me to sell them. She also advised me that every distributor should take the vitamins themselves to experience how great they are, and wear the lovely make-up.

Because I was working around all the stores in lots of areas for TKL, I had a massive amounts of contacts, so I managed to book lots of demonstrations in peoples homes and took lots of orders. Even Phyllis, my manager had a great big Shaklee party in her house for me. Norma Gay was correct, the vitamins were excellent. I got to a stage where I kept running instead of walking I felt so full of energy. In only a few months, I became a supervisor for Shaklee and had to go on stage in Manchester's Midland Hotel to receive my diamond and sapphire supervisor's pin. I had recruited sixteen girls selling Shaklee for me.

Four of these girls were running Shaklee slimming clubs; one of the slimming clubs was being run by one of my neighbours, Margaret Harley, who is still a friend of mine. I had demonstrations at my own home, which were attended by some of my sisters and cousins. My sister Elizabeth arranged that I do a demonstration and a clothes party in the Co-op in Stockport where she worked, plus I was kept very busy supplying all my distributors with stock for their customers orders, and slimming clubs.

I was part of a great group of girls. One girl was a hairdresser who also applied false nails, another a chiropodist, and one a beautician, who used to visit homes and apply false eyelashes, another girl did reflexology. I myself when Parviz had gone to live in his flat in Manchester had worked for Oriflame, a Swedish company and I used to do make up demonstrations in people's houses, so between us we used to say, we could make anyone feel and look lovely, if only we could find the time.

I was also doing clothes parties, a lot of which were done in the lunch break in the Tesco canteens, so all told I was making an absolute fortune. But instead of admitting how well I was doing, or how hard I was working, Parviz kept grumbling at me "what do you need to keep making all this money for?" and he kept telling me I should give up all the jobs!

He really could not bear me to be successful and popular.

Margaret, my friend since 1970 and Graham Taylor, had been living in Peterborough in Cambridge, but had last year moved to Blackpool and had bought a hotel. They invited us and our children to come over and stay for a few nights, and said they would not allow us to pay, but if I wanted to invite any friends they would have to charge the friends. It was now winter so there were no bookings at the hotel and all the rooms were available.

I had the brilliant idea of inviting my sisters, and some of their friends, also Sid and

0

Sylvia who had a caravan on our site, and who used to get lots of duty free alcohol so brought hundreds of pounds worth of booze down for everyone to buy. I invited Olwin Cash and her husband John, who lived across the road from us in Macclesfield, and completely filled the hotel, twenty-two of us all together.

We were the first to arrive that afternoon, as I wanted to set up the clothes and vitamins, for my family and friends, and expected to sell quite a lot.

Margaret and Graham had given us a room on the second floor, which Parviz hated; he said it was too high up and too cold, I told him we could not complain as we were not paying, he then chased me into the bedroom next door and kept banging my head on the wall and thumped me in the face, he then in temper knocked over a single wardrobe and knocked a big piece of plaster out of the wall and he said he was going to bed as it was too cold to stay up. He demanded that I sit in the room and do not go down stairs. By the time he had woken up, the other guests had arrived and taken their rooms so I could not ask Margaret to change our room then. The foul mood continued. Margaret had cooked an evening meal for us, which everyone enjoyed, except of course my husband who sent his back and said "it was rubbish and he cannot eat it."

The next morning we were all served a cooked breakfast. Margaret did the cooking and Graham waited on the tables. Parviz sent his breakfast back as he said the bacon was over cooked so they gave him another breakfast, but he sent that back too saying it was undercooked. This was like the way he had treated the chef on his site in Iran, and he seemed to think this behaviour made him look like a big important man. He finally ate the third breakfast, which they patiently served him, but probably felt like throwing at him.

Everyone kept going on about my bruised face, which I said had been caused by a fall, but some people there knew differently as this had not been the first time I'd had bruises.

A few years earlier, two of my sisters had been visiting us at our home in Peveril Walk, Macclesfield; when Parviz got annoyed and was about to hit me, one of my sisters, Jacqueline stood up to him and said "don't you dare lay a finger on her, or you will have me to deal with." He retaliated by telling them to get out of his house but fortunately for me, Jacqueline was not easily intimidated, so they sat there for hours until he gave in and went to bed.

On another occasion, my cousin Patricia was blow-drying my hair upstairs in the bedroom, when Parviz came up grabbed the hairdryer from her and said that "as we were talking so quietly we must have been talking about him. Pat was terrified, as I had rollers and hairpins in my hair and she later said she had imagined there would be blood bursting from my head, as he looked as if he was going to beat my head with the dryer. She kept shouting at him, "Parviz in the name of god, leave her alone, she has not said a word." So he had shown himself up on many occasions, and lots of people were aware of his unreasonable and uncontrollable temper.

After our breakfast in Margaret's hotel, we went for a walk around Blackpool and did not speak, whereas everyone else was laughing and joking and having fun just as we should have been. I had by now made my mind up that I could not continue like this, but was not willing to say anything whist we were with all these people as I did not want any further trouble nor did I want to spoil anyone else's weekend. Later that evening everyone arranged to go to the local pub, so we all set off together but all of a sudden Parviz told me that we were not going. He turned back and kept demanding me to do the same but two of my friends, Olwin and Sylvia, told him not to be such a spoil sport, and one at each side they linked me and made me walk with them, which I was glad about.

When we got to the pub, the girls had a great laugh and were pretending to the bar staff to be an all-girl singing group, singing in a show in Blackpool. Much to their amusement everyone believed them.

We only stayed about an hour and a half in the pub, as it was then closing time, so we all piled out and were about halfway back to the hotel, when Parviz appeared from nowhere. He had been hiding in a shop doorway and said he wanted to see my face to see if I would be happy and smiling, enjoying myself with my friends, whilst knowing he was in a bad mood. We got back to the hotel, and he managed to fall out with most people. My sister Anne's friend had taken his wife Margaret her breakfast up to bed to her that morning, he even lit a cigarette for her and left it on the tray with her breakfast. Parviz told this man that he was nothing but a fool and that his wife would only treat him like a fool if he did things like that.

It was winter, so we were all trying to sit around the fire, but there were not enough chairs so I sat on the floor. When I went up stairs Parviz followed me and accused me of sitting adoringly at Graham's feet!

We now argued for the rest of the night. In the morning Margaret and Graham told me that they could hear us during the night, and that I was crazy to stay with him, as he would never allow me to be happy. Margaret pointed out that I am now almost forty and if I don't leave him now, then it will be too late. A few of my other friends made similar comments.

I gave the situation a lot of thought on the drive home from Blackpool. I knew that Iranians are not known for their predictability, and that being hit was not a daily or weekly occurrence.

But Parviz was a mentally and physically abusive husband and I had read about these types of people; you become their whole life, they focus on you, and you end up feeling condemned by them forever. I recognized and felt all of these symptoms.

Parviz always used to pour out his insecurities to me, I was his friend, his physical and physiological support, I was living his life, I did not live by my own feelings, I was always trying to cope with his. I once told him I felt like his siamese twin only without being joined at the hip.

I also thought back on many years ago, when Parviz would hit me and then deny it, and when Doctor Alexandra took photos of my bruises and told me to go to the police.

I remembered how many times poor Mark had phoned the police, and even made a poster and walked into Macclelsfield in protest at the way his father was treating his mother. All these thoughts were flooding through my brain.

I had been married for twenty years and had lived in the hopes that things would get better, but now they were actually getting worse, as he now thought he had got me forever. But that might soon change!!!

On the motorway going home, I pulled the car to a halt on the hard shoulder and told Parviz that I had no intention of putting up with this behaviour for the rest of my life and that I intended to divorce him. I felt a bit safer doing this in the open rather than at home, as I did not want another black eye. That night I went to sleep in the spare room, and in the middle of the night Parviz came in and started battering me in my sleep (as my father had done so many years earlier.) There was no way I was going to change my mind after that; this was a new level of cruelty he had not used on me before.

The next day, I went to the estate agents and told telling them to put the house on the market. A few days later they came and put the for Sale notice board up in the front garden. The next day Parviz went to the estate agent and told them we had changed our minds and were not selling, so they came back and took it down again.

I made an appointment and went to see our doctor, who told me he believed that Parviz had a psychotic disorder, which could be schizophrenia, or could have a split personality, but this would be treatable.

The Doctor went on to explain that people with this disorder usually try to distort their partner's reality in the relationship. He also said they are a bad role model for the children, and if Parviz would not accept treatment, then I should get out and stay out.

I felt sorry for Parviz again as usual, and thought maybe he couldn't help his moods.

I went home and talked to him about it and asked him to please talk to the doctor, which he agreed to do. Everything was fine for a few days, until he suddenly blew up again and said he was not seeing any bloody doctor about anything, and he was not allowing me to divorce him.

When this happened, Mark said to me, "Mum please don't change your mind about the divorce, because if you don't leave him, I will have to leave both of you."

Chapter Nine

I DECIDED TO GO TO Sillioth for a few days to think everything through but the next day Parviz turned up unexpectedly. We were barely talking but I thought maybe he is trying to make an effort. I told him I was just about to visit Liz and he could with me come if he liked.

We called to see Liz who said she was incredible lonely and as missing Joe, so I invited her over for a meal. After the meal Liz said there was a good show on at our club on the lido and maybe it would be nice if all three of us went and enjoyed it together. We drove up to the club as it was freezing and raining and, once inside we ordered the drinks. Liz usually drinks a shandy. I told Liz she was right about the show, it was very good, and enjoyable and she kept saying, "thanks for taking me!" After a while, Denny the man from the caravan in front of ours came over to say hello. His wife Brenda was a nice person, but I usually avoided Denny as he was very nosy and a gossip, and I knew Parviz did not like him. Parviz had told me in the past that Denny was very jealous of Liz and Joe because they had a big hotel and because Joe was chairman of the Round Table, so I did not invite Denny to sit down with us. Later in the evening Parviz went to the toilet and we saw Denny followed him in.

When Parviz returned, he picked up the end of the long table we were sitting at and overturned it, throwing it on its side and spilling everyone's drinks on to the floor. He completely lost control of himself swearing and kicking the table. A group of men got hold of him, put him outside and told him he should not drink if he could not handle it, which only made him worse. Liz and I followed him outside and got into the car to drive Liz home. Parviz insisted on driving, and then told Liz he did not want her or her husband near our caravan again, and in fact he was putting it up for sale tomorrow. He drove down the wrong side of the road, swerving like a lunatic all the way to where Liz lived. Liz kept screaming, "please Parviz stop the car and let me out" but he would not.

When we got back to the caravan he said that three men in T-shirts had told him in the gents' toilet that Liz and Joe and their girls came to visit our caravan, and that he should put a stop to it.

The next morning, when I tried to discuss all this with Parviz, first of all he denied it, as he usually did with everything else, so I reminded him of what he had said to Liz, who he admitted is a very kind and gentle person, I said he should go and apologize to her as she was having her driving test today, so I did not want her to be upset. He agreed, which was unusual, as normally it would take him days to come around.

We went to Liz's house; her eyes were puffed up as she had cried all night long. Parviz told her that three men in T-shirts had wound him up, and she said "Parviz I will forgive you for Maureen's sake, but there were no men in T-shirts in the room last night, I was sitting facing the gents' toilets and only you and Denny went in and out of the toilets at that time."

When we got back to the caravan, I told Parviz, "I know it is Denny who has caused all the trouble, and I asked him to please admit it. Parviz then swore on his children's life that it was three men in T-shirts whom he had talked to, but I knew these men were non- existent.

When Parviz fell asleep, I went over to Denny and Brenda's caravan and told Denny I knew what he has said, and I also knew that the three men in Y-shirts did not exist but his reply was "I told Parviz not to tell you, as I do not want to fall out with you, so I made the three men up!" My husband had lied to me, and sworn on my children's life to save a total stranger and a person he did not even like. I would never be able to trust his word again.

Very calmly, without any argument without any temper or emotion, I told Parviz I had found out how he lied to me, and I was never going home again. AND I NEVER DID.

I drove down to the phone box, at the gates of the caravan site, and phoned Phyllis my manager and friend, to tell her I had left home, and for the foreseeable future I will be living at the caravan. Phyllis sounded quite shocked but she knew me well enough to know that if I said something I meant it. She just said we will miss you, I hope everything works out for you, and please keep in touch.

I went back to the caravan and told Parviz I had given up my job; now he was shocked that I had gone through with it, as he knew I loved my job. He then started to realize that he was not going to manage to talk me around this time.

It was a very difficult thing to do to love someone and to know that you must leave them.

But if I did not take this step now then my children and me would never have of life of our own.

I asked Debbie did she want to go back to Macclesfield or did she want to stay with me and go to school in Sillioth. She said she definitely wanted to stay with me. The next day we went to the school in Sillioth and enrolled her as a pupil, then we went to Maryport and ordered a school uniform for her.

The caravan might be ok for weekends and holidays but to live there permanently was the most boring existence I could think of, as I was so used to being busy, but I fully knew this split had to happen. Now I had taken the first step and would never go backwards.

Mark had been given a place at the college in Macclesfield, so could not jeopardize that, by staying in Sillioth, but he said he would come up to visit as often as he could, and he also kept telling me I was doing the right thing. He told me that he and his dad did not speak, so Mark just looked after himself. Mark has always been my friend as well as being my son, and I knew I was going to miss him so much, as we had always been able to talk about anything and everything.

I went out to look for a job, but in the far north of England there was not much employment at that time. I found work in a television hire shop, but they said I would have to live in Workington, which was a long way from Sillioth. I went everywhere to try to find a house to rent but could not find one. I even tried the council, but they said that as I owned a house in Macclesfield, and it was my decision not to live in it, I could not be put on their list. So I had found a job, which is the hardest thing, but could not find anywhere to live. What was I to do now?

Liz her, mum and the girls were due to fly to South Africa, so it would be even more isolated when she had gone. I was really going to miss her. I bought her a dress ring with her birthstone in it, as a going away present, and she was delighted and said no one had ever bought her anything like that before. Finally the day came and they left Sillioth for the last time.

My sister Elizabeth often came to visit us at the caravan, and she had decided to come for a visit before I close up for the winter. Elizabeth was always a good laugh and full of fun, we decided to go out for a drink and she decided she would wear my black hat.

We went to the Queens Hotel bar in Sillioth, as I knew the new owners John and Sandra. Whilst Elizabeth was up at the bar ordering drinks an elderly couple started to chat to her, Sandra warned Elizabeth they are usually after free drinks. So Elizabeth told them she was wearing the hat as she had just been to her husband's funeral so they came and sat with us and devoted their evening to cheering her up. And we bought all their drinks. They told us jokes and funny stories. Elizabeth was bursting trying not to laugh then finally she gave in and started to smile, and the old couple were over the moon that they had cheered her up. After a few more drinks and a few more jokes, she was killing her self-laughing and by the end of the night they were saying she was the merriest widow they had ever seen! She did eventually give in and told them the truth that her husband is alive and kicking, which they said they had known all the time.

I continued to sell Shaklee and do a few clothes parties, just until I got rid of all my stock, as business was not brisk up there, and people did not seem to be particularly interested in vitamins.

It was almost winter and the days were becoming shorter, so Debbie and I drove down to Macclesfield to get some of our belongings. When we got back to the caravan, it had been broken into, all my jewellry had been stolen, along with the television, which was our only company, also lots of other electrical items. This was dreadful, as life was really tough enough with no job, no proper home, and now this. I went around to the police station when it opened and reported what had happened.

One of the policemen came to visit me, and wanted a description of all the stolen items. He told me they were probably now on the way down to Blackpool to be sold.

A record came out at this time, called 'This Town's Becoming Like A Ghost Town' and this felt so appropriate; with no holiday makers around and now Liz and her family gone as well, there just did not seem to be any signs of life. I did go to visit Anne's mum Elsie every week, she used to bake lovely pies and cakes and insist that I take some back to Debbie.

One evening I came home to find my kitchen window had been broken, seemingly with a brick so this became a nerve racking week as I thought some one had tried to break into the caravan again. The site was completely empty, we were the only people in the middle of all these fields and were so vulnerable, as caravans have such great big windows. I was terrified both for me and for Debbie but we had nowhere else to go. I put tacks around all the edges of my curtains in case anyone threw a brick through the window and hoped the curtains would restrain the brick, and every night I sat up in my bed until daybreak, terrified, without a telephone and with no television to watch, and no police station open. I cannot express how daunting and nerve wracking this was.

A few years later, Debbie admitted that she had broken the window. If only she had told me that at the time, she could have saved me a lot of fear and stress.

The site was due to close in October for the winter and then no one would be allowed to stay in their caravans, so I looked all over Sillioth for a house to rent but there was only one and it was damp and horrible. I knew there were no flats in Macclesfield, so thought if I went to Blackpool we might find a winter let.

While Debbie was at school I drove down to Blackpool and bought a paper. There were lots of flats and I found a great one on Dickson Road. I then went around to see Margaret and Graham, who only lived about two streets away, and to tell them we were coming to live in Blackpool for the winter. They were both incredibly kind and said I did not need to rent a flat as we could stay at their hotel free of charge, but I said I would rather be independent, and it would be nice that they are close by.

Back to Sillioth and to pack up. I could not wait to get to the new flat. The landlady had said she did not want children as they encouraged other children around the building and became a nuisance, but I told her Debbie was very grown up and would not be noisy, so she agreed to break her own rule.

On the Friday evening after school, we drove away from Sillioth and down the motorway heading for Blackpool. As we drove past the 7 miles to Blackpool sign, I said to Debbie, "This is the beginning of a brand new life for us, we could be very happy, or it could go wrong, but please remember I am doing my best for us." Debbie just looked at me and said "mum I always trust you to get it right." I still always remember that day whenever I drive pass that 7-mile sign.

We moved in to the flat, unpacked and everything felt pretty good. Debbie and I were sharing a bedroom but the landlady said she would give us a two bed-roomed flat when it became vacant next week. This flat was on the first floor and was very nice but the other one sounded even better. We had gone to bed and were just dozing off when outside we heard a very drunken man singing Christmas carols even though it was the last day of September. I got up and looked out of the window and saw he was sitting on the pavement in the street looking quite settled. Debbie said "welcome to Blackpool mum", so we then both got the giggles and took ages to get to sleep.

I got in touch with the estate agents to see if any progress had been made with a sale of the house. They told me they had sent a few people around to look, including a man who stars in Coronation Street, but very often they could not get in to show anyone around, and Parviz would not let them have a key. I told them I now lived in Blackpool and would be willing to come down in future when a viewing was required, and I gave them my landlady's phone number.

A few days later, I received a phone call from them, saying they had someone who wished to view, so I phoned Parviz and told him what time I would be there. He said he would also be there. I showed the couple around the house and gardens and a sale was agreed, I sold the house for over double what we had paid for it some six years earlier. Then I sold them some beautiful blinds I'd had made for the bathroom, but I had not managed to find anyone to put up. The man told Parviz that he was the Managing Director of a large sales company, and that I was a far better sales person than he himself or any of his salesmen, and he would give me a job any day. I thought that was a great compliment but of course Parviz only glared at me. It really did not matter any more, as at least I had made the sale, and was beginning to see some light at the end of the tunnel.

Mark, Debbie, and I had a very nice Christmas together. We spent most of our time around at Margaret and Grahams hotel. They had a lot of guest in for the holiday, so I suggested we have a drag night when all the men would dress up as ladies. Margaret and I got Graham ready and I put my wig on him. I think he quite fancied himself dressed up, and we had a brilliant night, with lots of fun and games and laughter.

At the beginning of October, as soon as I had arrived in Blackpool, I had gone around all the estate agents to look at businesses for sale. I had looked at lots of hotels, most of which were leased properties, with just the business for sale. I also looked at a lot of newspaper shops but all the ones that I liked I could not afford and ones that I could afford I did not like the living accommodation.

Every week I used to go into the estate agents, to see if any suitable properties had come on the market. One day I went in and the girl in the office said "I know it is not what you are looking for but, a leased property Rest Home has just come on the books." She told me that the business alone would cost £30.000. Because I am a Cancerian and an avid homemaker, the word 'home' always appeals to me, so I said I would go and look at it.

I made an appointment and went to look at the rest home on Waterloo Road. The owner Maureen was in hospital and a lady called Edna showed me around the building. She told me she worked until one o'clock five days a week, then Maureen's husband Roy took over, until the two sons came home from school in the evenings. The estate agent's description had said that the property consisted of two private bedrooms, and I knew I needed three as Mark would later come to live with us, so I do not know what made me go to look at this property, yet when Edna showed me around the owner's accommodation I could not believe it but there were three bedrooms, just what we needed. The house desperately needed re decorating and a good clean, yet I had a strange feeling, as if the house had wrapped itself around me and I was meant to be here. Edna then showed me the cellars and lastly she introduced me to the seven residents.

They were all sitting in the sitting room, and one lady called Betty asked me if I was going to buy it. I said "probably," and a few of the residents said thank god for that. Another resident said "will you let us have two slices of bread at tea time as we are only allowed one and a half now?" I replied "if I do buy it you can have as much food as you can eat." I told Edna to tell Maureen that I would be buying the business.

When I got outside, I remembered my mother once saying, "that surely there must be a place where people like her could go to be looked after." I thought this must be one of those places, and often wondered since, if she had sent me there.

I went to Margaret and Grahams hotel I told them I had fallen in love with a dump, but would make it into a palace. Margaret asked me what it was called and I said I seemed to remember seeing the word 'Iona' near the front door, so we got the yellow pages and found out it was called 'The Isle of Iona.' I thought it was a beautiful name, inappropriate at the moment, but I would make it appropriate. I knew there was an island near Scotland called The Isle of Iona, which was the first Island that Christianity had come to.

My next problem was the price of the business so I made an appointment to see Mr Tennant at the Yorkshire Bank. He and I hit it off immediately. I told him about the Rest Home and that five residents pay £55 a week and the two in single rooms pay £65 each per week, and to buy the business I would need to borrow ten thousand pounds. He said even though it is not his job to do so, he would go along and have a look at the rest home and see what he thought about it. I went in to see him a few days later and he said, "Why don't you just buy a nice house and get a job." I told him I had set my heart on getting the Rest Home and if he did not let me have the money then I would get it somewhere else. He said give him until Friday at four o'clock and he would see what he could do. On Friday I walked around town waiting for four o'clock then from a phone box outside the British Home Stores I phoned Mr Tennent and he said, "I still think you should buy a house but you can have the money for the Rest Home." I felt like jumping for joy, I was so very happy.

I went along to see my solicitor, to tell him he could proceed with the sale. He said "I have some good news for you, and bad news. The good news is the divorce is going through and the bad news is some other people who were interested in purchasing the Rest Home have made a offer which has been accepted." I was absolutely devastated, as no one had mentioned another buyer.

About a week later I received a letter from my solicitor, asking me to get in touch with him. I assumed it was about the divorce so I made an appointment but when I got into the office, he said the other people had backed out of the Rest Home deal as the man has lost his job, so and I can now proceed with the sale. I said I was still interested but wanted to re negotiate the price, so I went to see Maureen and offered her one thousand pounds less, which she eventually reluctantly accepted, and we agreed that I would take over on the 26th January.

I then had to go to meet Mr Carr the Manager of Social Services, to give him my references and be approved by him. I called in to the offices without an appointment and when I got there the staff were just having their office Christmas party. Mr Carr and I got along extremely well and he said it would be a pleasure working with me. I paid him the registration fee and he said he would send the certificate in the post. Our new life would soon begin.

On Boxing Day we flew to Majorca and stayed in the Santa Maria Hotel in Magaluff. Mark fell in love with Spain and kept asking could we get an apartment here and buy a jewelry shop but much as I would love to have pleased my son, I knew I could not live in a hot country again, as I had found out in Iran that the extreme heat does not suit me.

We made friends with a pensioner called Doris who had run a Rest Home when she was younger, so she spent a lot of time giving me advice, which I appreciated. A few months later she came to stay at my Rest Home for a holiday.

We also made friends with a Scottish couple called Grace and Doug, who later came to spend a weekend at our caravan and a few times came to stay at the Rest Home.

Whilst we were in Spain, I had read in a newspaper that three policemen in Blackpool had been drowned trying to rescue a man who was trying to rescue a dog. Any news of Blackpool interested me, as it was where we were going to settle permanently in our new business. We had lots of laughs in Spain, we went to the Caves of Drac and on lots of trips and it was good to relax with both of my children, after all that had gone on in the last year.

Chapter Ten

THE NIGHT BEFORE WE MOVED into the Rest Home, I sat and contemplated what I considered as the end of my old life.

I had now got my heart back, my body back, and my mind back, and could not help feeling how pleasant and argument-free life was without a husband.

In the early years I had thought there was a chance he could stab me. My mother and I had even discussed this, and I had never kept any sharp knives in the house, but I had now escaped, and did not have to think like that anymore. My freedom felt precious.

With the confusion of a dreadful childhood, then an unhappy marriage, I had never seemed to have a clear view of what life was going to throw at me next. I now felt as if my own life was about to begin, for which only I would be responsible. I found the prospects quite challenging and exciting, and knew I only had myself to depend upon.

So I would leave the bad memories behind and hope to make some new and happy ones. One thing I was determined about was 'that my crying was done.'

I had read that what makes us strong is how well we rise after falling, and after all the pain, life somehow seems to make us stronger. Sometimes we become more strong than the people around us. Because we are now strong, when we need a shoulder to lean on, we can suddenly find we have nowhere to go, as there is no shoulder broad enough to support us. I now wondered if my situation has given me more strength but I do believe that it has.

I am now ready to move on to a new chapter in a new life, and ready to embrace the future.

I always try to keep things in perspective. I have always tried to make allowances for the imperfections in others, but now it is time I set out some ground rules for myself.

Rule No1 - The past is the past and must stay there, so I will now only look very enthusiastically ahead to my bright and hopefully happy future.

Rule No2 - I am not looking for a man, but if a man should find me – I have promised myself I will never give my power to any man ever again.

I then decided I would continue with more rules when I have more time to think about them, but these will do for a start.

I went to bed really happy and full of anticipation knowing my new life would begin tomorrow morning.

January 26th 1983. Wearing a navy blue business suit I entered my Rest Home 'The Isle Of Iona' for the first time as its new owner. This Rest Home was to remain mine for over twenty years.

Maureen the previous owner, introduced me to all the residents, four men called Clifford, Fred, Big Tom, and three ladies called Mary, Betty and Lillian. There was also another resident called Little Tom who was over ninety years old, and who had been admitted to hospital. Maureen then told me that Lillian is extremely ill.

After the introductions, I started cleaning out the kitchen cupboards, as everything was so filthy, Maureen said to me, as she was just about to leave The Isle Of Iona for the last time, "I am surprised you are cleaning in your good suit." I felt like saying, I was surprised that anyone would hand over a house in such a dirty state, but I bit my tongue and said nothing. I went across the road to buy some cleaning products but there was only fairy liquid in stock, so I cleaned the entire kitchen with fairy liquid.

Two of my residents asked for extra blankets for their beds as the weather was freezing, but there were none in the cupboard so I gave them my own, as I did not envisage I would have time to go to bed that night, plus I had ordered a new bed for myself which had not yet been delivered.

Edna, who worked from nine am until one pm, told me that when I had renegotiated the price of the business and offered Maureen one thousand pounds less than her asking price, which she had accepted, Maureen then proceeded to strip the place, only leaving the bare essentials. Every thing I touched needed repairing, or just throwing out, but I was not worried about that, as I was happy to start from scratch and replace everything eventually.

There was a big chest freezer in the kitchen, which in the afternoon started to leak.
I called a repairman who told me it was not worth repairing.
The weather was incredibly windy, and the TV Ariel blew down from the roof into the front garden, which meant the residents could not watch TV for the next few days.

About four pm, I heard Betty shout twice "Maureen she's gone," meaning Lillian had just died. When I went up to the bedroom, Clifford was waiting for me on the landing and said, "if you are nervous I will come in with you. I considered this to be a thoughtful and kind offer so I accepted.
I called the Doctor to confirm the death and to issue a death certificate, then I notified the next of kin, and the undertaker arrived to remove the body. A great start to my new job (and my new life).

At this point the hospital phoned to say they were sending Little Tom back to the Rest Home. They warned me that he is doubly incontinent and could not feed him self. I told them I had only moved in to the home today and could they please keep him until tomorrow but they said "sorry no as they needed the bed that night."

In the middle of all of this, my furniture arrived and was delivered upstairs to the second floor flat, which was the floor Debbie and I would live on. The entire house was in chaos, with only me to cook the meals, look after the residents and cope with this resident's death.

When Debbie came home from school, I said, "Debbie, I just wish I could walk out, close the door and never come back".

Debbie at least got busy cleared the dining room tables and washed up after the teatime meal. I offered her a wage if she would do the tables every evening after school and she was delighted to earn some money. It was a great help to me.

On our first night, someone came along and smashed the wing mirror on my Rover car and next morning the man in the shop next door said "that is because the car is too posh for around here." I was not sure how I going to deal with this problem, but decided I had enough to worry about at the moment.

I asked Edna to work Saturday so as I could go out and stock up. I remember thinking that whichever direction I go in or whatever type of shop I walk past we will need something from it. The first purchase I made was a great big TV for the residents lounge, which they were really excited about.

I discussed menus with my residents to find out what they would like, and just knew I was going to enjoy spoiling them, but that is down to my Cancerian birth sign, as we love to look after people and be generous with the people we care for; they call us cancerians the Mothers of The Earth! So this was a perfect type of job for me.

I asked the residents if they would they like me to cook chicken with rice one day just for a change but Betty told me quite firmly, "we do not eat rice for dinner, we only eat it as rice pudding" so that was me told!

I decided to put an advertisement in the Evening Gazette for staff. I employed a hotel owner, as her hotel was closed in the winter months; she was a great help and a good cleaner. After her first week, she said, "Do you mind if I offer you some advice? "She told me I was feeding the residents four and five star meals of pork chops, leg of lamb or best steak every day instead of once or twice a week which she said was not practical, and the business could not afford it, with residents' fees only being fifty five pounds per week. She of course had experience from her own business. I explained to her that this is the way I have always fed my family, and I was sure our resident would benefit from all the fresh meat fish and vegetables, nor would I enjoy cooking cheap or frozen food.

I ordered television sets for all of the residents' bedrooms, and a stair lift to carry anyone upstairs that needed assistance.

Sometimes some of the ladies would object to having a bath or to having their hair washed, so I had to find a way around this. We had a very large square landing on the first floor leading to all the residents' bedrooms; in fact it was as large as a bedroom.

I bought a hairdryer on a stand and every Wednesday I would set up something like a hairdressing salon. I offered to do a shampoo and set, shoulder massage for the ladies, and paint their nails all for one pound. With the one pounds I would buy two womens, magazines, and a box of chocolates to be enjoyed whilst their hair was drying, and a variety of different colored nail polishes. This worked amazingly well, as they thought that they were paying for the treatments, they did not feel forced, and I would hear them discussing who was going to be done first. Betty would come to me on a Tuesday and ask could she make an appointment to be first, the atmosphere was wonderful and they seemed to be much younger and were being much nicer to each other.

I introduced a 'happy hour' once a week when most of them would enjoy one or two glasses of sherry and chat about the old days. On one of these days I asked them to show me photos of when they were young. Each one of them had a photo of them-selves in their early twenties and I was amazed at how glamorous they had all looked, so

I put all their beautiful photos up on a shelf in the sitting room for visitors to admire.

I had a look through my wardrobe and offered Betty and Mary some of my clothes, so we had a bit of a fashion parade, and they chose what they wanted.

When Social Services came to do the annual inspection, they said they were like completely different residents, so smart, confident and happy. I found all of this very fulfilling and worthwhile; I was certainly enjoying job satisfaction.

I asked Hughie, a friend of mine in Scotland, to come down to Blackpool and decorate the entire house, starting with our flat at the top of the house and working his way down until the whole house was completed. He arrived in Blackpool with his brother and said it would take them about three weeks just to do the inside of the house, and the outside needed to be left until the weather got warmer.
My friends Margaret and Graham were wonderful they let Hughie and his brother stay at their hotel for bed and breakfast free of charge, I would provide their lunch and in the evening they would go out for a meal, and have a few drinks in the local pub. They enjoyed making some new friends and my sister Elizabeth went out with them a few evenings for a laugh. At last the Rest Home was beginning to look as if it belonged to someone and my next job now was to buy new beds, furniture and carpets, which I took a great pride in doing and really enjoyed.

In June I had to attend a court with my solicitor to obtain my divorce. About twenty other people were there, all getting divorced at the same time. It took about fifteen to twenty minutes and I remember thinking that if I had known it was that easy I would have done it a long time ago.
When I got back to work, Debbie said they had had a Social Services inspection, done by Mrs Jean Tytherington, and that Mrs Tytherington was leaving Social Services this week to open a private Rest Home of her own in Preston.

I was just so happy to be divorced, that I kept dancing up and down the long kitchen, and singing, 'this my life,' and 'I am free.' Debbie was laughing at me, saying "I did not think you would be this happy, especially with all these old people being such hard work." But that was no problem to me.

I had managed to talk Margaret and Graham into having a Rest Home too so I phoned all the estate agents to try to find one for sale. I finally managed to find one and in the evening I drove them to view it. as they did not have a car at the time. After viewing, Graham said "I now know exactly what I want, but do not know how to get it," so the three of us had a long talk and they decided to put their hotel on the market. A few months later the hotel was sold. I had heard that The Chaseside Rest Home was coming up for sale, as the owner was in poor health, so I phoned up and made an appointment for the three of us to view. I picked Margaret and Graham up and drove them to St Anne's. They both immediately fell in love with the place, not surprisingly as it was a beautiful building. They agreed to purchase, so long as Social Services would register them. I had an excellent relationship with Social Services, so I said I would be guarantor for them, and would give them any help they might need. The next week, we all had a meeting with Social Services at Chaseside and sometime later the business changed hands.

Before Margaret and Graham moved in to their Rest Home, we decided to have a day out to celebrate their last days of freedom. This was also to be my first day out since buying my rest home. We left home at eight o'clock in the morning and went to Alton Towers in Staffordshire; we arrived at ten am as soon as the park opened.

We started off by going on the corkscrew, which was a new ride at the time and by the end of the day we were shattered, so Margaret and I fell asleep in the car on the way home. We soon awoke with the car running out of control on the motorway, when Graham who was driving had also fallen asleep at the wheel. We were all really shocked at what had happened and at the realization that we could have been killed.

I had been a member of the Rest Homes Association since my first week and had always attended the monthly meetings.

The chairman, Eric Allcock, now asked me to become the Association's secretary, which would involve taking the minutes of all the meetings, typing them out and posting them to all our members. I did try to decline the job, as I thought I had plenty to do at the Rest Home, but somehow Eric managed to persuade me. Soon after I had accepted the position, he then made it my job to start going to various meetings with different branches of Social Services, sometimes in Blackpool, sometimes in Preston or Lancaster, as lots of new legislation was being discussed. This job was now talking a lot of my time, but I was really enjoying it. With all my newfound knowledge I was able to help a lot of other Rest Home owners; I never saw the others homes as competition, I just thought we are all working together to improving the industry and the quality of care.

I went to visit Mr Carr, the Social Services Manager, and told him that I would like at my own expense to take all my residents on holiday during the summer months. I asked him would I be allowed to close the Rest Home for a week and do this. Mr Carr said you will have your hands full but if you are willing to take responsibility for them, then we will agree. He was always great with me, as he really appreciated the good job I was doing. He actually offered me the loan of a Social Services bus with a lift in the back which would accommodate little Tom's wheel chair and he also said he would provide a driver, as the bus would only be insured for a Social Services registered driver.

In July, I closed down the Rest Home and Debbie and I set off with our seven residents for a happy holiday to the five chalets I had booked at Pontins in Morecambe.

This proved to be a much harder task than looking after them in the Rest Home.

Every mealtime, breakfast, lunch, and evening meal we would push little Tom in his wheel chair to the dinning room, which was situated quite some five minutes walk away, and the other residents would walk beside us chatting happily, but once inside the restaurant, Debbie and I would queue up for every ones meals but by the time we got them all fed and was about to have our own meal, some of them would have finished eating and would start asking to be taken to the toilet, so I would usually leave my meal and queue up with them. This proved to be a great way for me to lose weight, not that I needed to in those days.

After a nice walk, we would then get them settled back into their chalets as some liked to have an afternoon nap. Then it would be time for a afternoon cup of tea so I would run into each chalet and put all the kettles on, then run around each one and brew the tea, then again run into each one to pour the tea, add milk and sugar and serve to the resident with biscuits.

In the evening we had the same routine as lunchtime, but we would dress them in their best clothes and get them up to the dinning room safe and sound. After most meals, little Tom would complain that he preferred the food at the rest home to these meals.

After the evening meal we would always take them to a show but little Tom would then complain again that he would rather have his telly and Coronation Street. One night we got a bunny girl to sit on his knee for a photograph and he was so excited, that every evening afterwards, he happily came to the shows hoping the bunny girl would show up again.

My guardian Angel must have been looking after me at this time, as a young man approached me, introducing himself as John. He told me he could see that we were from a Rest Home and he was on holiday on his own. He said he was nineteen years old, a fully qualified care assistant employed by Social Services at a County Council Home, and if I needed any assistance with residents toileting, or lifting, or help in any other way, he would be more than happy to help me.

I told him I would have to phone Social Services before I could let him help, and he readily agreed. When I did phone, his manager at Social Services gave John a glowing report.

Our residents really, liked John and he proved to be an excellent hairdresser, so he would do my hair and the ladies' hair before we all went out together for our evening meal and to watch the show. John started to have his meals with us and would walk to the shows with us, letting two of the ladies link him. This young man was an incredible blessing. How many young men on holiday would volunteer to do all this? Plus the residents really liked him. I offered to pay him for helping but he totally refused.

The holiday finally came to an end, the residents said their goodbyes to John, and invited him to visit them in Blackpool. We all got home and the residents seemed to be pleased to be back in their familiar surroundings, with lots to talk about.

After the holiday, Mr Carr came to visit the home to see how successful the holiday had been and some of the residents proudly showed him their photos. He told me he really admired how brave I was to take them all away, and he said I was the only private Rest Home he had ever heard of to do such a thing. He then told me we were front runners in Lancashire in a quite few ways, the first home to have a stair lift, the first to have TVs in residents' bedrooms and the first to issue staff uniforms, as Debbie and I were wearing ours at the time. He said we gave a totally professional image and had an excellent reputation with the Social Services team; this was all like music to my ears.

This was 1984 and there were not many Rest Homes in Blackpool, but new ones were beginning to open up in the area, so with my position in the Rest Homes Association, I was very pleased to be seen to be leading by example.

I was always on a mission, always driving myself, but I think this was because of the way I was brought up. Maybe I was going to spend the rest of my life proving myself to myself, but I was certainly enjoying this challenge.

Some time later I employed a very experienced care assistant called Heather.

Heather enjoyed all aspects of the job, including cooking and baking. After about six months, Heather said that if Debbie and I would like to take a holiday, she would move into the Rest Home with her two children and take full responsibility. This sounded good to me, as we had never even considered taking holidays before, we had not been used to them in the past so had not thought along those lines.

I booked a hotel on the Havre De Par in St Heliers in Jersey for two weeks for Debbie, myself and my sister Elizabeth.

We got a train down to Dover then sailed over to Jersey on a ship. We disembarked about five in the morning and caught a taxi to the hotel but it was still closed for the night! I thought they would have a night doorman but no, so we had to sit on the front doorsteps until seven o'clock with all our luggage.

The rooms were large and nice and airy, the food was good and we went on lots of coach trips, but Elizabeth was not very well so we did not bother to go out at night.

At the end of the two weeks, we boarded our ship to return but the sail was delayed by about three hours due to the severe weather conditions. Finally we set sail. Lots of people around us were being sea sick, as the sea was extremely rough but Debbie and I found a quiet corner and lay on the floor to try and sleep. In the morning I went to the dining room for breakfast; even though there were over one thousand people on board, only four of us had a cooked meal.

When we got home, Heather had done an excellent job and all our residents were happy and well looked after.

I did of course bring each one of them back a nice present. Betty being her usual outspoken self said that the presents were only bribery, so as we will let you go on holiday again.

Chapter Eleven

Quite some years ago, when I had bought the business, I had enquired if the property could eventually be bought. Maureen had told me that the building belonged to a church and could never be purchased, as the church refused to sell.

Now in 1986 I went to the estate agents in town, where I always paid my rent and asked for the name and address of the owner of the property. The man in the office said they were not allowed to give it, but any comments I wished to make regarding the property needed to be put in writing and would be given to the owner.

(I had decided to try to buy the property, as for the last four years I had been continually spending money on the building and yet it was someone else's property, and all I was doing was increasing the value for them.)

Heather, a member of staff, had been sitting in the kitchen eating her dinner, when two legs of the stool she was sitting on disappeared down through the kitchen floor, so now the entire kitchen floor had to be replaced as the wood was rotting, and then of course new floor covering bought yet again.

Two men from the fire department had come to do the yearly inspection and they told me that due to new legislation, in case there should ever be a fire and people had to run down stairs to escape, I would have to have the stair lift removed or have the stairs widened.

If I had the stair lift removed, Little Tom would not be able to get downstairs each morning. I certainly would not let him be confined to his bedroom for the rest of his life and I knew he would never agree to go into another Rest Home, as The Isle of Iona had been his home for a lot of years, and he was very happy with us. Another important point was that Little Tom never had any visitors, from family or anyone outside of the home, so all the friends he had lived here in the home.

I eventually found a builder who agreed to widen the stairs and he also had to make the landing on the next floor narrower, so this was a major job, and while the job was being done we had no hand rails on the landing or stairs for a few days, so I slept on the landing on a garden sun bed at night, in case any of the residents went to the toilet during the night and might fall.

I also had to have the entire house re-wired and brought up to the 16th edition for the latest electrical certificate. I had an intercom system fitted through out the house and at every resident's bedside, so as to hear if a anyone needed us day or night. At first some residents treated the intercom like a new toy buzzing me in the middle of the night to ask what time is was, or to tell me what they would like for breakfast!

I had also got the builder in to open up some attic space on our floor and build a private bathroom for us, as at the present time we were sharing one bathroom with the seven residents, and this was most inconvenient.

The lady Mayor Mag Hoggart lived across the road from us, so I paid her a visit and asked her how I could go about finding the owners of the property and I also explained the whole situation to her. Mag said she remembered the house being built when she was twelve years old and she said that the estate agents would not want the house to be sold, as they would be paid commission for collecting the rent.

Mag went on to tell me the history of the house, and the story of the two brothers who were both called Mr Saville. One of the brothers was a builder; in 1922, he built the three-storey house on the corner of Waterloo Road and Saville Road, (which was now the Rest Home).

He built this house as a large residence for his brother, who was a very wealthy property developer. The top floor was to be used for the servants and they also built three shops at the side of the big house.

They then went on to build one hundred and six, large and mainly semi-detached houses on Saville Road, built of stone. The builder then built himself a very nice detached house in stock brick next door to his brother's house.

Saville Road had been named after Mr Saville and his brother.

I finally managed to trace the Mr Saville who was now living in Poulton Le Fylde and told him that I was interested in buying the property. He replied that he would be interested in selling it to me if I would agree to buy the whole block, as he was now eighty-four years old and did not want the responsibility. The block consisted of the three-storey Rest Home, with three two-storey shops, each shop with a store room upstairs, which could be, used as a flat, and at the back of the building, three toilets for the shop keepers use, which if demolished would give me lots of car parking space.

I asked Mr Saville how much he would be expecting for the block and he gave me a very favourable price, so without any hesitation I agreed to go ahead with a sale.

Even whilst talking to Mr Saville, I was already planning to turn the whole block into a fabulous big luxury Rest Home.

My mind was now racing. I would have extra ground floor and first floor bedrooms, an extra bathroom and at least two toilets on the ground floor, smoking and non-smoking sitting rooms and a office. I would also be able to utilize the car parking spaces outside all the shops to make a beautiful big garden extending all the way around the side of the house, plus car parking at the back when the toilets were removed.

I phoned and made an appointment to see my bank manager, Mr Tennant.

I borrowed big Tom's cap, went and bought an apple, and arrived for my appointment in Mr Tennants office with an apple in one hand and the cap in the other. Mr Tennant roared with laughing when he saw me, he said" I think on one hand it is bribery and on the other hand it could be begging" so I told him he was right in both cases." I then showed him a sketch of my plans, and told him I would get planning permission! But even if I did not get it, then the shops would still be paying rent, which would repay the mortgage, plus I would not be paying rent on the rest home, so I could not fail.

Mr Tennant agreed but said that head office could have the final say.

A few days later Mr Tennant phoned me to tell me that I had got the money, and that a customer of his who was also a friend was willing to do all the building work at a reasonable price. I remember thinking 'Mr Tennant sounds almost as excited as I feel'. What a brilliant bank manager to have.'

I stayed up all night drawing up detailed plans and realized that I should be able to accommodate twelve residents, with more than adequate day room space and car parking space, which I knew, was a new requirement. Also in the new legislation, bedrooms would have to be larger, but this was not going to be a problem as I would have plenty of room. I was really in the swing of it all now.

The next morning I went to the town hall and presented my plans to the planning department, who told me I must have them drawn up by a qualified surveyor.

I had a friend called Mel Stevens who was a surveyor, with an office in Bispham, so off I went to visit him clutching my precious plans, and within a few weeks the plans were back in the town hall.

I was informed that a planning committee was coming to survey the site on Tuesday morning, then a few days later I received a letter saying the planning had been passed, and they especially liked the four large bay windows I had designed all around the house, and the large garden this would enhance the area, and I was now free to start on my project.

This was it! I was on my way! I now had to let the tenants of the shops know that I would not be renewing their leases, but would be willing to help them to find alternative premises.

The shops in my property consisted of a newspaper shop an antique shop on Saville Road, and next door to them a great big double fronted shop on the corner of Saville Road and Waterloo Road selling wooded doors.

I found a big bathroom shop on Waterloo Road displaying a poster for a closing down sale. I decided that this shop would be excellent as a newsagents, as it did not have any parking restrictions outside and even had its own car park. I made enquiries about the rent and the lease, and then went to visit Stan who with his wife owned the paper shop business. I told him I had found a shop on the main road, with a long lease which would be coming up for rent and would definitely increase his business, plus there was a large three bed-roomed flat over the top, which he could live in if he chose to. A few days later, Stan came to see me and said the shop would be perfect but would cost him £10.000, which he did not have, as it would need fitting out with shelves and fridges and so on, so I told him I would talk to my bank manager which I did. Mr Tennant offered Stan a ten thousand pounds business loan, which he accepted. The newsagents business did so well in the new shop, that a few years later Stan and his wife bought that property, which included the shop and the flat.

The people in the antique shop had already told one of my residents, Ena, that they would soon be retiring, so I did not anticipate any problems with them, but needed to put my mind at rest that they would be happy with the situation.

I put on a headscarf and some sunglasses so as they would not recognize me, then Ena and I went into the antique shop. I had told Ena to enquire what they would do when they retired, as I wanted to hear the response for myself. I would pretend to be a customer looking at a vase. Ena asked the question, and they told her, "The lady from the big house around the corner wants the shop back, so she is doing us a favour, as we travel all the way from Poulton every day to open the shop just until the lease runs out, and we cannot wait to retire."

I was so pleased with what I had heard that I bought the vase, but did not reveal my identity, so I now knew I would have no problem with them, as they could not wait to get away. Two down, one to go!

I found a very large double-fronted shop on Lytham Road, which was a very busy main road. I thought the doorman could put all his wooden doors outside on display so once again I thought this move might increase his business.

This man proved to be more crafty, however he said he would move out if I gave him £3.000 as he still had time left on his lease. His shop was going to be made into a massive lounge with two big bay windows, so I gave him the money and off he went.

The building work took about three months. All the side of the house was propped up with big girders, and the large shop windows removed, to be replaced by new walls and bay windows, and then the shops were knocked through into the Rest home and completely rebuilt.

The door shop had become a large sitting room, while the antique shop became a no- smoking lounge and a telephone room so as residents could make phone calls in private.

The paper shop had become two ground floor bedrooms, a bathroom, and a second toilet, and all the storerooms over the shops were knocked through into the rest home to make more bedrooms and toilets.

I found all of this incredibly exciting, choosing fitted furniture, curtains, and carpets, wallpaper and bedding. I also bought television sets for each of the new bedrooms, and had the latest nurse call system installed throughout the house. I was doing what I am most happy at, 'Homemaking.'

Social Services manager Mr Carr and assistant manager Bill Harris came to do an inspection so as to re-register the home. Mr Carr said he was amazed with the transformation, he was delighted and proud to have my home in his area and was sure I would soon fill my new rooms.

Maureen the previous owner also phoned me to say she finds it hard to believe what I have managed to do, so complements all around.

Now that I had lots of private car parking space, I decided to buy myself a gold coloured Jaguar Sovereign Car with beautiful leather seats, which would be easier for our residents to slide in and out of.

I thought I deserved it, after all the building work and the complete renovation of the home had been completed.

'The Isle of Iona' was now a very busy rest home, with twelve residents, me, a few care staff, night staff and a cleaner all rushing about, plus most of the residents having family and friends popping in to visit and expecting cups of tea and biscuits.

We had always had birthday parties for our residents but now there were a lot more residents so a lot more parties. We always took photos and put them up on the doors for everyone to enjoy. We now started having afternoon bingo, and the residents were offered a glass of sherry if they fancied it. We had a hairdresser visit every week, and a chiropodist visit every two months.

I some-times hired a twelve-seater coach and would take the residents to Granada studios to the Coronation Street set. We would have lunch and then they would have a drink in the Rovers Return Pub. Other times I would hire a large coach, and to fill the seats we would take residents from the Westfield Rest Home or the Burnside Rest home and have tours out into the countryside and discover lots of lovely places, one being the Troughs of Bowland. In the wintertime, I would hire a small coach and take them through the illuminations, then stop at a fish and chip shop on the way home.

Some of our residents would enjoy going to the Waterloo Pub, which was next door but one to our rest home, so within easy walking distance.

One night a fancy dress party was held in the pub, so Debbie hired a nun's outfit for herself and we also dressed up some of the residents. Jack asked to go as a baby with bib and dummy, one lady went as Hilda Ogden wearing an apron, rollers and a headscarf and one went wearing a hairnet as Ena Sharples from Coronation Street. It was lovely to see them joining in and enjoying them-selves.

Every Thursday evening, after they received their spending money, Big Tom and Jimmy would go to the Waterloo Pub and have plenty to drink, but the landlord would discreetly phone me when they would be leaving his premises, so as I could watch them walk home. I used to have to smile as I watched them leaning on each other or holding each other up and singing their heads off. These two guys were brilliant friends and really enjoyed each other's company. Tom's son Eddie was a policeman, so he used to say to Jimmy, "don't let me fall in case some one calls the police and that bloody Eddie turns up".

Big Tom and little Tom shared a twin bedroom and little Tom in his mid-nineties used to go to bed about nine pm. When he was all tucked up, he would often say he could see his wife's face up in a corner of the room near the ceiling and he would chat away to her for hours. We would often hear him say, "Hello darling I wish you were down here in this bed with me." Big Tom would go up to bed later, and we would hear him shout, "shut up and go to sleep."

We also had another great resident called Lennard who was just sixty years old and could not read or write. Jimmy or Tom would ask Lennard to go to the shop for their cigarettes or to put a bet on a horse at the bookies across the road and they would each give him ten pence for going.

Lennard later gained confidence and started going around to all the other residents, to offer to do their shopping, but he would charge them ten pence before he left the house, in case they would forget to pay him when he came back. I would usually go shopping for the residents or would sometimes take them shopping, but they liked Lennard to get the small items for them as they would say he was running his own business and they liked to support him. What lovely loyalty!

Most of our residents usually got on very well together, and were often good fun to be with. We did of course have a lot of sad times when one of them would pass away due to old age. On the day of a funeral, I would usually request that the funeral director would stop the hearse outside the rest home, so as our residents could stand outside on the steps and pay their last respects, as I thought it would be to depressing for them to have to attend funerals, unless they particularly wanted to. I would always go to the funerals and take any members of staff who would like to attend. Occasionally a resident would have outlived all their family and friends, and so we would be the only people there.

On the whole, the residents were like a big happy family. Any new lady that would come in would have her photo of when she would be about in her twenties, added to the others on the shelf in the lounge. Staff and visitors alike could see that they had not been born old, but had once been young and beautiful.

With my residents' permission I used to keep a list of where our people had lived when they were young or first married and what type of job they had worked in. I asked members of staff to cut any clippings out of books or newspapers referring to these places and we could then chat to them about it.

We had a few married couples, one was called John and Doreen who had only been married for a year. Doreen's mother had been a resident in my rest home years earlier. John and Doreen used to go out to the Waterloo Social Club and get quite tiddly then come home. Some times they would giggle and be romantic, but other times they would fall out and argue, then when they made up they would go out for another drink to celebrate being friends again. Sometimes on a Saturday in the summer, John and Doreen would have a car boot sale in the garden, with a bottle of sherry under the table, and after a few drinks they would start to sell everything half price!

We had another couple, Annie and Bill, who had been married for sixty years, so I made a lovely party for them and ordered a large cake to help them celebrate their anniversary. I also invited their son and daughter to join in the fun. About a week later they had an argument and on the Sunday morning, Bill went out got into a taxi and told the driver to take him to any rest home as far away from his nagging wife as possible. It was quite funny later that afternoon when their son, who was in his fifties, came to visit and kept saying jokingly "all I am worried about is who is going to get custody of me."

A few years later we had a couple called Margaret and George. Margaret used to tell me that if George went out to buy a bottle of whiskey for them both, he only bought it to have his wicked way with her.

An Irish lady who lived in the Rest Home called Josephine had fallen out with her son over some land in Ireland so she changed her name to Ena so as her son would not be able to trace her. Another Irish called Rose sometimes would go out and buy a bottle of Vodka, and later tell us she would have to drink the whole bottle as it was only cheap so you need twice as much to have any effect. We also had May who had two men residents fighting over her, but one of them Bill had a car so she usually seemed to favour him.

Lots of staff training would take place. I would get two members of staff to play the role of carer and resident and they would then practise on each other how to sit directly in front of a resident to feed them correctly, whilst making eye contact and quietly chatting.

New staff were usually amazed when I would demonstrate how dreadful it felt to have a care assistant stand at the side of them, rushing food into their mouths and saying, "can you hurry up and eat this as I have a bus to catch." After these training sessions, the staff had then at least felt the implications of how horrible this would feel to be rushed with their food.

We would practise handling and lifting a resident, and helping them to get in and out of a chair or a bed. Staff training also included food hygiene, first aid, practical use of fire extinguishers, and lots more. This all gave our residents a feeling of security, knowing that if they were ever ill or feeling vulnerable, they would certainly be treated with patience and kindness by trained confident staff.

I could no longer close the home to take the residents away on holiday, so quite a few times, if they were self-caring I would pay for two or three of them to go on holiday together. I would book a holiday, usually in Pontins or Butlins and when the day came, I would drive them there, check out the accommodation and put the luggage in their rooms for them. Then I would pick them up again at the end of the holiday, and hear all the stories of what they had got up to.

In 1984, I had sold my caravan and bought a new three bed-roomed holiday home in the beautiful area of Grange-Over-Sands in the Lake District. I did not get much time to spend there, but had a telephone installed, so that if I was there, the rest home could contact me in case of an emergency.

I would like to have let my residents have holidays there, but was nervous in case they put the gas on and forget to light it, or in case they might fall down the steps and injure themselves. So if they went I would go and stay with them.

I had a great birthday party at our holiday home one year. Mark and a few of his friends were there with Debbie and two of my sisters, quite a few of my neigbours, and lots of my friends, including Mal and Eugene, an Irish couple, who cooked us all a fabulous barbecue. The champagne really flowed and after all his barbecuing, Eugene later made a video film of the party and guests. The holiday home was near a field, where people in parachutes would jump out of airplanes and land, then Eugene would film them as they jumped, making a commentary and pretending they were quests arriving for the party, which was really funny. The video shows us all singing happily until four am and I must say I still enjoy watching the video.

My son Mark had once done a parachute jump into this particular field for charity.

Debbie had mentioned to me, that she would like a monkey as a pet. Maybe it was because of my deprived childhood, but I always had to make sure my children had everything they wanted, plus I also enjoyed spoiling the people I care for. So I decided to visit the pet shop to enquire about owning a monkey. The man in the shop said they could be very noisy and would often wee on the walls of the room they were in, so of course I decided against a monkey. There was a beautiful blue and gold parrot in the shop and the owner said he bred them and had one of six weeks old for sale, so I decided to buy Debbie a parrot as a nice surprise. The parrot cost me over £1.000 with another £500 for its perch and cage. I just could not wait to see Debbie's face, so I took the parrot on my shoulder in the car and drove to Topping Street where Debbie was a hairdresser in Pineapple Hair Studio. She seemed amazed and delighted with her present and it was nice to hear her say to the girl she was working with, "We are lucky that my mum is always so generous and loves to give us surprises."

The last time I had bought Debbie an animal as a surprise was just before Christmas 1983, our first Christmas in the rest home. I had gone to buy a Burman kitten for Debbie for an Christmas present but when I went to pick the kitten up, I realized that there would only be one kitten left on his own, so I bought them both, the girl for Debbie and the boy for me. When I got home with the kittens, Debbie asked me what they had cost and when I told her they were one £135 each, she said you must be mad.

Debbie called her kitten Toyah and I called mine Mishca. Toyah used to sleep in Debbie's bed at night, and tap her on the head in the mornings to wake her up for work. She lived to the age of eighteen years, which is a great age for a cat.

Debbie named the parrot Tika. Tika and the cats gave us a lot of pleasure over the years.

We kept the parrot's perch down stairs in the residents' lounge and each day we gave it a small amount of the breakfast, lunch and evening meal that the residents were served, plus of course he would have all the usual parrot food.

The residents just adored the parrot and taught him to say all sorts of funny things.

Ena taught him to say "hello" and to talk in a very posh voice. Jimmy taught him to say,

"Ello love, are you all right? in a Blackburn accent. Then Mark used to come to visit and teach him to speak in Spanish, so this parrot had a very wide vocabulary.

We all loved that parrot so much; all the visitors, including social services, used to go in and talk to it, so it was the centre of attraction in the home.

At six o'clock precisely it would slide down off its perch, walk across the floor out to the hallway, then climb up two flights of stairs, one step at a time to its cage then, after spending some time in our sitting room with Debbie, he would go in-to his cage and stay there for the night.

Each morning I would bring Tika down-stairs on my shoulder and he would say good morning to everyone we would meet on the way down.

Years later, poor Jimmy became a double amputee, having both his legs cut off and every afternoon the parrot would slide off its perch like a fireman, then toddle across the floor and sit on the arm of Jimmy's wheel chair. Jimmy really loved the parrot and the parrot loved Jimmy.

Debbie had trained as a hairdresser when she left school and had become a very good one, but Pineapple Hair Studio, the shop she was working in, was to close down as the owners were going to live abroad, so Debbie decided to join our team at the 'Isle Of Iona'

She had always had free board and lodging at the rest home, and no bills to pay so her wages were all her own to enjoy herself with. Now that she was working on the premises, she would not even need transport, so with her rise in pay, she would be very comfortably off. She said she intended to have great holidays abroad, which she did, and I was delighted for her that she could. She went off to Florida and visited the theme parks and had a wonderful time, and on another trip to New York with an empty suitcase.

I became registered with Manchester Social Services, so that we could take residents from Manchester into our home for one or two weeks' holidays by the seaside.

Each year Manchester Social Services used to book in a lovely lady called Rosie who was already living in a care home in Manchester as a permanent resident. On her first day, I took Rosie in a wheel chair down to the promenade to see the sea. On the way, we bought an ice cream and when we arrived on the beach, the donkeys were just having a rest after giving the children a ride on their backs. To Rosie's delight we spotted a donkey called Rosie so we went and gave the donkey half of Rosie's ice cream, which it seemed to really enjoy. Every day I would push Rosie to the shop for two ice creams, one for her and one for the donkey and when she went back to the care home in Manchester, the Matron phoned me to tell me that on her first day back, Rosie had cried for her donkey.

Another one of our holidaymakers was a man called Arthur who used to come in to us several times a year. Arthur lived with his daughter-in law in Levenshulm. I used to drive down and pick him up, and then I would drive him around Manchester town centre and point out the new buildings. We would then carry on to Blackpool where, Jimmy and all the other residents would be waiting to make him welcome, and Debbie would have a lovely meal ready for him.

Arthur on previous visits, had made lots of friends with our male residents and he would bring them lots of stories of what was happening in Manchester, including being able to describe the new buildings! He used to get them singing all the Neil Diamond songs, and the parrot would join in with happy chirpy noises.

I feel very nostalgic thinking back on all these people, and how easy it was to make them happy if you just cared enough to put the effort in.

A delightful Irish lady called Ella was another regular holidaymaker. Ella lived on her own in a flat in Manchester and she had written to me to see if she could come to us for a holiday. She explained in the letter that she had had a stroke, was in a wheel chair and would need dressing, undressing and toileting as she was paralyzed down one side.

I wrote back, sending her the homes brochure with all the details. When Ella received my reply, she was happy and gave the letter to one of her care assistants and to ask her to book her in. What she did not know and neither did I, was that her care assistant was my sister Jacqueline (good resident confidentiality).

Ella was loved by every one of our residents. Even though she did not drink herself, she would always arrive for her holiday with a bottle of sherry for the ladies and a bottle of whiskey for the men.

She would ask me to take her on a shopping spree down Waterloo Road in her wheelchair, so off we would go, Ella sitting all excited with her shopping list in her hand.

Ella had five or six care assistants visiting her in her flat, as she was totally dependent on them for all of her care needs. She would buy a pair of slippers for each of the care assistants; all their favorite colours and the correct sizes would be written on her list. We would then tour the handbag shops and again great effort would be put into choosing the correct bag for each girl. The shopping done, she would now insist on buying a cream cake for each of our residents. I would protest and tell her I would buy them, but I was wasting my time as she would not listen. Other days I would take Ella to the pleasure beach or down on the sand to see the donkeys. Twice I took her to a show and a meal at Blackpool pleasure beach, and a few Sundays I took her to mass, but not often, as I almost always had to work on Sundays, since most of the staff had children and wanted Sundays off or they were single and would want to go out on Saturday nights, and get up late on Sunday mornings.

Ella often told me that she thought it was wonderful having two sisters looking after her, one in Blackpool and one in Manchester. It made her feel like part of the family. She always complemented Jacqueline and said that when she was at home she only allowed Jacqueline to bath her. Ella had a lady and her husband in Manchester, who would always drive her door to door, from her flat to us and home again end of her holiday. She was a very organized lady. Occasionally, on her way to a football match, Debbie would visit Ella in her flat, which was near Manchester United Football ground.

Ella is now in a rest home in Manchester as a permanent resident and when I visit Manchester I sometimes go to visit her. I always get a lovely warm welcome and she usually says she would like to go back to Ireland with me, Ireland being her country of birth.

I was always very proud of the fact that these people and many more would come to us for their holidays and treat the Isle Of Iona as their second home, and it was also great for my residents, as they used to get excited when I would announce that one of our holiday makers would be coming in next week, there would be a buzz about the place in anticipation.

Chapter Twelve

THE REST HOMES ASSOCIATION WAS a wonderful way of meeting other rest home owners.

I made friends with Carmel and Brian, who had a rest home on the promenade, Anne and Jim, whose rest home was in north shore, as did Mike and Dorothy, and I met lots of other people. After our association meetings, which would always take place in a social services hall loaned to us for the evening, we would all go for a drink in the pub where great discussions would take place regarding new legislation for rest homes. Then once the business was out of the way, we would always have a good laugh. We all became very good friends and it was nice for each of us to feel that we had the moral support of other rest home owners.

Brian and Jim used to play golf, so were members of the North Shore Golf club, whereas like their wives, I was a social member and two other social members were Neil and Jean, who shared a partnership in a rest home in south shore.

Once a month we would all meet up at the golf club for a candlelight dinner. Our circle grew until we also had Noreen and Sam, a delightful couple who spent eight months a year in America and four months a year in Blackpool, so provided different topics of conversations, also Anne and David, who were not rest home owners, now joined us on our table. These were wonderful nights out as we always had maximum amounts of fun and laughter.

Margaret and Graham were not members of the golf club, as there was now a six year waiting list for new memberships, but we often went out for meals together and we would visit each other regularly. They then also joined the rest homes association, and I introduced them to Cathy and Jim. And they managed to form a new friendship, which I was delighted about, as they did not have many friends, and these new friends would be other people they would have something in common with as they were in the same line of business.

1987. I had now been the owner of 'The Isle of Iona' Rest Home for five years; it was also five years ago since I became a member of the Rest Homes Association and it was four years since I became the secretary.
It had been a long five years, with many changes in the legislation for all rest homes.
Most of my friends, like myself, had built big extensions to their rest homes, plus a lot of new people had come into the business, and some of them had now also become friends of mine, as I had always gone to a lot of trouble to help new members in any way that I possibly could. Sometimes I would show them how to do the paperwork, or how to go about hiring and interviewing new staff or I would send them new residents to help them fill any vacancies they might have.

The rest home business had really grown fast, since the Member of Parliament Norman Fowler 'lifted the lid' on charges for residential care, and said that anyone of retirement age could automatically knock on the door and go into a care home if they wished.
I was considered as a forerunner in this type of business, as when I had bought my rest home there were only seven in the area. Now in our association we had one hundred and twenty two registered homes as members, which meant I would have one hundred and twenty two set of minutes after typing, to photo copy and write envelopes for, then send out, informing all members of all the changes of legislation, changes in fees and all sorts of other things relevant to the business discussed at our meetings.
Social Services set up meetings once a month for any person interested in setting up a care home or becoming a care home manager.

I would attend these meetings as an officer of the association and a knowledgeable care homeowner.

Social services and myself would tell these people all the rules, answer any questions they might have and also explain the requirements of how to apply for registration to become a care home owner or manager.

New associations were forming all over the country. In some cases I would attend and advise them how to go about forming an association in their particular area, and in other cases I would attend national associations to see if there would be any advantage in our association joining or amalgamating with them. I did finally agree that our members could benefit from also becoming a member at their own discretion, of the British Federation Of Care Home Proprietors.

I always attended all the new registration information meetings at the Social Services office in King Street, at which each month there would be eight or ten people hopeful of becoming registered. The people considered suitable would then have lots of checks done on them and would be required to produce a number of references.

At one of these meetings I met a lady called June Hewitt. June had told the meeting that she had a lot of experience and had worked as a care assistant for a friend of mine called Pat Bruce in Pat's care home, and would now like to become a registered manager for Neil and Jean in a second care home which they had purchased.

June gave a very good impression and seemed to be a very genuine person. At the end of the meeting, I told Social services that I would consider June to be an asset to any care home as a manager.

I offered June a lift home, and on the way we chatted a lot about Junes' residents and her commitments to them. I really liked her as a person and told her that I only lived five minuets away and if she ever wanted any help or advice she could ring me at any time.

When I got home, I phoned Jean and told her I was very impressed by June, and that she would in my estimation be a very trustworthy and hard-working manager.

June and I went on to become longstanding friends. As time went by, we found we had such a lot in common; we had both suffered in our childhood, both lost our first babies, both had very unhappy marriages, and later had both ended up in the care business. Now in recent years we had both each lost a sister in similar circumstances. June and I are still wonderful friends to this day, and I always enjoy her company and her amusing opinions on life. June later on went on to buy her Care Home from Neil and Jean.

One of the members of our association, Jeff suggested that we should start a supper club. This idea received a great response, and lots of discussion took place. It was finally agreed that each member of the supper club would take it in turn each month to arrange a good restaurant of their choice within a five-mile radius of Blackpool tower.

Whichever member was to choose the restaurant would also phone up and book the venue, then book a coach for the transport and also collect the money from each person to pay for their meal. We would then each buy any wine or alcohol ourselves, but not from the kitty. When the transport and meal had been paid for and a suitable tip left for the waiters, whatever money was left over was then put into a social savings account until the end of the year, when all our supper club members would use it to take a trip to London to see a show and stay in a nice hotel.

The super club had been an excellent idea and we discovered some wonderful restaurants. We all looked forward to these nights with great excitement. If any of us had any friends visiting we were welcome to invite them along, as I did when my friends Liz, Joe and Alana came to visit me from South Africa. Each month after our supper club outing, there would be more money enthusiastically added to the savings account.

Liz and Joe were very impressed that we were all such good friends and commented that even though we were in the same business we did not consider each other as competition, and most of us would try very hard to help each other.

Once a year, Jeff would arrange a day out for us. One year it was a boat trip to the Isle Of Man, as he said, "we rest home proprietors work very hard in our chosen vocations taking on major responsibilities and commitment and deserve a bit of fun and relaxation in our lives."

We also had lots of garden parties and Fun days to raise money for the Blackpool Hospice and other charities. We would invite some of the stars from the shows in Blackpool, such as The Platters, The Grumbleweeds, Cannon and Ball and Little Mo.

The Lord and Lady Mayor of Blackpool would usually open these events.

My job would be to meet and greet these people, offer them a glass of champagne and generally chat to them, explaining why the event was being held, who would have been involved in the organizing of it, and where the money would be donated to.

I would then take them out into the gardens and introduce them to the public, there would be stalls selling homemade cakes and jams, tomb olla stalls and much more.

We had each asked a local business to donate raffle prizes; some were very generous and donated a television set or a weekend away for two or a meal for two in a good restaurant. We always invited the local press on these occasions, and we would then invite them again some weeks later when as association secretary I would be presenting a cheque to the chosen charity, so my photograph would appear in the Blackpool Gazette. On one occasion we presented a cheque for £3.000 to the hospice.

Jeff came up with another great idea, that we visit complexes designed as apartments for elderly people, in case one day they might wish to go into a care home, so that they would know exactly what to expect and to realize just how much care and love and support would be given to them in one of our care homes.

About ten of us agreed to take this idea on board, so we made a video film with Dorothy Bessey, explaining all the care procedures, and exactly what a potential resident could expect from any care home in our association.

Each one of us visited elderly complexes in our local areas and made appointments to provide a film show and a free supper in the local community centres

Each of us made and took along meat pies, or potato hotpot, or apple pies, and all sorts of other appetizing suppers. After the film shows and the free supper, we would then provide bingo, to make this a night out for the elderly people and we would distribute our brochures as well as being able to provide information and answer any queries or concerns they might have regarding their future care.

I had a special telephone installed in my rest home on behalf of the association, to be used as a 24-hour help line for elderly people in the community. I advertised the number in all the local newspapers, so that if anyone wanted any information about care homes, I would be able to advise them, and to let them know which home would have a vacancy.

I did sometimes get elderly people who would phone me in the middle of the night because they were lonely or felt vulnerable, so I would simply chat to them until they felt better, but this was not meant to be part of the service.

Every year, we organized a free Christmas party for any elderly person in the Fylde Coast who would like to attend. All they had to do was phone my 24-hour help line to book a place and I would then also arrange transport for them on the day of the party.

We booked the York House Hotel, and then put an advert in the Evening Gazette advertising a free Christmas dinner with a present from Father Christmas and a party afterwards. Most of us arranged to pick up the elderly people from where they lived, and would then drive them home afterwards.

Members of our association would be very active selling raffle tickets and raising money to pay for this event. Also each month we would buy a bottle of whiskey or vodka and sell raffle tickets at our monthly association meeting, and then all monies raised would go into the Christmas fund.

Edwin Jacks was appointed as the new Director of Social Services in our region, and he proved to be very popular with everyone.

Mr Jacks called a meeting to introduce himself to everyone. He said that he and his wife some twenty years ago had run a local authority care home, and he appreciated that it could some times feel like living-in a gold fish bowl.

He told me he had been told that I was not just the secretary of the Rest Homes' association, but that I was the Association! He said he had heard about all the good work I did, so that was he and I off to a good start Mr Jacks asked me to find a good hotel in St Anne's, as that is an upper-class area and to organize a seminar on his behalf, which was to be called 'Who Cares for the Carer?'

This seminar went down wonderfully well with care homeowners and managers alike, as Mr Jacks seemed to be a person who appreciated the long hours and difficult job of running a care home. Mr Jacks told us all that we were all in this care business together and we had to care for our residents, care for our staff and care for each other.

Sometime later, the chairman of our association retired. Mr Jacks tried his hardest to get me to take the chair, as he said I would be excellent for the job, but I kept telling him that I preferred to be the power behind the throne, not to sit on the throne. He just used to laugh and tell me I was a very unusual person, and he had a great regard for me.

Even though it was quiet an unethical thing to do, as the role of the social services was to police our care standards, Edwin Jacks offered to be the temporary chairman of our associations meetings until a new Chairman could be appointed.

The meetings were always fully attended, as Mr Jacks was a very interesting person and was also held in high regard. As a fellow Cancerian he certainly knew how to bring out the very best in people, and to do every thing in his power to help them. I went to Edwin's leaving party when he retired; hundreds of people attended, and in front of all those people he gave me a big hug and told me he would miss me. I was very sad to hear a lot of years later, that after his retirement Edwin Jacks had died of cancer.

Chapter Thirteen

DEBBIE HAD PLANNED TO TAKE me on a trip to Paris as a birthday present, so in September 1987, we travelled down to London and stayed overnight in a hotel. At six o'clock the next morning, we caught our coach in the centre of London, to take us to the ship in Dover for our crossing to Paris for four days. We were booked into an Ibis Hotel and it was a lovely trip. We did lots of sight seeing we sailed down the river Seine, we went up the Eiffel Tower and we had a meal in the Latin Quarter where Debbie later had a caricature painted. We were taken on a 'Paris by-night trip' on our coach, we also found time to do lots of shopping, and Debbie bought herself a few gargoyles.

On the third night, I went out for a meal with a few of the other people on the trip. Debbie had decided to stay in the bar with some young people she had made friends with. Later, when I came back to our hotel room, there was a great party going on. Debbie and her newfound friends were having a party, so of course I joined in. It was a great last night in Paris, and the whole holiday was a really great birthday present.

Then back to the rest home, back to working day and night, and back to all the rest home association meetings.

Now only two months until I was going on what had been advertised as 'a trip of a life time' which would include five nights on The QE2 sailing to New York, four nights in the Waldorf Astoria Hotel in New York, then to fly back to England on Concord.'

One hundred of us were to enjoy this holiday, as our travel company had chartered Concord. and Concord only took one hundred passengers.

I had bought lots of glittery sophisticated clothes, lots of gorgeous jewellry, shoes and handbags; it was the Concord and the QE2 after all, so no expense was spared.

On Friday November 6th we left Blackpool on two luxury coaches, taking us to Southampton where we stayed overnight in a hotel. There were one hundred people in our group, mainly business owners from Blackpool and most of us knew each other, so we had lots of laughs.

On Saturday after lunch, we boarded the QE2, which was to be our home for the next five nights. This was a new and exciting world and it was very impressive. I shared a cabin with a girl called Marilyn. Every evening, we would get dressed up in our glamorous eveningwear and put on our new makeup and exotic perfumes, which we had purchased on the QE2 duty-free. Then off we would go into the exquisite Mauritania restaurant for the most wonderful meals served by very charming waiters. We were really treated like royalty and after dinner there would be a wonderful show for us to enjoy.

During the day I used to love to be on deck. When we would pass other ships, our ship would sound her horn and the other ships would salute us. I found it incredible exciting and was so proud of our ship, one of my friends used to say to me "anybody would think you are the owner or the captain."

Later we would wander around the nightclubs. There was a band called ONYX LIVE who would sing and play every night in three different venues.

They used to sing a song called the QE2, which told the story of the great ocean liner, which was known as the Queen of The Seas, and all the QE 2's history, including when she took men to war. I just fell in love with this song and would visit each of the clubs each night until I had heard it sung, and then I would happily move on.

One night I approached Onyx Live and asked them if they would make me a tape of the song. They said it was only meant to be played on board the ship, but agreed to make a copy for me. They said that they could not record it for me at the moment as the sea was to rough, but promised to record it later and send it to my home in England. True to their word, they did exactly as they had promised. When I received the tape I made a few copies of it incase it ever got destroyed or lost and my granddaughter Sharn is the proud owner of one of the copies.

We all went to the Captain's party and each one of us had our photo taken with Captain Bennett. He told me that this is the ship's six hundred and forty first voyage across the Atlantic Ocean, and that he was a very proud man to be her Captain.

On Thursday 12th of November, we were approaching New York and had been told we would be due to sail past the Statue Of Liberty at 4am. We were all up, dressed and standing on deck in the dark at 3.45am, in freezing conditions and on a rough sea, we were so determined not to miss the statue. When we finally sailed into New York, the Big Apple everywhere was white with snow. Two coaches were waiting for us, and drove us to the Waldorf Astoria Hotel, which is located on Park Avenue and 49th.

We were to stay in this fabulous hotel for the next four nights.

We had read about all the fabulous shops and could not wait to explore them, but I had a very strange longing to go down to the Grand Central Station, which was only a few minutes' walk away. Marylyn kept saying, "I do not know why you want to go down there as it is not a safe place," but I insisted I just had to go.

We walked into the Pan Am building which is now no longer there, next to the station, but when we got down there, it was very intimidating and quite frightening; there were a lot of drunks and drugged people lying on the ground, and lots of beggars, so we just kept walking very fast, from one policeman to the next, all the way around the station. I read a wall plate, which said the station, had been completed in 1913. I had absolutely no idea at the time why I was so drawn to the place, but I really felt compelled to visit the station. A lot of years later I found out that the Grand Central Station is where my grandfather had worked in New York for six years.

We explored the department stores, and then on our second day, the coaches took us to Washington, where we visited the White House and saw the President take off in his helicopter for the weekend. We went inside The United Nations building on 1st avenue & 46th, we walked down 5th avenue to Tiffany's and Trump Tower, then over to the Rockefeller Center, then on to the Empire State Building, Times Square, and St Patrick's Cathedral. We also managed to fit in a horse and coach ride round Central Park and stopped at a restaurant for lunch with great big green chandeliers, called the Tavern in the Park We took a cruise around Manhattan Island, which is only 13 miles long and 2 miles wide, and we passed the Statue of liberty. The next day we all took helicopter rides over New York and flew over the 'Statue of Liberty'.

I really had to smile when I thought of us freezing up on deck on the ship waiting to see the statue, where-as now we had seen it every day since we arrived, and were yet to see it a few more times.

On the Sunday night, we were all taken on our coaches down town to the World Trade Center, to the 'Windows On The World Restaurant' on the 107th floor, in one of the Twin Towers, where we had breathtaking views of the New York skyline, and of course the Statue Of Liberty. Another evening, after an exciting day out, we took the subway to Chinatown for a meal, then as it seemed to be the done thing, we walked across to Little Italy, where the ice cream and Italian delicacies are very popular. This was an extremely busy five days, with some wonderful sightseeing, but I was determined to see and do as much as possible.

On November 16th two luxury coaches transferred us to John F Kennedy Airport, to the Concord Lounge. We took photos of Concord and were each presented with a model of the plane and there was a cocktail party laid on for us before boarding the supersonic jet.

It really was a flight of a lifetime, the plane was all done in gray leather and was super luxurious. This was a most amazing experience with the most wonderful food served with a 1955 white wine called Chateau Latour Pauillac costing £135 per bottle.

Three hours and twenty minuets later, we arrived into Manchester Airport, where my son Mark had arranged to meet me. The only word to describe the flight was 'magnificent.' In fact the whole holiday was just wonderful.

Concord and the QE2 are no longer in service, and the Windows on the World in The Twin Towers is now longer in existence, so these are precious and poignant memories.

This was only the beginning of lots more wonderful holidays. Two years later, in November, we did a tour of South Africa. On this trip there were fifty-two of us, which was one coach full. For the first few nights we stayed at the five star President Hotel in Cape Town. On our first evening, there was a jewellry auction in the hotel ballroom.
I bid for and then purchased a diamond ring and an emerald ring with a beautifully cut emerald, encircled with six diamonds and six smaller emeralds. These are still my prized possessions.
We visited Table Top Mountain and had lunch in The Wooden Bridge restaurant then we moved on to visit Pretoria, Port Elizabeth, and Cape Point. where we saw the meeting of the oceans. We spent a few days in the Beverley Hills Hotel in Durban and our next port of call was Zulu kraal in Zululand, then the part I did not like was the Kruger Park, with all the snakes and spiders out-side the bedroom door, even though it was a high-class hotel. Finally near the end of the third week, we arrived in Johannesburg to stay in the hotel for three nights. My friends Liz and Joe, who had moved there from Sillioth, came to visit me at the hotel. They were coming to pick me up in three days time, and when the rest of the party were flying back to England, I was staying with them for a further week in Springs in Transvaal.

Going to Ascot Races for two days each year was always a great thrill. We would buy beautiful outfits, then travel down on the Royal Ascot train enjoying a champagne breakfast. At Ascot, we would wave to the members of the royal family driving past us in their coaches, and then on the second day we would go to Ladies Day.

At different times of the year, we would go to Haydock Races and sit at the high round champagne tables to eat oysters and prawns and drink champagne. I believe that life is for living, I always worked hard and did my best to play hard, but thank goodness I had been blessed with having plenty of energy and a love of life.

My son Mark bought his first house in Stockport in January 1989. I went to visit him to help him move in and we spent the whole night sitting up chatting, but then Mark and I had always been very good friends and had always, been able to chat about anything and everything, and had always enjoyed each others company. Sometimes when it was a special occasion we would go off to the Coach House in St Anne's and have lobster and champagne together.

Mark decided he wanted to have a house warming party, so I arrived from Blackpool with a few surprise presents. I bought him a microwave, a Hoover vacuum cleaner, and a cordless telephone. He was really happy and excited by the time his guests arrived, which included my sister Elizabeth with her daughter, some of our cousins, and lots of his friends. We had a lovely night. Mark kept telling his guests my mum is great, and we are such good friends, we are like two peas out of the same pod.' It made me so happy to hear him being so proud of his mum.

Over a year later, Mark left the Insurance company he was working for and got a job as a holiday representative with Thompson's, as he had always wanted to live in Spain. He came back to Blackpool and spent the last week with me before flying off to his new life.

Mark's first job was in Majorca; every six months the reps were transferred to a different resort. Marks next transfer was to Gran Canaria, then onto Barcelona on the Costa Brava. Mark learned to read write and speak Spanish fluently. Every time he moved to a different resort he would telephone me and "say you must come and visit whilst I am here," so off I would go, and with free accommodation I was getting to explore all the resorts and only pay for my airfare.

Mark was always busy going on the coaches to the airport to collect his holiday makers, then dropping them off at the various hotels, sometimes working until 4 in the mornings, then after only a few hours sleep he would be out doing his welcome party meetings, telling his guests all about which-ever resort they were in. He would do this with great confidence and enthusiasm and he would then sell them lot of trips and excursions. He seemed to be extremely happy and was excellent at his job.

Whilst Mark was working in Spain he would phone me at home at least once a week. One time he phoned me and told me he had lost his bag containing over £700 which he had taken for the trips he had sold that day, but a few hours later, one of the holidaymakers had found the bag in a phone box and had handed it into the office. Other wise Mark would have had to repay all the money. What a wonderful and honest person the man who did that proved to be!

Having worked on all the Balearic Islands and the Canary islands, Mark was then transferred to Greece to work in Chania in Crete, I had never been to Greece, so this was a great opportunity for me to visit and explore another island for two weeks and this time I took my friend Jean. Mark's company had arranged for Jean and I to have a villa each, free of charge, next door to Marks villa, which was on the edge of the Mediterranean ocean. It was a very beautiful area. The Greek hoteliers and restaurant owners adored Mark and treated him like family, and I was so proud to see how highly thought of he was. Every night we went into a different restaurant and none of the owners would let us pay for our meals, as they kept telling me that Mark was like a son to them.

Chapter Fourteen

A FEW YEARS EARLIER I had bought the house next door to the rest home. This was a stock built detached house, which Mr Saville the builder had built for himself, so it was extremely well built, with nice large rooms.

I had rented the house out to tenants for a few years, but now decided to completely renovate it for myself, so as I could invite friends for dinner parties and to stay over night, which of course we could not do whilst I was living in the rest home.

I started by having all the chimneybreasts pulled out, then all the ceilings pulled down and re-plastered. Georgian beveled glass double doors replaced all the doors on the ground floor and all the windows were replaced by triple glazed leaded windows.

The big wide staircase was removed, to make way for a very ornamental spiral staircase, which gave lots of extra space to both floors of the house.

A new luxury bathroom was built and a Jacuzzi was installed. The master bedroom had its own en-suite and dressing room.

My dear friend Barry introduced me to a company in Manchester who built me the most wonderful bedroom furniture, which included a pull out ledge on the bedside cabinets on which to place a glass of champagne whilst sitting in bed, so the house gradually became my palace.

Lots of parties and fun took place in that house, and I had the greatest of pleasure in having somewhere beautiful to invite my friends.

We would have lots of barbeques on the patio in the back garden, and with its high walls which had been painted and covered in lots of lovely wall boxes containing flowers, some people used to say it felt like an open air night club.

I was in my kitchen one day when Debbie came in and asked me what I would be doing for Christmas. I said I would be working as usual, and she then said, "well you will have a extra present to buy, as I am pregnant." I ran over to her and gave her the biggest hug, as this was the most wonderful news that she could have given me.

Seven months, later I was at Manchester Airport seeing Mark off as he was going on holiday. I was just coming out of the lift when a member of staff at the rest home phoned me and said Debbie had gone into labour. I was out of the airport and drove all the way to Blackpool at over one hundred miles a hour, as I had experienced what it was like to be left in labour on my own, and there was no way I wanted my daughter to suffer that.

When we arrived at the hospital, Debbie told me she had booked me in to stay with her during the birth. Nine hours later, at four fifty one on Sunday morning, I was there waiting for my granddaughter as she arrived into the world. I had watched this beautiful perfect baby been born after her long tough journey. I was so very proud of Debbie; this was one of the most exciting days of my life.

On the previous evening I had planed to go to my friends Mike and Dorothy's wedding anniversary party and I had bought a dozen red roses and a bottle of champagne, which were in my car, as a present for them, so I thought this must have been fate, as I could now present them to Debbie as soon as her baby had been born, as a thank you for the wonderful job she had done.

After presenting Debbie with the champagne and roses, I dashed back to the rest home to get my camera and to telephone every one with the wonderful news. My friend June came back to the hospital with me, and we took photos of the proudest mum and grandmother in the world with this beautiful new addition to the family. I felt as if life could never be better than this.

I was at this time very interested in politics. When we used to go to the House of Commons on Thursdays to hear Prime Minister question time, I used to buy a bottle of House of Commons gin and it was the best gin I have ever tasted.

Just one of my jobs was treasurer of the Conservative party in Alexandra Ward. I used to go around all the shops, local traders and private businesses, in the area and sell advertizing space on my Alexandra Ward Christmas card to raise money for the party. After having the cards printed, I would then go out and deliver them to every house in the constituency.

The canvassing was an experience in itself. I will never forget my wonderful friend Barry, coming out knocking on doors with me canvassing for the Conservative party even though he was a Labour man himself. What a true friend! On election night, Debbie would come down and watch the votes being counted, which was a nerve-racking experience. When I got lots of votes she kept patting me on the back and saying "well done Mum" Margaret kept saying "don't call her mum, call her councillor"

Mark was now working in Bangkok in Thailand. He telephoned me and said it is a very safe country, and I really should visit it, as there are lots of wonderful things to see. He then arranged a holiday for my friend Jean and me, to spend a month in Thailand, Hong Kong, Singapore and Bali.

All the hotels were five stars, plus he got us a massive discount. We bought four different currencies and set off on another wonderful experience.

We spent a week in Thailand with Mark; he took us the golden palaces and the floating market, which were fascinating, and the night markets where lots of bargaining went on.

Mark then came to Hong Kong with us for a week, so as well as a wonderful holiday, I was getting time to spend with my son, plus he was a professional tour guide.

Some time later, Mark changed his job and became employed by British Airways as flight crew, flying long haul, so now when I flew British Airways I would get virtually free travel, only paying airport taxes, and on a few occasions whoever I was travelling with and I were upgraded to first class.

A friend of mine and I flew to America, where we arranged to meet my dear friends Margaret and Peter in New York. We all stayed in the Waldorf Astoria Hotel for few days before all flying to their home, which was a small hotel in Vermont in the ski resort. Whilst we were there, they lent us one of their cars, so we travelled around Canada for a few days, which was another nice new experience.

Margaret and Peter had got married on a yacht a few months earlier in Florida. I had travelled over for the wedding, taking my friend Christine, who had been my hairdresser when I worked in the shop in Salford a lot of years ago. The wedding had been a wonderful affair, and afterwards we all went on honeymoon together, including Margaret's daughter Maria and her husband. We had a fabulous week together in the theme parks in Florida.

On another trip to the United States, I went to visit my wonderful friends Noreen and Sam in California. They live in one of the most incredible houses I have ever been in and they even have Reindeers in their garden. After leaving Noreen and Sam, we drove down most of route 66 and a few days later arrived in Las Vegas and stayed at one of my favourite hotels, the Golden Nugget. I have stayed in lots of different hotels in Vegas but really enjoy this hotel most of all.

I will only write about a few more holidays, otherwise it will sound as though I never worked and spent all my time on holiday! When I was at work, I would work day and night and not bother about days off, but I was at the rest home for twenty years, so had fitted in quite a few holidays.

I always knew I was leaving the home in safe hands as Debbie had been working there for quite a few years, and had proved to be very reliable and punctual. The residents all loved her and always complemented her on her cooking.

I had applied to Social Services to have Debbie registered as a manager of the rest home, so she was interviewed and obtained references from the priest at the Catholic Church, who used to visit our home, and a Baptist minister Pastor Mc Lowed. Debbie passed with flying colours, and was awarded her certificate.

Mr Carr, the manager for Social Services, said to Debbie "Congratulations, you are now a Registered Manager of a rest home which has an excellent reputation," so now we always had a manager on the premises, as Debbie like myself lived in.

I had decided to take a friend of mine to visit my friends Liz and Joe in South Africa. After staying with them for two weeks, Liz lent us her car, as we had wanted to spend a week in Zimbabwe (in the past called Rhodesia). We wanted to see some of the country and to visit Harare and Victoria Falls.

The last holiday I will mention for a while, was when another friend Carol and I went on a trip to India for four weeks. We started off in Delhi, then went on to Agra and Jaipur. This was a wonderful experience, as we toured the country on our coach, we rode on elephant's backs up a mountain and into a palace, we saw ladies in the most beautiful coloured saris digging on the road works, we saw cows sitting on the motorway, and they being a sacred animal in that country, all the buses and cars would simply drive around them. And a few days we had lunch in palaces.

My favorite place was the 'Taj Mahal', built a few hundred years ago by Emperor Shah Jahan as an immortal tribute to the memory of his beloved wife. I visited the Taj Mahal on three occasions. The first time I went there at eight o'clock in the morning, when there were no tourists about, so took some wonderful photos. I also had one taken of me sitting on the bench, which Princess Diana had sat on a year earlier.

I found there was the most fascinating atmosphere in the gardens of this hauntingly beautiful building and it was a feeling that I shall never forget.

I found Bombay slightly depressing as we saw lots of people begging in the street, and they would have only one arm. Our tour rep told us that the other arm would be cut off at birth so as they could later earn money by begging.
After our fascinating time in India, we then travelled down to Goa and had a beach holiday for a week, going shopping and out on the boats, then coming back and having a massage on the beach by four Indian ladies.
I found India a very impressive and fascinating country and we enjoyed the four weeks we spent there immensely. I would certainly recommend the Taj Mahal to anyone who would have a chance to visit it.

With five of my girl friends in Blackpool we used to have a girls' night then out every Friday night, sometimes we would go to Mad Harry's in town and have fancy dress parties. One of these parties was called 'What were you wearing when the Titanic went down?' I went dressed as the captain of the Titanic and I made my friend Deny's a mermaid's outfit in which she looked stunning. Val Doreen and Judy all dressed as high-class passengers in cocktail dresses and cigarette holders.

Another party was called 'A thoroughly bad taste party.' We all wore a variety of colours in our outfits such as a pink camisole, green skirt, blue jacket, red handbag and yellow shoes, with lots of cheap jewellry, with beauty spots on our faces.
We used to have the most incredible laughs when we were dressed like that, as how could anyone possibly keep a straight face when we could see how funny each other looked.

At Mad Harry's we usually ended up dancing on the chairs with or without alcohol.

Blackpool was always a fun town to live in, with plenty going on.

My son Mark was now living in London and working out of Gatwick Airport, so I used to go to visit him in his apartment, and we would have some very nice days out visiting places such as Brighton which I had not been to before.

Mark eventually transferred to Heathrow airport, which he seemed to enjoy much more, and he moved back up to the north of England so was much nearer to his family and would then travel down to Heathrow from Manchester Airport by shuttle.

I had taken my residents up to Garstange Marina, as they loved to sit and watch the boats. All of a sudden a cruiser called Kingfisher took my eye with a 'For Sale sign' on it. I of course went and inspected the boat, which was four berth and was only a few years old I was very impressed. I wrote down the owner's phone number and when we got home I telephoned to find out the details. I had a few years earlier been interested in buying a boat with a friend of mine, but we could not find one which was suitable, and all of a sudden Kingfisher looked very appealing. After talking to the owners on the telephone, we agreed to meet up and they took us out on the canal in the boat. It was a beautiful evening, so we had the hood down; Debbie and I just loved Kingfisher so a sale was agreed.

We were now the very proud owners of a very nice boat which had been completely renovated. It had a proper shower, toilet, electric fire, television set and was all done out in my favorite colour, royal blue. Debbie was the first one to spend a night aboard.

Each winter I would have my boat taken out of the water, winterized and housed in a shed until the springtime, when she would be floated on the water again. She gave us a lot of pleasure and even Sharn when she was about three or four years old used to steer Kingfisher and happily keep saying "look Nanny I am driving the boat on my own."

I made some very nice friends on the marina and had some happy times there. I took my friend June out on the boat and we sailed down the canal to one of the local pubs for lunch. June fell in love with the boat, so she and Len bought an old one, which Len renovated himself. We planned to have lots of boat parties and barbecues and after the parties the girls would sleep on my boat and the guys would sleep on June and Len's boat.

I kept my boat until I decided to move to Ireland, and then reluctantly put her up for sale, when a friend of mine who owned a photography business bought her and enjoyed her as much as I did.

I was extremely devastated when Princess Diana died, as I had the privilege of meeting her twice, on both occasions in Blackpool. On one of these occasions, I shook hands with her and talked to her and when I got home I said to Debbie I know now how people feel when they say I will never wash this hand again, but of course working in the rest home that did not last for long!

I had a surprise telephone call from Parviz. He said Hilary, the girl he had been living with for a few years, wanted to meet me, so I invited them both to the rest home, and I made a nice meal for them with salmon, prawns and white wine.

I wondered what the meeting was about and thought maybe they wanted to get married, but I made them both very welcome. After a few glasses of wine Parviz went down-stairs to the toilet and Hilary started to tell me that Parviz hit her, he was in continuous bad moods and she was totally unhappy. She wanted to see me to see if I could offer her any advice, or to find out if there was any chance of him getting any better. At this point, Parviz came in and had been listening at the door, so dragged her off home, I knew that feeling well but did not make any comment as I did not want to get involved.

Some years earlier, just after Parviz and Hilary had first met, my son Mark was selling a gold coloured Capri, which was only two years old. Mark's father, Parviz, had said that his girlfriend wanted to buy the car and that he was going to pay in cash and she would repay him so much a week until the amount was repaid, but of course this was nothing to do with us. A price was agreed between Mark and Parviz, but before the car changed hands, Parviz suddenly said I am going to pay you twenty five pounds less as the arial is broken. Mark said I have already given you the car at a special price so I think that is very unfair, but Parviz deducted the twenty-five pounds. This was his way of impressing his girlfriend and he did not seem care about the fact that Mark is his son and that is where his loyalty should have lain. Poor Mark was very upset about this behaviour and said he very much regretted selling him the car in the first place.

After Sharn was born I decided to resign as secretary of the Rest Home Association as I had done the job for eleven years and wanted to spend more time with her. All the members got together and decided they could not let me go as I was to valuable to them, so they created a new position as President, and they said this would be less demanding and a lot less work. We had never had a President of our association so this was a great compliment. They then bought me four crystal brandy glasses and a lovely silver tray, as a 'thank you,' for all my hard work as secretary. The members voted that every Christmas in future we would call our Christmas Dinner Dance 'The Presidents Ball'

One hundred and twenty two people attended the first Presidents Ball.

Jean would make me smile when she would often say, "I am so proud to be the president's best friend."

I used to stand near the door and welcome all my guests then after dinner I would go on stage and give an after dinner speech, which was my least favourite part of the evening. Margaret and Graham often came all the way up from Peterburgh to attend our dinner dance at Christmas.

One of our members Neil was a Mason, so we would be invited to 'Ladies Night' at the Masons hall in Fleetwood usually once a year. These were quite grand occasions when everyone would wear evening dress, and each person would receive a gift from the Masters Lady. The glasses would be raised, lots of toasts would be drunk and these were always very enjoyable evenings.

Jean was the friend that I spent the most time with, we went on lots of holidays all over the world together, even though I would sometimes go on holidays with other people. Jean would always be agreeable to go to where ever I suggested and I would then do all the arranging. In eighteen years we never had a wrong word between us, she would also come to the golf club nights with me, she was great company and always dressed beautifully, in fact I used to tell her, that she looked like a film star!

On a few occasions I would book a show in London with a company called Four Seasons, as they would also book a hotel for us. On one occasion they arranged a limousine and a chauffeur to take us to the theater and a bottle of champagne in the fridge for when we arrived at the hotel as I had told the manager it was my birthday. When we arrived at the theater the chauffer as he was helping us out of the car kept saying to people in the queue 'no photos please, no photos! Then he whispered to us that will really make them wonder who you are.

Every New Year's Eve Jean would have a fabulous party at her home, which I always looked forward to. At midnight someone would have to bring a piece of coal into the house for good luck, the party would usually go on until the early hours of the morning. .

One afternoon whilst I was on duty at the rest home, Jean's daughter phoned me to tell me her mother had collapsed a few hours earlier and she went into great detail to explain everything that had happened and how an ambulance had been called and how Jean had been resuscitated. It took her a long time before she could tell me that my dear friend had died. I was devastated because it was so unexpected and such a shock and because we had spent such happy times together.

Debbie had been on a day off, and just happened to come home after I got the dreadful news, she was very kind and said to me "I will take over and do the evening shift for you." The next few days were very sad days; grief is a strange thing, it ambushes you, and unexpectedly it comes like waves over you.

Mark and my lovely friend June, who was also a friend of Jean's, was great at this very sad time and we all went to the funeral together.

I always remember June sitting holding my hand in the church as my tears flowed when they played Jeans favorite song, 'A Spanish lullaby'

Association President

Chapter Fifteen

In 1999, my aunty Mamie, who is my father's sister, phoned me up and told me that my first cousin John in Galway in Ireland had a cottage he wanted to sell. Even though I knew nothing about all of this, she had told him that I might be interested in it as a holiday home.

Mamie and I sailed over to Ireland to view the cottage. This was the first time I had met Bridie and John, as John had not been born when I was last in the village. They were delightful people, with a lovely Irish laid-back attitude to life.

The cottage was next door but one to where my father had been born; it was also the cottage that I had been in trouble for chasing the cat into when I was four years old, which was the last time I had been in this village.

My cousin John had inherited the cottage from his father. John's father and my father were brothers. John had no need for the cottage himself, as he had had a lovely bungalow built some twenty years earlier on the other side of the village.

There was a large field at the back of the cottage, which I thought would make a wonderful garden. The cottage itself needed extensive renovation inside and out, so I told John I would give the whole project a lot of thought.

The village had not changed in the fifty-six years since I had last been there, and two of the cottages still had working farms at the back of them. The cottage my father had been born in had now fallen down, but looked very ornamental in the way it had collapsed.

I went to visit all the neighbours who all still lived in the same houses, only they had now become widowed elderly ladies in their eighties and nineties. They still remembered me being there as a child and one of the ladies told me that, I had left a lasting impression!

My father still had a younger brother living in the village at that time, he lived alone as he had never married, but seemed happy and contented enough.

Later that day after we left Williamstown, I drove one hundred and thirty miles up to Glencar in County Leitrim, to visit my mother's sister Liz and two brothers. This was the farm that I had always been so happy on as a child when my grandfather had been alive. It was lovely to see them all and they made us incredibly welcome. The next day we drove to Dublin, then sailed back to England.

A few weeks later, Mark and I went back to Galway to have a second look at the cottage, as I had always valued Mark's opinion.

I had a nice feeling about the village of Shanbally and especially to have John and Bridie as neighbours so close by. So the decision was made. I told John I would buy the cottage, and would be applying for planning permission to build a large extension.

I went to work on drawing my plans, but I had done all this before at the rest home so very much enjoyed it all.

In the year 2000, I received my planning permission to build, so I hired a local builder called Norman, who was excellent and did a most wonderful job. Norman had built his own cottage so was very familiar with this type of structure.

I had chosen a new fitted kitchen, a bathroom suite, wallpaper, tiles, and floor coverings before going back to England to work in my rest home.

Norman built a beautiful large bedroom and luxury bathroom for me, then fitted my chosen bathroom suite. A new kitchen was fitted including a luxury stove and a dishwasher (the first in Shanbally), new double-glazed windows and doors were fitted, and the entire cottage was renovated with only the best of everything.

Leaving a wild perimeter, a one-acre split-level garden was developed, with beautifully manicured lawns against a backdrop of beautiful ornamental trees. A delightful patio and barbecue area was built, surrounded by double walls with flowers in the middle and it all slowly but surely became my paradise.

My garden used to feel like being in heaven. I used to sit in it and think this is my precious space, the only place in the world where I cannot worry about anything.

My granddaughter Sharn and I would sail over for long weekends at the cottage.

Sharn learnt how to herd the neighbour's cows from the fields into the barn in the evenings, she also learnt how to milk them, and she would often come running up to the cottage with a pail of milk to show me how much milk one of her favourite cows had given her. Sharn was so lucky she just got there before the end of an era, as only two years latter most people in Ireland had stopped milking cows, so she just got a glimpse of life the way it used to be. These were happy days and Sharn loved the country life; also these would be happy memories for her to savour for the rest of her life.

Whilst I was at the cottage, before going home to Blackpool I would always call up to Glencar to visit my mother's two brothers, Owen and Vincent, and her sister Liz. My mother's sister Liz was one of my favorite aunties and we would spend many hours enjoying each others company and chatting away about the old days when we would have been out on the farm together looking after Liz's hens. Liz had never married or left home, she often said she wished I lived nearer to her as she was short of female company, and because we had always been such good friends.

She often said I should buy a piece of their land, which had been my grandfather's land when he was alive, and I could build a house on it when I retire. Her brothers Owen and Vincent were all for this and said I could use part of the house as a shop, and that they would always support me as customers.

My cousin Patricia invited me to stay with her for a week's holiday. She was also living on what had been our grandfather's land. Every morning when I woke up, I used to have the most wonderful feeling waking up on granddad's land again, just as I had done as a young girl. This is when I decided I would eventually build a house here.

On January 25th 2000, I received a phone call from the nurse in charge at Ennsingham Hospital in Maryport, telling me that Elsie Armstrong had been admitted the previous day. She said that Elsie was very seriously ill, was deteriorating fast and that she kept asking for Maureen in Blackpool. I told the nurse to please tell Elsie I would be there as soon as I possibly could. It took me almost two hours to drive to Maryport. I called to see Elsie's son Thomas on my way and he told me that Elsie did not have long left to live and that he would come to the hospital with me.

When we arrived on the ward, the nurse said that Elsie had been drifting in and out of consciousness, but that she knew that I was on my way and she had kept asking for me.

Elsie was in a cot type bed. I took the side of the cot down and told Elsie that I was going to give her a big hug. This was the lady who had told me twenty years earlier 'that she loved me like a daughter'

Elsie had lost both of her daughters; Anne had died of a brain tumour August 23rd 1980 (I have already written about this in chapter eight), then a few months later, Elsie's other daughter Margaret had drowned herself in a river.

Elsie lay with my arms around her and she talked non-stop for over an hour and a half. She talked of her childhood, of her parents, her marriage and her children, and of course the two daughters she had lost.

She talked and talked and talked, and when she had finished she said, may God bless you lass for being here with me, then seeming to have got everything off her mind, she just closed her eyes and went to sleep. She then died peacefully in her sleep.

Thomas had stood at the end of the bed and witnessed all of this. When we got back to his house, he told Marjorie his partner, "If I had not seen all that with my own eye's I would not have believed it." Thomas then told me "My mum certainly loved you lass and she definitely waited for you."

I was going to miss Elsie a lot, as in the past I would some times drive to Maryport and take her to my holiday home for a few nights as I knew she was very lonely. Every night she would enjoy a bottle of Guinness, as she said it would help her to sleep. Other times she would get a bus down to Blackpool and stay with me at the rest home for two weeks at least once a year and she considered this as her annual holiday. She would book a pensioner's day trip from Maryport to Blackpool, so all her friends would be on the bus. I was always waiting in the car park when the bus would arrive and Elsie would be the first off the bus. We would then wait and I would have a chat with a few of her friends whom I had known for years, then when we drove away everyone would wave her off. She used to say " I feel as important as the Queen with that lot seeing me in your posh car." Elsie would make lots of meat and potato pies, lots of apple pies, and potato hash. We and our residents all loved Elsie's baking.

Elsie was an extremely heavy smoker, but was it any wonder after all that she had been through? Before she would leave Blackpool, we would go down to Waterloo Road shopping, where she would buy all her family presents and Blackpool rock, and I would always buy her 200 cigarettes, then off she would go back to Maryport on the bus, happy and smiling in the knowledge that she was loved and appreciated.

I may have been like a daughter to Elsie but she was also like a mother to me! And I was certainly going to miss her.

July 4th 2000, I was visiting my aunty and uncles in Glencar, when my uncle suggested that I could buy a field from him if I want to build a house in the area. We went around in my car and looked at the field, with a river flowing at the bottom of it, and I agreed that if I could get planning permission to build a house then I would purchase the field.

So off I went to see Eugene Kelly the surveyor, and asked him to apply for planning in my name. This was the beginning of a long drawn-out process which went on for almost three years before I actually received the planning.

One of my cousins daughters Lisa who I have always been very fond of phoned me up on April 7th 2001 and said that she and her partner George were looking for a rest home to purchase and would I consider selling mine to them.

Lisa from being a young girl had always visited me in my home, so was very familiar with the place. I told her they should come over for a meal one evening and we could discuss it.

When Lisa was a teenager, she used to come to see me in Blackpool and I would dress her up in some of my glittery evening wear and jewellry and take photos of her. She always used to say Aunty Maureen when I grow up I want to be just like you. She had now grown into an extremely glamourous young lady in her mid twenties.

Lisa and George came to visit, then after the meal I showed them around the home and all of the thirteen bedrooms. George who had not been in the home before said he was very impressed at the extremely high standard, and they both agreed that they were very interested in going ahead with a purchase, so we agreed on a price.

I had been studying Astrology for over a year, I found it to be a fascinating subject.

Kathy and Kevin held Astrology meetings in the Waterloo Hotel every Monday evening, this was a great venue for me as it was next door but one to the rest home so virtually on my doorstep. In July the founder member Barbara Giles who had done readings for me in the past agreed to do a reading and told me I would sell my rest home next February 2002, I knew that if Barbara said it, it would definitely happen so became quite excited about the change it would make to my life, but February was six months away so plenty of work to be done yet.

I would go and ask the residents would anyone like to go to Fairhaven Lake and three or four would usually agree to go. On arrival, we would go into the café and have tea and cakes, then we would go and feed the swans on the lake. Sid, who was ninety-nine years old, never missed these outings, which were usually about once a week. He used to sit and talk to me about his wife and how they had loved to spend time at Fairhaven Lake and how happy they had always been together.

Sid was a wonderful artist and spent a great deal of time drawing pictures of beautiful cottages and lots of lovely buildings and gardens. I made a gallery on the ground floor for Sid's paintings, so all our visitors, including doctors and chiropodist used to go in and admire them and Sid usually told them to their delight that they could choose one and take it home. Every morning Sid would read the Daily Mail, so he would then have plenty to discuss with people during the day. One of the most amazing things about Sid was that even though he was ninety-nine years old, he did not need to wear glasses for reading or for his painting.

I had always told him that when he reached his one hundredth birthday, I would take him out in a Rolls Royce, which he really looked forward to and could often be heard chatting to visitors about. Sadly only four months before he reached his one hundred birthday, Sid passed away in Victoria hospital.

In January 2002, Lisa and George came to stay at the rest home for a few days to learn the procedures and they were both upset to hear that Sid had died, as they had really looked forward to looking after him.

Debbie had agreed to stay on as Rest Home Manager for a few months at least until Lisa and George themselves would become registered.

Finally on February 2nd 2002, I walked away from my rest home. It was the strangest feeling, after having spent just over twenty years there.

My son Mark had just bought a house in Heald Green and he suggested that I share his house with him until my house in Ireland was built.

Heald Green is a lovely area and quite close to Manchester Airport, so it was very handy for Mark to catch the shuttle down to Heathrow for his flights with British Airways.

At the beginning it felt strange and I was not quite sure what to do with my newfound freedom. I joined an art class and found it very relaxing, learning to paint in watercolours. I used to think I wished I had done this whilst Sid was alive and then sometimes we could have painted together, but I simply did not know that I would be capable of doing it, so now I used to teach Sharn what I had learnt and we would paint away happily together, as she would usually stay with me at the weekends

I have framed a lot of my work and given a lot away to friends. It is a great compliment when I go to visit them and see one of my paintings hanging on their wall.

Now that I did not have to go to work, some weekends Sharn and I would just take off to the cottage, she would sit on the back seat of the car with her feet up and watch programs on the car television set and other times we would sing all the old 1950's songs. Some weekends we would go on a coach trip somewhere, or we would simply visit the Manchester Museum where Sharn bought lots of unusual items in the Museum shop, then we would usually go sight seeing and end up on a shopping spree.

One Saturday we went into Marks and Spencers in Heald Green. After doing our shopping we returned to the car, I got into the driver's seat and as soon as I sat down a man got into the car beside me, calmly picked up my handbag which contained my phone, my house keys, my money which was just over £200, (I would not often be carrying that amount of cash but we had just come back from Ireland the night before), and my bankers cards, he then got out of my car and into a white car driven by another man, which was parked behind my car blocking me in. I could not retaliate as Sharn was still standing outside of the car. I drove as fast as I could to Marks friends house as knew he had a spare key but he was not at home. The house next door happened to have a van parked outside with a set of ladders on top. I knocked on the door and explained the predicament I was in and asked the driver if he would climb in through my upstairs window and open the door for me which fortunately he agreed to.

As I got into the house, the telephone rang and a man's voice said to me "I have found your purse in the street with your phone number in it, and if you come to met me at B&Q car park, I will give it back to you." I just knew that this was the man who had robbed me, or his accomplice, and they now wanted to rob the house.

The man with the ladders was still there at the house, so he said that if I wanted to go and meet him' he would stay outside the house and make sure the man did not get in.

I took Sharn to the next-door neighbour's house in case any harm might come to me and I went to B&Q car park but sure enough he was not there, because he had turned up at the house.

When I told my sister Anne what had happened she said, "you should not carry that amount of money in your handbag, as you have now given that man a taste for robbing other people." I did remind her that she tells lots of people that she carries all her takings from her shop in her handbag, and that we are all be free to carry whatever we chose in our handbags. I could not help remembering the old saying, 'You cannot choose your family'

Chapter Sixteen

I HAD AN IRISH FRIEND living in Perth in the west of Australia called Anne Smith, she was a few years older than me and had immigrated to Australia when she was a teenager.

I met Anne when she came on holiday to Blackpool to visit her brother who was a resident living in my care home. She and I had become good friends and had kept in touch. Anne had for years been inviting me to go and stay with her for a month in Australia. I always promised her that one-day when I sell the rest home and retire that I would visit her.

Sometimes it is strange how things work out, because I had joined Friends Reunited on the internet and received a message from a girl who said we had been at school together until we were eleven years old, and she wondered if I still remembered her. She gave me her name as Barbara Beckett and she said that she and her husband had lived in New Zealand for over thirty years and that she had photographs of she and I walking in the Whit Week Walks together in Manchester. These photos had been in The Manchester Evening News in 1950 and her mother had sent for copies, which she now sent to me.

We chatted a few times on the phone and kept sending each other e-mails then she invited me to New Zealand to stay with her and her husband Dave for a week's holiday.

This seemed like a great idea as I have a first cousin Winifred living in New Zealand. Winifred is the cousin who lived with my family for about six months when we were teenagers, and I had promised to go and visit her some day, so now it seemed like a splendid idea to go and visit all three of them.

In October 2002, I went to stay with Anne in Australia for four weeks. We had a great time together, we went out in Anne's car almost every day or quite often with friends of hers. Anne took me to some wonderful places sight seeing, we went on a boat trip down a river and had a delicious lunch, she took me to some fabulous restaurants and for the best chinese meal I have ever tasted. We also had a day at the horse racing with all her friends from the bowling club; I decorated our hats in an Ascot style and we entered the best hat competition.
Anne really put herself out and nothing was too much trouble for her.
After one month I then flew to New Zealand and stayed with Barbara and her husband Dave in a brand new house they had just had built. New Zealand is an incredibly beautiful country and we again spent a lot of time sightseeing.

I then went to visit my cousin Winifred, her husband Roy and their two sons, who live in a very beautiful split-level beachside house with three terraces one for each floor.
We had such a lot to talk about and so many photos from the past to look at. This was precious time spent together, as we have known each other all of our lives. They then also took me out to see the local sights.

After all this, I flew back to Australia and spent one more week with my friend Anne. She invited all her friend around for a barbecue as a leaving party for me. Anne was a lovely and good-hearted friend. I am so glad I went to see her for that extra week, as she passed away one year later.
In December, Sharn and I flew to Lapland and went to visit Father Christmas at his house. Lapland was incredibly cold; we went on a reindeer ride and on a snowmobile and lots of other things. All the children were given a present of a bell usually worn around the reindeer's neck. This was a delightful trip to see all the children so happily enjoying themselves, and I must say all the parents too.

Sharn and I had a few days holidays travelling all around London. We stayed in a very nice hotel and she was very excited as we went to see all the sights. I took her on the open top bus and we just kept hopping off to visit lots of different places. Sharn fell in love with Big Ben. I was glad as I have always been fascinated by it and we took some great close up photos of it. I bought her a watch that she decided to name big Ben's little Ben. We went to Buckingham Palace. I would like to have taken her inside but it is usually only in August and September when tourist are allowed inside. I did a trip there a few years earlier and it was well worth the visit. By the time we went on the London Eye, she really knew her way about and could point out all the tourist attractions to me, which proved to be a good geography lesson.

The planning permission for my new house had been deferred on three occasions, first of all because they said I could not have a two-storey house, then it was deferred again as they said I couldn't have Georgian windows nor a slanted roof at the back of the house. They again deferred it, saying I must build further back to the west and closer to the river, which is where I had wanted to be in the first place. It was a real uphill struggle trying to get the planning passed, as one neighbour said it would be easier to roll a boulder up a mountain. I often wondered if it was my English accent that was making it more difficult, but I was not willing to give in. Finally, after a long struggle, I was granted planning permission for a six bed-roomed house and a large conservatory.

On March 12th 2003, after winning my battle, I went to the solicitors in Manorhamilton with my uncle Vincy and signed for the land, which I had agreed to buy almost three years earlier, on consideration that I received planning permission to build a house on it.

So now it was all systems go.

The next day I was saddened to hear that the war in Iraq had started, as I had marched in Manchester in protest against this war.

On April 1st 2003, the foundations were put in for my new home in Ireland.

I kept flying over to Ireland to check on how the building was going on. I already had a car at my cottage in Galway, so I would fly into Knock airport then my cousin John would pick me up in my car and I would spend a night there and enjoy the cottage and then the next day I would drive two hours up to Glencar. It was exciting to see how fast the builder was erecting my house.

Desmond the builder had said to me months earlier " as you are coming back to Ireland to live for the rest of your life, I am going to build you a fine house and will only use the best of everything" and it was obvious he was keeping his promise.

I would then spend a lot of time looking around at kitchen and bathroom show rooms, also tile showrooms, seeing that the prices were massively more expensive than in England, but of course I already knew this, as I had done all this in Galway two years earlier when my cottage was being renovated.

When back in England, I was making the best of my last few months before moving away. With some of my friends, we hired a stretch limousine and went to Ascot for a few days, I went to see all the shows and did all the things I knew I would not be able to do once I moved to live in Ireland.

We had a lovely elderly lady Eula Platt living next door to Marks house, her and I would have a chat over the garden fence every day. She would often tell me she does not know what she will do when I move to Ireland. Mark used to love to walk Eula's dog Sandy. One morning I woke up about 3.30am and heard a dog whimpering. My room was at the back of the house, I opened the window and knew that something was wrong but could not see anything in the dark. I put on my coat and went down to our garden and could see Eula lying on the ground at the bottom of her steps next door.

Eula's legs looked badly injured so I covered her up with a blanket and called an ambulance and I then phoned her brother. The hospital later told me that as well as her injuries Eula had hypothermia, and had she not been found soon she would almost certainly have died. When she recovered Eula bought me a great big plant for saving her life, I brought the plant with me when I moved to Ireland

I was all packed and ready to start my new life and everything was arranged, but at about nine o'clock the evening before I was due to sail, I received a phone call from Kristine, who is Liz and Joe's daughter in South Africa.

Kristine had phoned me to tell me that her mother had been shot in the head and had died a few hours earlier. I found this news very difficult to take in, in fact I felt devastated, as only the week before Liz had sent me a e-mail telling me that I was like her guardian angel and she often thinks of me as her earth angel. How could something so dreadful happen to such a kind and lovely lady as Liz?

I cancelled my arrangements to move, as how could I start my new life at the same time as my friend's life had ended? A few days later I still had to travel to Ireland, as I had appointments with various tradesmen. When I got there, I was not capable of choosing which tiles and carpets I wanted fitting, as I was totally grief stricken.

My son Mark was also very upset by the tragedy, as he had spent a lot of time with Liz and Joe in South Africa. Only a few weeks earlier, Liz had been discussing with Mark their plans to sell up in South Africa and to come to Ireland, and either live in the top floor of my new house or to live in my cottage in Galway until they decided if they liked Ireland, and if they did, then Joe would build them a house of their own.

Liz and I had spent hours on the telephone chatting about these ideas and about employment, as she was working as a secretary in the hospital in Johannesburg and said she had hoped she would be able to find something similar over here. She had also said Joe was hoping he would be able to set up a business here in Ireland.

This was all planned for November, so they were also on the threshold of starting a new life.

Mark got compassionate leave from British Airways and flew to join me in Ireland.

He then helped me to choose all the carpets and was a wonderful help. After a few days of sorting things out, we travelled back to England, and I remade my plans for a few weeks later to move across the Irish Sea.

Chapter Seventeen

On September 8th 2003, I finally sailed to Ireland to begin my new life. I had hired two removal vans to take all my furniture and belongings. We sailed from a port called Moston in Wales at 10pm to arrive into Dublin port at 6am. I had not sailed from this port before but it was a very nice ship and the food was good, so after a nice meal the removal men went to the bar and I went to my cabin. There were two single beds and plenty of space, whereas a lot of these ships have only bunk beds.

At 5am a breakfast was served, after which we drove off the ship and drove across Ireland from the east coast to the west coast. After stopping for lunch in a nearby town called Ballymote, we arrived at the new house.

I had expected the house to be all ready to move into as the builder had promised it would be ready, but in fact it was in a unbelievable state.

As we arrived, the builders were just concreting the front, back, and conservatory steps, plus they had just laid all the concrete around the house. We sat there in disbelief as one of the builder's men told us "you can't get in there today, you will have to come back tomorrow". I tried to find the builder but he was nowhere around. I eventually got inside the house by walking on a plank of wood, I had expected that I was moving in today!

I was shocked to find that it was completely unlivable, with no electricity, no water or heating and none of the five toilets had been fitted.

The four removal van drivers got together and had a meeting in the garden, then decided to build a large wooden ramp propped up on bricks to try to unload the two large vans. This was going to take three or four hours or maybe more and they were beginning to worry, as they would later have to drive all the way back across country before sailing back to England on the ten o'clock ship.

The removal men stored all my furniture and belongings all the way up to the ceiling in two rooms, then left, so now what was I to do? I was actually homeless, so I decided to book into a B&B. I was very aware I could not live in a B&B for the next few months, so the next day I went down to my cottage in Galway, but it was not realistic to live there either as it was a two hour drive away from my new house, and I realized I was going to have to be on site every day if ever the house was to be completed.

I went to find the builder Desmond, who everyone called Dessey. Dessey was building a new housing estate in town consisting of fifty-seven houses and he was a nice and very popular man.

I told Dessey I was extremely upset that he has let me come all this way with all my belongings and now I had no where to live!

Dessey said "follow me to town and I may be able to solve the problem of accommodation for you." Dessey showed me a brand new house in Manorhamilton which he had just finished building so as to rent it out and he told me that I could have the house free of charge until mine was ready to live in, so I moved a lot of my personal belongings into the new temporary house which became my home for the next three months. This was a very kind gesture, but seemed such a waste of my time as I could have still been in England, spending this time with my family.

In October, I received a phone call telling me some upsetting news, that my daughter had been involved in a motorcycle accident and had badly broken her ankle. As I had always been so protective of my children, I felt dreadful that this should happen while I was living away in another country.

Debbie is a very 'tough cookie' and never once complained about the pain or the discomfort, staying positive and cheerful throughout her recovery, even though it must have been very hard to deal with. I guess she must have a high pain threshold where as mine is very low. I asked her would she like me to go back to England to help, but she said no as everything has been arranged.

I kept going up to the house every day, waiting for the joiner to come and fit the skirting boards, but usually he would not turn up. I would phone him and he would say next Monday definitely but next Monday would come and no joiner. I would be on the phone again and he would say tomorrow, then tomorrow I would be on the phone and he would say next Monday. After three weeks, he actually did put in an appearance and did some of the work.

This was not only the joiner, it would be the electrician the tilers, in fact most of the workmen, but apparently this is not unusual in Ireland. When I would tell my friends that I had waited in a empty house for three weeks for some workman to turn up, most people would tell me that I was very lucky they turned up that fast. By the end of October a lot of the builders work on the house was almost completed.

I had a electrical company come down from Northern Ireland to fit a music system throughout the entire house, and whilst they were wiring, I thought they may as well wire for a burglar alarm system, even though this is a relatively safe area. I just wanted to get all the wiring out of the way for the future. I then got lots of wall lights fitted which I had bought in England, as I think lighting is important to the ambiance of a house.

I had spoken to Michael, who is one of my cousins, when we met at a family dinner in England a few months earlier and he had told me that he and his wife would be moving to Ireland later in the year and as he would be looking for work, he would be happy to do my decorating and any jobs around the house. Well now Michael had arrived.

It was amazing just how much there was to do, curtain rails and blinds to be put up in all rooms, five bathroom cabinets with electric lights to put up, wardrobes to erect, mirrors and pictures to hang, towel rails and toilet roll holders to be put up. The stairs and all upstairs floors were varnished twice with a special varnish. Michael had to wear a special facemask, as the smell of the varnish was so strong. The entire house of fourteen rooms, a very large hall, a porch and the upstairs landing waited to be decorated.

On December 4th 2003, I at last moved in to my new home. Michael still had lots to do but that was OK since at least the house was now livable, and every day I was busy emptying boxes, finding a new home for ornaments and setting up all the rooms in the house. Michael's decorating and interior jobs lasted for just over three months.

I had bought some beautiful Italian tiles for the hall and had chosen lots of others for the conservatory, bathroom, and kitchen floors and was really looking forward to having them fitted.

My next job was to have a very large kitchen fitted, also a second kitchen, which could be used by guests for self-catering when I eventually opened as a guesthouse.

I had a whole wall of mirrored robes fitted in my bedroom, which was lovely as it reflected the garden into the room, it was slowly but surely all coming together and looking quite grand and I was very proud of my achievements.

As this is a six bed roomed house and far too large for one person to live in, I applied for registration to make it into a guesthouse. After a very thorough inspection, which I had expected, on May 13th Failte Eireann approved me as a registered B&B.

I would now put all my self-discipline and skills into operation, as I was just about to enter into a new arena, performing my communication, hospitality, and cooking skills for a world-wide audience as I was now on the internet and receiving enquiries from countries all over the world, for the coming summer months.

This was a very exciting experience, as I was receiving enquiries from America, Australia, New Zealand, Israel, not to mention France Germany and Spain.

I now had to decide what I was going to do with my land, which had previously been a field and was thick with rushes. I felt as if I would need a magic wand to turn it into a garden. I had done something similar at my cottage but this was massively worse, as the field at the cottage did not have rushes.

After a lot of searching I finally found a man called James, who said he could do the job and gave me a price for it. He told me he would need to remove about 30 lorry loads of earth to get rid of the rushes, then I would need to find someone who would sell me approximately the same amount of soil.

I went to a few garden centres and enquired about the purchase of soil, only to be told by each one that they did not sell soil. One suggested I try to find a building site where new houses are being built, as they sometimes sell the left over soil.

I drove for days looking for building sites with a pile of soil. On about the fourth day I found a site on the far side of Sligo but of course the site manager was not there. I was told he would be back tomorrow. I had by now realized that the word 'tomorrow' is one of the most used words in Ireland!

The next day, I drove almost twenty miles back and saw the site manager, who told me "we do not know how much soil we are going to need for the gardens when the houses are complete, so come back in six month's time and we may have some to spare, but then again we may not." What a waste of time that had been.

I found it hard to believe that I was driving around Ireland looking for soil and it being so hard to find in a country that is full of it! I continued the search and eventually found a new housing estate being built and a builder who agreed to let me purchase the soil. As I needed such a lot, I had to bargain on the price, to which he finally agreed.

James, who owned his own lorry, removed the old soil and rushes and I had to pay for it to be put in a tip, in god knows where. We then found that the land was extremely water logged, as the land survey had shown that the land was fractured rock on top of solid rock. I had not anticipated this problem, so now a massive drainage system had to be installed. These were expenses I had not allowed for. Finally the new soil was collected, placed on the ground and rollered, and then grass then seed was sown.

James later told me that he had found a water spring in my garden and had blocked it off. I was quite upset that he had done that without my consent, as I was using water from a neighbour's well about quarter of a mile away and sharing it with quite a few other neighbours in the vicinity, I was continuously worried that the well would run dry in the summer when my visitors would arrive. Maybe I could have used the water from the spring for the house or maybe I could have made it into a water feature, but it was too late now.

Three years earlier I had paid £1500 to a mains water scheme, but this had not yet been connected in this area, as I was the only person that had agreed to join the scheme and I could not get any sort of answer as to when the water might be installed. In the meantime, I had a large motor installed in the garage to pump the water from the well into the house and to the water tank upstairs in the loft.

Eventually the garden was complete and a fence was put up. As a river flows at the bottom of the garden, I also had a stile built over the fence as even though the water flowing is beautiful, I considered it could be a danger if any of my guests brought children.

I can still visualize my uncles as young men standing on the bend in this river and catching the fish with their hands. I remember my aunty Liz used to lie on the bank at the side of the river and wash her hair. She would lie with her hair in the water with the river flowing through it. It must have been a wonderfully relaxing feeling. I also remember my grandmother bringing the washing down to the side of the river and sitting there for hours until all the washing was clean and ready for drying, so now when I look at this river these are all the scenes, which I smile at and remember so well.

I now had to find a company to make road signs for the B&B, not easy in a strange country and not having any contacts in these things, but finally I designed them and then ordered them from a company which was based over one hundred miles away. Quite a few weeks and several phone calls later, my signs arrived, only to find that they had been made pointing in the wrong direction, I then had the hassle of finding a company to pick up and return the signs to the company that had made them. Weeks later and at a great expense, my road signs were erected on the main road.

The house was now ready, the gardens were ready and I was open for business. I named my B&B Glencar House as I lived in Glencar and I had some very attractive business cards printed, which included a picture of the waterfalls.

Glencar is an area known all over Ireland for its beauty, its lake, its waterfalls, and is only eight miles away from Lough Gill and the Isle of Innisfree. It is sometimes compared to the Lake District in England.

The fact that I was now in a different country opening a new business did not unnerve me in the least. One thing I have learnt about myself is I can trust my own judgment, and I knew I could do it, because I believe that if you care deeply enough about something and work hard enough at it, it will work. I must admit that some mornings I would wake up and think what in the world am I doing here? And I was missing my family dreadfully.

Lots of my guests would comment that I was very brave, being out here in the country and never knowing who was going to knock on my door, but I did not worry too much about that either, as being on my granddad's land I felt somehow protected, and thought maybe he was up there looking after me.

The road signs had only been up for about eight months when Leitrim County Council sent a man with a lorry to take down all the signs displayed on the N16 roadside. This included the estate agents who were trying to sell properties, the local restaurant and of course mine and many more. When I went to the council offices to ask why my signs had been removed, they told me I needed to apply for planning permission before they could be re erected, which would cost me one hundred euros, and that I could not have the signs back until I paid thirty euros handling fee for each sign. I applied for the planning permission instantly.

After six months, I had still not received my planning permission, so I telephoned the planning office and was told that they were so busy with planning for houses that they had no time to work on planning for road signs. I was now very annoyed at this attitude, so wrote and told them that if I did not receive my planning within the next few months, I intended to sue them for loss of earnings.

So eventually the planning arrived, but I was told I could only have one sign at the top of the road instead of the two I had previously had, so now I had to start all over again, get my sign reworded, add my phone number and the name of the B&B to it, and then have it re erected at the road side; more expense.

I joined an art class and enjoyed doing the watercolour paintings. We went out and painted castles, church windows, Glencar Lake and all sorts of interesting things.

Some-times when the weather was bad we would stay in the classroom and paint objects brought in by Liz, our tutor and when Sharn would be over on holidays she would come to the art class with me and we would paint away quite happily together.

I also joined a computer class and did an advanced course on computers. At the end of each computer course we would all go out for a meal together, which I would arrange.

I would book a table for the evening at a wonderful newly opened restaurant called The Fillet of Soul, which was owned and run by a man who had won The Chef of the year award, helped by his wife who was restaurant manager. They kept my business cards on their bar and used to recommend customers visiting the town to stay at my B&B.

I in return would recommend my guests to The Fillet of Soul for a splendid evening meal. It helps people to enjoy their holiday when they have a good B&B with good beds and luxury surroundings, where they can enjoy a good-home cooked Irish breakfast in the mornings, and in the evening to have a good restaurant such as The Fillet of Soul to go out to.

My visitors' book soon became full of lovely compliments on my warm welcome, my cooking, and my beautiful home in the perfect setting.

I was very proud to win the 2005 Irish Welcome Merit Award from the Irish Tourism Industry for my Irish hospitality and they also sent me a certificate, which I have displayed in the dining room and is much admired by my guests.

Ireland is very much into further education; we are so very lucky here in Leitrim to have so many courses, a lot of which are free as they are funded by the Peace and Reconciliation Fund in a hands across the border initiative to help to reunite the people on both sides of the border in Ireland. What a wonderful idea, and it is working wonderfully well.

We have lots of classes on all sorts of subjects such as health awareness, bone density awareness, and nutrition. Another course was called 'The Right To Question' where each week all twelve of the class would sit around a table with, the first week a doctor, the next week a practice nurse, another week it was two pharmacists from the local chemist, then on the last week with a guarda from the police station. We had the right to ask any questions and get a well-explained and detailed answer.

We also have courses which we pay for. I joined a photography course, which was extremely interesting, and there was even a belly-dancing course, which I was not tempted to join. These evening classes led to quite a few social functions and at one I met and had my photo taken with Mary Mc Aleese, the President of Ireland.

When we win our awards and certificates, our photos are published in the local newspapers, which gives you a feeling of belonging.

I then discovered the organic centre where there are courses on growing your own herbs, making medicine with your own herbs, and cheese making courses, just to name a few.

I joined lots of these courses and found them to be extremely beneficial.

I had by now made quite a few friends in Ireland, and some of them I introduced to the organic centre. Friends are very important to me, I am a person who is always willing to help my friends, as well as enjoy their company, and I always stay loyal to them.

One of the friends I made on one of the courses is a doctor of psychology; one day she told me that I am one of the most well balanced people she had ever met in her life, and that she wanted to spend more time with me to get to know me better.

Another place which does wonderful courses, is Belle Isle in County Fermanagh in Northern Ireland. People go there to learn how to cook for dinner parties or barbecues or even just to learn how to make scones and bread and cakes and at the end of the class the pupils eat the meal that they have cooked with a few glasses of red or white wine in the lovely dining room.

Joe, my friend who still lives in South Africa, came to Ireland to visit me for two weeks and he made it very obvious that he was looking for a wife, even though it was only just over a year since Liz had died. He kept singing an old song to me called 'The Story of my Life' and some of the words were, I want the world to know when I take you for my wife! He sang this for most of the two weeks.

He told me repeatedly that his daughter Alana had kept telling him that she and I could run a business together in Cape Town and that she would welcome me into the family but after lots of conversations on the subject, I told Joe that marriage was not for me and neither was Cape Town, as I would never consider living in south Africa. A few days later, Joe then told me that he was coming to live in Ireland and would open a business here. He even told all my friends and my uncles that he was coming to live here and he looked extremely surprised when I eventually told him that I would be selling up here and would be moving back to the UK so he would be here on his own. I do think he finally got the message but after his holiday, he returned home and kept sending me text messages telling me that I am a very special lady.

I do realize that Joe would have possibly have been a good help in my business as he and his late wife Liz had run a large hotel in Sillioth, and being a builder he would be very handy, but I had convinced myself that I was too young too marry, and too used to being my own boss.

Chapter Eighteen

On January 20th 2005, I decided to go over to Blackpool to look for an apartment, as I was now planning to spend the winters in England so as to spend more time with my family and friends. I am now blessed that I have a few close friends in Ireland and lots of acquaintances, but my friends in England are very longstanding, so I would now enjoy spending more time with them, and free to go for meals and to see some of the shows for which Blackpool is renowned.

I went to view an apartment in a new development in Blackpool, on the first floor, in a very nice safe area, and within walking distance of a very good supermarket which sells high-class food and wine and homemade bread, they also sell newspapers, cards, and stamps and just about everything you may need and they also have an all day restaurant. There was also an excellent bus service close by. I decided the apartment would be very suitable, and was looking forward to the contracts being signed in a few weeks.

Now back in Ireland and with three homes to support, I decided that I needed to get a job, but it would have to fit in with the running of the B&B.

I saw an advertisement in a newspaper in Galway advertising a business opportunity as a distributor for Kleeneze. This turned out to be an excellent idea, as I could choose my own area to work in.

I knocked on every door in the area that I live in and introduced myself, and then in all the surrounding areas. After I had made a sale and written the customers orders, I would tell them about my B&B and promote my business.

I then went on to knock on all the other B&B's doors in these areas and made friends with most of them. These were valuable connections as over the years we all sent guests to each other when we ourselves would be fully booked. I also made new friends in my neighbourhood and one of my friends introduced me to The Irish Country Women's Association, of which I became a member. Life seemed pretty full and very busy.

After about six weeks being back in Ireland, I decided that I needed to take a week off from everything to go to England to sign my contracts and get the keys to my new apartment. I had difficulty finding the time but finally managed to get away.

I am always in my element when home making so really enjoyed the time spent choosing the furniture, curtains, carpets, and so on, then all of a sudden another home was created.

After my exciting week away, I returned to Ireland. The outside of the house was now due for painting, so off I went to Roscommon, which is almost two hours' drive away, as I had seen a nice unusual coloured paint which I had decided to use, but was not sold in Manorhamilton or Sligo. I will go to the ends of the earth to get something that I have set my mind on. The outside of the house and garage were painted and that was that picture completed, then to my surprise I was also connected to Lough Gill Water Scheme, which was a major relief and a big worry less for me, as I always worried in case the water in the well would run out, and I would get the blame, as had happened in the past.

Every few weeks, I would drive down to my cottage in County Galway which would take me two hours then when I would get there, it would usually take me about three hours to mow the large lawn with a big powerful lawnmower. Very often my cousin John would have mowed it for me, for a fee, which we had both agreed upon, so I would usually then find other jobs to do, like weed the flowerbeds and tubs.

In July 2005, Debbie and Sharn flew to Ireland, as Sharn usually spends six weeks of the summer holidays with me. Debbie also brought her father Parviz, who had previously written to me and said it sounded so nice over here he would like to book in, so I agreed, as I do not hold grudges.

On the Wednesday I drove to Knock airport to pick them up. I took them to a few of the sights to visit Lough Gill and on the boat trip, and then we went to the waterfalls.

For two days Parviz was OK, then on the Friday I drove Debbie back to Knock airport as she was returning to England to resume work on the Saturday. As soon as Debbie was out of the car, he changed and started his usual unreasonable behaviour, which came as quite shock to me. He said he wanted to see my cottage as he had been told I had decided to sell it and he might want to buy it. I knew he had no money and was always pleading poverty but I did not want to mention this to him as I had no wish to hurt his feelings.

I drove the extra thirty miles to the cottage but, when we got into it he started, saying, "come here Mo and look at the thickness of these walls." As though we were viewing the cottage for the first time. I said, "yes Parviz I do know the thickness of the walls as it was me who decorated them." He then started banging on the wall with his fist and saying "I said come and look at the wall."

My cousin John came over and invited us to his house for a cup of tea with him and his wife Bridie.

This was the first time they had met Parviz. As we sat in their kitchen, Parviz started talking about an old man that he knew who was over sixty who had a younger wife who had just had a baby. The old man was having an affair with a young girl who he insisted his wife should employ as a nanny for the baby. Parviz then proceeded to demonstrate how the old man was stroking the young girl's leg and thigh at the interview. I was embarrassed and Bridie and John looked very surprised at this conversation, also we had Sharn sitting listening to this unnecessary nonsense.

I said that I must get back to the B&B as I had guests booked in. I must say Bridie and John looked relieved when I said we must go, so we left and drove back to Glencar.

That evening, I had a married couple from Israel staying in the B&B. The next morning after breakfast, as they were leaving, the lady said to me, "you are a lovely person, don't ever change". Parviz immediately started to mimic the lady in a loud and exaggerated voice, which the lady and her husband could hear. I found this very embarrassing as she would probably think that I was married to him, and that he was living with me at the B&B. When the guests had left, I told Parviz that I would no longer tolerate his bad behaviour and that I would not allow him to ruin my business, but he was jealous again because I had received a compliment, just like in the past.

He went from bad to worse and continued to argue about all sorts of nonsense. I remember feeling drained, and feeling as if I had a massive weight on the back of my neck and on my shoulders. I suddenly remembered, that this was how I regularly felt when I was married to him.

He then started to go on about the expensive wood that my kitchen was made from. He was trying to pick arguments which I cannot even begin to describe. I then told him that I did not intend to argue with him and would not have any further discussions about my kitchen, the wood or anything else for that matter.

When he realized that I definitely would not give him the satisfaction of arguing with him, he then started to demand that I drive him to Knock airport.

I told him that it was one hundred miles there and back, but he would have known this, as it was only yesterday that we went there with Debbie. I explained that I was not in a position to be away from home for so long as I had guests arriving from America in a few hours time. That drove him wild, and he kept telling me that these people must be more important than he was. I have now come to realize that with people like Parviz, you are only a victim if you allow yourself to be.

I suggested to Parviz that he go and stay in another B&B or a hotel, then get a bus to Knock airport on Monday morning when his flight was due.

Sharn and I drove him to Sligo as there is a hotel there, and when I dropped him off it was like the weight of the world was lifted from my shoulders. I kept thinking, how on this earth had I put up with his unreasonable behavior for over twenty years.

When you fall in love with a man, it has a permanent effect on you, and his brief re-entry into your life has its purpose too, leading you to the fresh realization of your own strength and how much you treasure the life you have created for yourself.

I feel very blessed that all my guests that come to stay here are always very nice polite people. They come from countries all over the world, they are very often highly educated and usually speak excellent English. I have never had any problems with any of them, only extreme politeness and good manners.

A few of my first cousins on my mum's side of the family have been to visit me. Ellen and Tanya, who are two of my favorite cousins, were the first, then Ellen came back and brought her brother Paul and we had a lovely time together. Paul is the youngest in the family of cousins and is forty years old, he has been married to his wife Joanne for twenty years and they have just had their first baby, Ellie Holly. What wonderful joy this baby has brought into their lives. Next week I intend to travel to England to Ellie's christening.

Other first cousins on my father's side of the family Maureen, Margaret and their mum Mamie, have been to visit a few times, sometimes bringing other friends with them.

Also lots of my friends from England come over to stay with me. My friend June came over with her two sisters, Maureen and Peggy. They both live in Scotland and are also friends of mine. I took them to Lough Gill and to the beautiful waterfalls and to visit the religious town of Knock, where Our lady is supposed to have appeared. Now a beautiful church has been built on the place and most tourists go there to collect the holy water. Also once a week there is a special service to help the sick and disabled people as they pray and hope for a cure.

Each winter I close the B&B from January 1st for two or three months. This is usually a good time to go on cruises with a few chosen friends. In January 2006, four of us went on a Mediterranean cruise on The Black Prince. We visited Madeira, Palma, Las Palmas, Gran Canaria, Lanzarote, Tenerife, Casablanca and Lisbon in Portugal. The Black Prince is a very old ship and proved to be very noisy, but the food and service were excellent.

We had also booked a second cruise for two months later, a Caribbean cruise on the Arcadia, which is a big new ship, so of course very modern. This time my friend and I had booked a suite with a large balcony and our other two friends had booked the same but on one deck above us.

The four of us flew to Barbados to join the Arcadia before sailing to Grenada, Dominica, Tortola, Antiga, St Johns Azures, Ponta Delgarda and we then sailed all the way back to Southampton, so no worries about over-weight luggage, then in Southampton a luxury coach took us back to Blackpool.

My daughter Debbie had joined the prison service then after lots of training, I am very proud to say she passed all the exams. We all attended her passing out parade, I had the pleasure of meeting all her colleges and the people in charge and we had a lovely day with lots of good food and lots of group photographs taken. I bought Debbie a lovely watch, to show her how proud I am of her and to commemorate the occasion, as this was a job that I myself would love to have done and almost did. This made the occasion even more special for me to see her achievement.

Debbie told me that day, that if I had been allowed to take the prison officers job all those years ago that she was sure that I would have been a prison Governor by now.

I now recognize that, because of my upbringing, I have spent most of my life trying to prove myself. I always sort of felt as though I had brought myself up. Because of this feeling, I tried very hard to build a strong foundation for my children to make sure they were confident and secure and that they always felt loved.

So now when I see them achieve what they set out for, as did Mark with British Airways and now Debbie with her prison career, I am just overjoyed for them, knowing that they are so happy in what they are doing is also very important, I am so very proud of the people they have become.

Lisa, another favorite cousin of mine, who had previously bought my rest home, had now moved over to Ireland and had met a delightful Irishman called Patrick. Patrick had fallen in love with Lisa on first sight, and they had now decided to get married.

I drove down to Kerry, as Lisa lives on the beginning of the Ring of Kerry, which is an incredibly beautiful place.

Lots of my cousins were there for this special occasion. As a wedding present, one of Patrick's friends had given Patrick the use of five holiday bungalows sharing a courtyard, so as the family could all stay together for the three nights.

The bride and brides-maids looked outstanding, and so did my cousin Mary. I told her I had never seen her look more lovely in her lavender outfit and hat.

It was a truly wonderful wedding, and the reception was in a five star hotel, all the guests were greeted with champagne in the beautiful gardens before having a absolutely wonderful meal with lots of wine flowing. Then everyone danced until dawn. It was a most enjoyable and perfect three days.

Chapter Nineteen

I ARRANGED A FAMILY HOLIDAY for my daughter, my granddaughter and Debbie's partner.

We had all always been such good friends that I knew we would have a great time together. I rented a lovely big house in Kissimmee in Florida with a swimming pool, a hot tub and a large four wheel drive car, as I had promised them we would have the best of everything. This was all arranged for August 2006. I also booked to have a very special, very expensive day at Discovery Cove, where the main attraction is swimming with the dolphins, this one-day cost as much as the flights to America.

I had agreed to pay for the all the flights, the house, the car, the trips, and all the evening meals eaten in restaurants. I also gave them some spending money.

Mark does not like Florida, so did not wish to join us.

Debbie agreed to do all the driving, and Sharn agreed to just enjoy herself.

We visited The Magic Kingdom, Bush Gardens, MGM, Pleasure Island, and Sea World, to name a few. On the day we visited discovery cove, it thundered a lot as it did on most days, so it was quite late in the evening when the swimming with the dolphins took place, then later that evening a very delicious meal was served in the very classy restaurant.

This would certainly not have been a holiday I would have chosen for myself, as I had been to all the theme parks eight years earlier with my friends Christine and Margaret, and Margaret's family, when we went to Margaret and Peters wedding, when all went on honeymoon with them.

Because of the incredible amount of walking, I knew it would not be suitable for me as I now suffer arthritis in my feet, but I desperately wanted to see them all enjoy themselves.

I had told the girls that they could choose a holiday of a life time, with no expense spared and that is what they chose, so I decided to persevere, as my feet would probably get worse in the years to come, so I decided to do it now whilst I still could.

Whist we were in America, Sharn and I went to Sarasota to stay with Margaret and Peter. Sharn was delighted when she saw that Margaret had a swimming pool and two fabulous parrots. On one of the days, Margaret took us to the Gulf of Mexico for lunch and a walk on the beach. Margaret and Peter wanted us to stay for a week, but it was a family holiday, so we said we would come back next year. Debbie later came to collect us and we all went back to Kissimmee. During the holiday Sharn started to say she might like a job when she leaves school, swimming with the dolphins.

In September of that year my sister Jacqueline came over to Ireland for one week and I decided to take a week off work and make it into a holiday so I took her to meet some of my friends, and we did a lot of sight seeing.

On the Tuesday, we drove 275 miles down to Kerry to visit our cousin Lisa and to introduce Jacqueline to Lisa's husband Patrick and to the new baby Aobha (pronounced Ava)

The next day, we went to visit Galway City and then drove down to Shanbally to see our cousins Bridie and John, the couple who live across from my cottage.

Jacqueline was very much at home in Shanbally, as when she was a young girl she often visited and stayed with our grandparents, sometimes with our dad and sometimes on her own. I then took her to visit one of our father's sisters, Nelly, who lives about thirty miles away from Shanbally. Nelly is now almost ninety years old. I remember her as a young lady when she used to work as a bus conductress in England. She used to be very attractive with long flowing hair, and when I was very young I remember she gave my family a photograph of herself in her uniform looking very glamourous.

Back in Manorhamilton, Jacky also had our mother's relatives to visit, and then later I took her to the farmers' market and to meet up with more friends of mine. We were kept really busy, then in the evenings we would sit and enjoy a glass of wine together and reflect on the day. It was a really lovely week, as Jacky is a really relaxed uncomplicated person and so easy to get on with. I really enjoyed her company and missed her when she went home.

I go to lots of B&B meetings, which are usually three or four hours drive away, so sometimes after a meeting I book into a hotel then go sight seeing in that area the next day before I drive home.

In the spring and summertime of course, I can not do this as the B&B is then too busy, there is lots of cooking and cleaning, and changing of beds to do, then the washing and ironing and shopping for the food. I also have to meet and greet the guests, and spend a little time telling them about the local attraction.

When all this is done, I then have all the three lawns to mow, which certainly keeps me very busy, but I am committed to any journey I embarked upon, and I do like to keep a very high standard.

I decided to spend Christmas in England with my family and at least two or three months away from Ireland. Ireland is a very beautiful country, especially in County Leitrim on the west coast where I live. I am living only twelve miles away from the Atlantic Ocean so I am living in a very damp climate however, which aggravates my arthritis. England may not be much warmer but at least it is not damp.

Both of my sisters Anne and Jacqueline had asked me if I would like to join them on a cruise on the Ocean Village 2. This is a ship I had not been on before. On all my previous cruises, we had to wear formal dress in the evenings and we would eat in a certain restaurant each evening for the entire cruise, whereas on the Ocean Village the dress is 'smart casual' and you may eat in any of the many restaurants.

On January 9th 2008, the three of us flew to Barbados. We had a very comfortable flight with First Choice and arrived on the ship on Wednesday evening.

The first day we were at sea all day, then on the Friday we woke up on the Isle of Margarita in Venezuela. After breakfast we went ashore and after some exploring, we went on a very enjoyable boat trip on a river. We dropped anchor and picked a starfish and a sea horse out of the water, which was a new experience, and of course we took lots of photographs. The next day we woke up in Granada where the port shops were not too bad, then on the Sunday we visited St Lucia, but being a catholic country the shops were all closed. That evening after dinner we had our photographs taken with the captain of the ship.

About seven thirty that evening, I went to the ladies toilet, but I tripped on what is called 'A lip' on the floor under the door. Just as I tripped the ship tilted, as the sea was very rough that night. I was thrown against a row of hand basins with a terrible force. I was very sore and bruised but thought it would be OK when the bruising went away.

We continued with our voyage, visiting Martinique, St Vincent's, Tortola, St Maarten, St Kitts Antigua, Dominica, then back to Barbados to fly home.

A few days after getting home, my fathers' brother in County Galway had passed away peacefully in his sleep at the age of 87, so I drove down for his funeral and stayed over- night with Bridie and John.

After the funeral, I went to a nice lingerie shop in County Roscommon, but whilst in the shop I started to get a stabbing pain in the left side of my chest.

I was concerned, as I had a two hour drive ahead of me, so I decided that in case I was about to have a heart attack and kill someone whilst driving and possibly myself, I called into the hospital for a check up.

I was still in severe pain so the doctor sent me for a heart trace a blood trace, and he insisted that I go for an x-ray. When he saw the x-ray he told me I had broken my Stirnum Bone which is the main bone across the chest. The doctor said he had not seen a stirnum bone broken across from side to side like this before, as usually they are broken from top to bottom. He told me he had sent for the heart specialist and for the medical team, and some time later three more doctors arrived.

They were horrified when I told them I had been carrying my luggage, and had even moved my washing machine, not knowing the damage which had been done.

One of the doctors then told me that I could not be allowed home, and I was admitted to the hospital. Lots of tests were carried out on me, blood traces, heart traces, and many more, as the doctors said they were very concerned about me as I had vital organs such as my heart and lungs lying on this broken bone.

They inserted a needle into my arm, which they left there for the entire stay and told me it was in case I had a seizure so as they would have quick access to my arteries. Two nights and three days later, they said that if the final tests were ok they would let me go home, telling me I must not drive, and for the foreseeable future should not lift anything weighing over five pounds.

By the time I got out of the hospital it was six o'clock in the evening and very dark and snowing, so I then had a nightmare drive home on the small unlit country roads, which took me three hours instead of two hours. I had to keep going as I was driving up to Larne in Northern Ireland the next day to get the boat back to England.

I could not afford to miss the boat, as I had booked a flight out of Manchester to California to see my dear friends Sam and Noreen, who had both been seriously ill lately. Sam had recently had a heart bypass operation, and Noreen has a decease called C.O.P.D. and is on twenty-four hour oxygen.

I had spoken to Noreen on the phone in December and she told me she did not think she has long to live, she had lost the will to fight, and that she would like to see me. I had asked Noreen if she thought she could hang on until February and then I would fly over to see her. So whatever happened I could not let my friend down now. I simply had to get there.

Noreen had also told me on the telephone that she was buying me a holiday in Las Vegas, in a top class hotel for five nights, which I told her I could not possibly accept.

My main problem now was, how do I get a flight to Chicago then a flight to San Jose without being able to carry my luggage. My sister Anne was very helpful. She drove me to Manchester Airport and lifted my luggage onto a trolley for me. After that, American Airlines were excellent and arranged to have my luggage lifted for me at both airports.

After seventeen hour travelling I arrived in San Jose at twelve o'clock midnight American time, and dear Sam was at the airport to greet me and drive me to their home in Saratoga. Noreen was too ill so had stayed at home in bed. When we got back I knew that Sam could not lift my luggage, so I got lots of carrier bags and unpacked my luggage in the car, as there are lots of steps up to the house.

Sam who was born in Jerusalem is one of the kindest most generous people anyone could meet. Some days he had trips arranged for he and I to go on whilst a wonderful Russian lady called Bella looked after Noreen.

Each morning after breakfast, Sam would set up his computer in his office then send me to answer my e-mails. We would often have lunch out, and then the three of us would have our evening meal together. This was very precious time we spent together, as I was aware I might never see these dear friends again.

April 2008. I am now back in Ireland and I have put my house up for sale. After my long break away, it is a pleasure running the B&B again, even though I am hoping that this is my last year of doing so. With my broken chest-bone, the jobs are much more of a struggle and mowing the lawn was painful, so I went and bought a more powerful lawn mower which does not need to be pushed so hard, but because it is bigger I cannot lift off the bag to empty the grass out. I usually lift it over the fence to feed it to the cows, which they queue up and wait for.

I went to see an osteopath who explained to me that the Stirnum bone is very flat and very thin so is very difficult to knit together to heal. He went on to explain that people who have a by-pass operation, after having the Stirnum bone broken as a means to get to the heart then have it tied together with wire as the only means of keeping it together to heal, so I must be extra careful.

Even though I sometimes feel as if I have lived several different lives, I have now learnt to face life on life's terms, to take one day at a time and to accept the things that I cannot change. On the strength of that, I have now booked another Mediterranean cruise for this October. This time I will take my granddaughter Sharn. It will be her first cruise so I have booked a cabin with a balcony, and she is very excited. My sisters and my niece Sharon will be joining us, so I am sure we will have a lovely time. I only wish my son Mark would come, but he thoroughly dislikes boats; in fact he will not even sail to Ireland on one, and always travelles by air.

My plan for the future is that I would like to buy a nice three or four bed-roomed house with a conservatory in the Blackpool vicinity in a good area. A nice private garden is a priority, so as we can once again enjoy barbecues on the lovely summer evenings. I have so much missed these barbecues whilst I have been in Ireland, as the climate is often damp and dewy in the evenings, so there are not many evenings when people can eat-out doors and by being so close to the Atlantic Ocean my garden is too windy.

A lot of my life has been about giving love to other people. I now know that by giving plenty of love does not guarantee you will get plenty back, but I always gave sincerely as much as possible to my family, my friends and my old people.

The simple things in life what I really wanted and would have been very content with were. A happy marriage, a nice house with large gardens, about four children as I have always loved children plus a few pets, that would have been my perfect life.

In the end people came from countries from all over the world to stay as guests with me in my B&B here in Ireland. I was regularly told that I am warm and welcoming, even by the lady who does my B&B inspections.

My guest would tell me that they loved my hospitality and good food. They would then write their comments and complements in my visitors book before leaving:

Strange though it may sound this has made all the hard work worthwhile. I also enjoy it at Christmas when I receive a Christmas card from some of these people who want me to know that they remembered their time spent with me.

So in the end I got the recognition here in Ireland that I deserved through hard work.

But isn't life wonderful that I got it through people who came from all over the world, who told me that they appreciated me, and wrote their thanks in my book.

I have not written about affairs of the heart as that would fill an entire book, or the three men who proposed marriage, the six month engagement which made me feel as if I had a dogs collar and lead around my neck, or about my on and off affair (for the last twenty two years) with the love of my life who is also my perfect soul mate.

Printed in Great Britain
by Amazon